D1025813

PLANET ON THE TABLE

PLANET ON THE TABLE

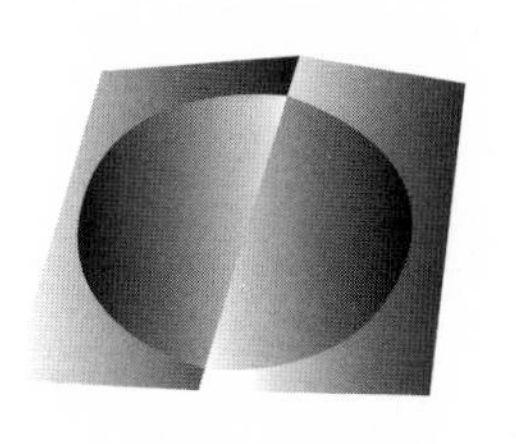

Poets on the Reading Life

Editors
Sharon Bryan
& William Olsen

Sarabande Books
LOUISVILLE, KENTUCKY

Managing Editor
Sarabande Books, Inc.
2234 Dundee Road, Suite 200
Louisville, KY 40205

LIBRARY OF CONGRESS CATALOGING-IN-PUBLICATION DATA

Planet on the table : poets on the reading life / edited by Sharon Bryan and William Olsen.— 1st ed.
p. cm. — (The writer's studio ; 4)
ISBN 1-889330-91-4 (pbk. : alk. paper)
1. Poetry—History and criticism. 2. Books and reading. I. Bryan, Sharon. II. Olsen, William, 1954- III. Series.
PN1064 .P56 2003
809.1—dc21 2002007234

Cover image: *Untitled* by Patrick Donley. Used courtesy of the artist.

Cover and text design by Charles Casey Martin.

Manufactured in the United States of America.
This book is printed on acid-free paper.

Sarabande Books is a nonprofit literary organization.

Funded in part by a grant from the Kentucky Arts Council, a state agency of the Education, Arts, and Humanities Cabinet.

FIRST EDITION

CONTENTS

INTRODUCTION

This book began in reminiscence, when the two of us were trading stories of our days as younger writers. We remembered devouring poem after poem and still wanting more, swapping authors and book titles, arguing passionately about styles, quoting favorite passages. We were all intent on making our various maps of poets in time and place: the Romantics, the first poets who broke with meter and rhyme, later poets who had to reexperience for themselves the implications of this break, New Formalists, Black Mountain poets, Deep Image poets, French poets, lyric poets, narrative poets—on and on and on and blessedly on.

In recent years we've sensed among many of our students and other young writers an erosion of that common ground and a loss of those maps—even of the impulse to make them. There are probably a number of reasons for the shift, from changes in English department curricula, to an exciting and necessary but sometimes overwhelming diversity of poetic voices and traditions, to the diminishment of reading skills in a sped-up, visually-oriented culture. We even wondered if some high-tech e-generation writers might feel wary of their own medium, might actually hold a kind of preverbal awe and dread of the written word.

Of all the books on writing poetry, not one we knew of dealt with reading. This other side of writing has been left as unilluminated as the dark side of the moon. It has been our experience that reading is at the very least the first part of the creative process, and itself a creative act—mysterious and fluctuating, alternately baffled and rapt, questioned and questioning: like writing. We felt the need for an anthology of essays by poets that would look squarely at reading, point to some common ground, offer at least some sketchy maps, and at the same time embody the passion that drives those of us who read and write poetry.

What we got goes far beyond what we had envisioned. There are, indeed, lists and recommendations (Bell, Hongo, Jackson, Kumin, McClatchy, Phillips, and others). There are also close readings that lavish attention on specific poems and poets (Gibbons, Gregerson, Hirsch, Lyons, Plumly, Wojahn). There are hybrid essays lyric enough to be poems themselves (Ruefle, McGrath). There are personal histories of reading (Behn, DeFrees, Dunn, Boland, Osherow), exhortations (Goldbarth, Zagajewski), familiar pairings (Behn on poetry and music), and surprising ones (Goldberg on poetry and murder). Some address and vibrate with the tension between wanting to read everything and wanting to read one poem a hundred times (Halliday, Rosser), and others talk more about how to read than what to read (Kumin, Macdonald).

These essays give voice and voices to the spirit of the unbrokered, teeming commonality of contemporary poetry, and give rise to the hope of an inclusiveness that resists mediocrity. They speak of particular poets with ardor rather than partisanship, and refuse to choose one "school" of poetry over another. They urge reading outside one's own comfort zone, reading on, reading further and further. And as a corollary, not feeling crushed under the weight of everything that one hasn't read, if only because to feel so crushed might stop one from reading further. Reading anything. Richard Jackson's reading of geographical maps. Carl Phillips's delight in *The Joy of Cooking*. Beckian Goldberg's love of detective novels that has her say "... if there isn't a dead body in the first chapter ... I'll move on to something else that's not going to waste my time." "Read Everything," Albert Goldbarth's first principle, leads him to muse, "What does it mean for your local bookstore to celebrate 'Banned Books Week,' but not tolerate *Outlaw Biker* or *Lesbian Witch* on its periodicals shelves?" "Read what you want to read at least sixty percent of the time," J. Allyn Rosser says, but also "Read what makes you want to keep reading." For the poet and the reader of poetry, Campbell McGrath says, "There is no poetry jail . . . and they cannot exile you from the Island of Language because, by definition, its limits comprise the limits of our world." Madeline DeFrees, who spent more than thirty years as a nun, is one of the few contemporary American poets who can speak directly to the experience of forbidden reading, of not having been allowed to read everything. Garrett Hongo's extensive list of philosophers, theorists, and poet-critics who have helped define the current intellectual climate carries the implication that poets who ignore such reading do so at the cost of the potential depth of their work. For Adam Zagajewski, the leading Polish poet of his generation, the ideal of reading everything ultimately implies some self-criticism, as this would include not only reading for inspiration but also reading "against yourself, for questioning." Eavan Boland's essay offers an example of this when she looks back at her childhood passion for patriotic English poems.

The useful suggestions for reading offered by some of these essays are also records of poetic advancement. There is Ed Hirsch's celebration of the middle-generation poets such as Lowell and Roethke and Berryman—a model generation for Hirsch, if only because it was "a generation who worked under the stimulus of each other." His essay lauds such unappreciated aspects of this generation as ecstasy, verve, compassion, and "grandeur." "Grandeur"—the very word that ends J. D. McClatchy's essay. For as much room as these essays urge we make for all aspects of readerly pleasure, they also advocate for a poetry of ambitious claims, a poetry that somehow embodies the tradition it must at the same time quarrel with. Keats,

Proust, Dickinson, Merwin, Szymborska, the almost impossibly ambitious Williams of the prose version of *Spring And All*, the Kafka who says that a book is as "an axe for the frozen sea within us"—these and other writers of tremendous striving especially populate these essays.

The gods of one's reading life don't always descend on these readers from on high; instead they sometimes seem to walk directly across the living room. Reading happens "unprogrammatically" (Dunn), even "chaotically" (Zagajewski) for nearly everyone here. In any case, as Hirsch says, "We are grabbed by these poets into art." For others, reading embodies nearly all of the permissions it did in childhood. Writing and reading, for Carl Phillips, are the private acts that they were then, "thereby confirming, at the least, anyone's right to dream." Robin Behn urges that readers "not abandon the dear and secret reasons we were drawn to hold the book in our hands . . . before anyone taught us to be self-conscious about the act of reading." It is that same self-consciousness that Mark Halliday worries over in his essay aptly titled "Perverse Reading," a defense of the very mistakes and reading tics and feigned sophistications that also make us the writers and the readers we are. Other poets worry neurotically that they are reading or have read the wrong things, or the right things at the wrong time. "Was I too young when I read Proust?" Mary Ruefle asks.

A shared hope of accumulating insight runs through the essays. Read, for example, Stanley Plumly's poignant and urgent essay on autumnal poems and you are encountering not just a "text," nor simply a close reading, but an intimacy between reader and poem that cuts across centuries. You are listening to a poet's lifelong engagement with a few cherished poems, a mind at work on matters of life and death. In short, these essays take us further into our own lives in their full complexity. The many reasons we read—for pleasure, learning, consolation, understanding, companionship, escape, to name a few—all seem to point to the possibility of profound change. "[Auden] saved my life," McClatchy says matter-of-factly. Or Ruefle: "That is why I read: I want everything to be okay." Or Osherow: "I'm not interested in reading poetry for the sake of writing poetry . . . but rather for the sake of living my life." Read McClatchy's description of his bedroom shrine for his tutelary spirits and you enter a sort of inner sanctum for both daylight truths and dreamwork: these spirits "seep into my dreams as I sleep and stand as models while I work." Or, as in a passage he quotes: "The process of reading is not a half-sleep, but, in the highest sense, an exercise, a gymnast's struggle. . . . Not the book needs so much to be the complete thing, but the reader of the book does." Read Cynthia Macdonald's essay for a unique and practicable way of approaching what one should read with the unconscious as much as the consciousness at the wheel. Read Goldberg's essay on the responsibility of poetry to the body and you go beneath even that, to the suggestion of "a language which desire speaks after death." That is another commonality here, one that, in the absence of poetry, would not exist as strongly in life: an unslakable human thirst for various forms of lastingness.

More than anything, these essays are love stories—not rose-colored romances, but love that includes doubt, violence, wrestling with angels and devils. Love of details, love that sweeps you away, batters your heart, drowns you, binds you—dangerous love, daily love, quiet love, devoted love. Love that calls us to the things of this world, love that reveals infinite other worlds.

The book may have begun with a look back, a kind of nostalgia, but the essays themselves bring us back firmly to the present. They are not wistful elegies for some lost golden age, but urgent, ongoing engagement with the world and what it means to be alive in it, here and now. And alive in poetry, too, in the solitude of the reading and writing of it, in the good company surrounding it. We hope this anthology helps to create the kind of exalted conversation that many of these poets regard writing and reading to be. We also hope younger writers read these essays the particular way Marvin Bell says the writer reads, "on the edge of his or her chair," ready to stand up and step toward the next book, toward the desk, toward poetry.

Sharon Bryan
William Olsen

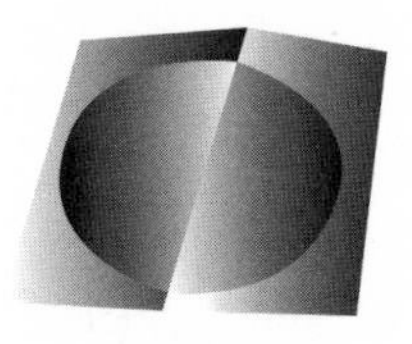

ROBIN BEHN

In the Music Room

I have been lucky. I grew up in a house of words. My parents met at Bay Shore High School where they were both English teachers. My father wrote a note to "Miss Walsh" asking her out, and had a student deliver it to her classroom. My father was thinking of the new blonde teacher, but the brunette, who turned out to *be* Miss Walsh, did not disappoint. In three months they were married.

Two teachers, friends of my parents, had a side business as carpenters. They built us a garage, repaired the cellar door where the coffins had been tumbled in and out—the house having been the undertaker's back in 1833—and built, in a little room off the living room, floor-to-ceiling bookshelves on two walls. This den served as my father's study—a plywood door rested on two two-drawer files against one wall of books—and my music room. There was a coffee table, purchased from a neighbor for fifty bucks, that opened to reveal a turntable and a place for storing LPs—my sister's Ella Fitzgerald, Art Garfunkel, Art Blakey, and my Shostakovich's Fifth, my Bach Sonatas, my Music Minus One. There was also a music stand, first a cheap folding one and then a high-quality black one permanently borrowed from the high school's orchestra room, and a flute, first a cheap nickel Selmer, then a Gemeinhardt open-holed silver, and then a Haines, serial number 30088—I still have it and I still have it memorized—and a shelf devoted to flute music. The music room was mine and the reading room was my father's and they were the same room.

My father kept the books divided into sections. Two copies of *Great Books*—my parents each wanted a fresh set for their own marginalia—took up several shelves. Then there were textbooks which spelled out what, to my English teacher father, was the only critical approach extant—*Understanding Fiction, How Does a Poem Mean*. Then the reference books: *American Heritage* and *Thorndike Barnhardt* dictionaries, *Roget's Pocket Thesaurus*, and an old set of Britannicas which held their own on a third wall in the petite built-in bookshelf original to the house. Then, wheeling back round to the fiction, everything by Katherine Mansfield, with whom my father was in love the way you can only be in love with someone you know in a book, and Faulkner, and Shakespeare, and Hemingway, all of whom he taught in his classes. And on down below that, poetry. The complete works of Dickinson and Frost, both of whom my father was fond of quoting—"Good fences make good neighbors," my father would joke as the twelfth or thirteenth child of our next-door neighbors rose briefly into view from the trampoline on their side of the barrier. And some E.E. Cummings, and Thomas's dogeared *Under Milk Wood* (brought out religiously every Christmas Eve, parts assigned to all), and X. J. Kennedy's *Nude Descending a Staircase* (how could a person be called "X"? and how was it my bow-tied father had come by a book with the word nude in the title?), and Eliot's *Prufrock*, thin and thumbed, and several high-school anthologies.

I knew the books by the look of their spines—the anthologies' horizontal ladders of graduated colors, their frightening prospect of more pages to read than there were hours in a life; paperbacks of all of Shakespeare's plays, thick inside with my father's inky trenches underlining passages; a ragtag assortment of novels, all colors, shapes, and sizes, and, among them, the mesmerizing, horrifying *Death in the Afternoon*, its wide, black, dusty, greasy spine embossed with a blood-red cape and crossed swords.

Next to these, the flute texts were ethereal, practically invisible, lying in a small heap on the one shelf that was mine. Long before I ever bought a book of my own, I made many pilgrimages to the Carl Fisher Music House on Wabash Avenue in Chicago to purchase flute scores. Practicing flute in the afternoons, or giving flute lessons to little girls who filed in one by one at thirty-minute intervals while their mothers kept the heat running in their cars by the curb, my visual field was filled by the head-high stand of notes and, beyond it, this sea of books. The words made a room. And the room was filled with music. When I think of my childhood that is what I see and that is what I hear and the seeing and the hearing are one.

Despite my bookish upbringing, I was, like everyone in my junior English class, at a bit of a loss when asked to write a report on a poet of my choice. The teacher had a stack of books on his desk for us to pick from. Of the dozens of poets on the approved list, one seemed to be a woman. It was embarrassing, walking up in front of everyone to find the woman poet. And the teacher, saying, Oh, I see, you've chosen the *woman*. Edna St. Vincent Millay. By year's end, I had purchased my first volume of poems, venturing into the Kroch's and Brentano's on Michigan Avenue after a rehearsal with The Chicago Youth Symphony, my flute bag on my shoulder. I took Millay's *Collected Lyrics* with me when I went to Interlochen Music Camp that summer, and read from "Renascence" to a cabinful of fifteen-year-old girls: "I saw at sea a great fog bank / Between two ships that struck and sank; / A thousand screams the heavens smote; / And every scream tore through my throat." I memorized the poem, ten pages long in my paperback edition. It was the first thing I ever read that had the vastness of feeling I had encountered in music and in life in a hundred unnamed ways, and then, that summer, when my best friend was brutalized and raped, encountered with a force that threatened to undo me. I did not hear this poem spoken to me, I heard this poem spoken as though from within me: "The Universe, cleft to the core, / Lay open to my probing sense, / That, sickening, I would fain pluck thence / But could not,—nay! But needs must suck / At that great wound, and could not pluck / My lips away till I had drawn / All venom out.—"

I began to write poems. Terrible poems, gushing poems, but poems, anyway, and I wrote them because Millay had written this and she was a woman, a very young woman, and she had said, "I saw and heard, and knew at last / The How and Why of all things past, / And present, and forevermore." A fair reading of the poem recognizes in its basic shape and narrative a spiritual as well as an emotional catharsis—"The heart can push the sea and land / Farther away on either hand; / The soul can split the sky in two, / And let the face of God shine through"—but for me, at fifteen, the religious part wafted over like so much smoke. It was that the woman had felt the pain of others to this depth and found words for it and lived that made me believe in the venture of poetry. Bach's *Sonata for Flute in E Minor* had always had the same effect on me, but it was a secret effect, the emotion without the words for the emotion. Millay's words were both more devastating and more healing.

Millay has been overlooked by the critics of our time until very recently. Two new biographies have ushered in an era in which, I trust, Millay will be brought back into the light she deserves. In all my undergraduate and graduate courses in the seventies and eighties, she was never mentioned, but *The Collected Poems*, a hardback, given to me by my father one Christmas when I was in college, has been on the shelf by every desk at which I have ever written a word. When I read "Renascence"—her juvenilia, really—I am not embarrassed, either for her or for me. She was learning how to write and I was learning how to read. We started by thinking big. We knew, or thought we knew, that for a woman's writing to be taken seriously, we should aim for the "universal," and what is more universal than all the human cries that ever cried? It is not a sin to overwrite. That is another thing she taught me: not to be embarrassed by large feeling, and not to be embarrassed to let your reader know of that large feeling.

Now when I read Millay, it is the sonnets I go back to most often. The bitter late sonnets: "Be sure my coming was a sharp offense / And trouble to my mother in her bed; / And harsh to me must be my going hence, / Though I were old and spent and better dead; / Between the awful spears of birth and death / I run a grassy gauntlet in the sun; / And curdled in me is my central pith / Remembering there is dying to be done." Or this, a cry for the age—a poem I turned to on September 11th:

ixxxvii

Upon this age, that never speaks its mind,
This furtive age, this age endowed with power
To wake the moon with footsteps, fit an oar
Into the rowlocks of the wind, and find
What swims before his prow, what swirls behind—
Upon this gifted age, in its dark hour,
Rains from the sky a meteoric shower
Of facts . . . they lie unquestioned, uncombined.
Wisdom enough to leech us of our ill
Is daily spun; but there exists no loom
To weave it into fabric; undefiled
Proceeds pure Science, and has her say; but still
Upon this world from the collective womb
Is spewed all day the red triumphant child.

Or this cry of the self:

iv

Not in this chamber only at my birth—
When the long hours of that mysterious night
Were over, and the morning was in sight—
I cried, but in strange places, steppe and firth
I have not seen, through alien grief and mirth;
And never shall one room contain me quite
Who in so many rooms first saw the light,
Child of all mothers, native of the earth.
So is no warmth for me at any fire
To-day, when the world's fire has burned so low;

I kneel, spending my breath in vain desire,
At that cold hearth which one time roared so strong:
And straighten back in weariness, and long
To gather up my little gods and go.

"And long to gather up my little gods and go." I have said those words over and over, a mantra for the spirit mired in its own defeats....

In that huge high school there was a wonderful Performing Arts department I considered my second home. I played in the orchestra and symphonic band, sang in the choir, acted on the stage, built scenery, sewed costumes, took music theory and acting classes. In the best of these, a teacher named Dick Johnson, who had been trained in the old schools of Oral Interpretation and Method Acting at Northwestern University, taught us how a character walks across a stage. "See," he would say, as each of us took our turn walking across the room, "one part leads." When Chris is Willie Loman, it's as if his back is going first, that burden is carrying *him*. When Lisa is Hedda Gabler, it's the proud neck. And, practicing, yes, we each could feel how the left hand, how the stomach, how the feet, how *something* in each character led. I think it is the heart that leads in Millay—her ability to feel emotion strongly—and her deft use of formal devices, her wild and sudden shifts from restrained to unabashed phrasing, that allow the heart to be revealed. A poem, like the actor's body, has all aspects to it, and, when it is spoken, there is a part that leads.

A flute can be both loud and beautiful if you open your secret throat in just the right way and use the air at the very bottom of the lungs. Or a flute can seem to be in another room, entirely, from the one you are playing it in, if you let the cheeks go just slack enough and almost speak a word at the same time the music-making air crosses the lips. Feeling crosses from music to words, and back again. When I was young I witnessed the crime that killed, for a time, the soul of my friend, and did not tell anyone. Feeling crosses from words to music, and back again. Speakable, unspeakable. Unspeakable, speakable. I played the flute to the walls of the room that was made out of books and they kept me company. The reasons we love books when we are young should be allowed to remain the reasons we love books when we are grown. We grow in our reading; we lead, perhaps, with *many* different parts of the heart and mind and soul and body. But we need not abandon the dear and secret reasons we were drawn to hold the book in our hands that was the source and the audience for feeling back before anyone taught us to be self-conscious about the act of reading.

I'm always stumped, tongue-tied, when asked who my favorite authors are; I have so many, and my allegiance to them is both steadfast and dynamic. When I think of other poets who have supported my need for immense feeling in poetry, Randall Jarrell comes to mind, a poem such as his "Seele im Raum," or Mark Jarman's "Questions for Ecclesiastes," or Neruda's "Melancholy in the Families," or Adrienne Rich's "Phantasia for Elvira Shateyev," or Akhmatova's "Requiem," Auden's "In Praise of Limestone," or Paul Celan's "Death Fugue." These poems slay me. All take on unthinkable subjects—annihilation, insanity, suicide, impending death, the weight of the world. Poetry need not take on such heavy subjects. But some poems must, and these do. And I think of Anne Sexton, a poem like "All My Pretty Ones"—she was the next poet I fell all the way in love with, reading from cover to cover until I came up against the fact of her death just days after it had happened and felt a great cliff, an opening, an absence sounding with her voice. I remember wandering the campus—I was at college by now—with a kind of grief I had never before experienced. She had rowed away to God.

As Millay says in "Renascence," "The soul can split the sky in two." Where I went next in poetry, over the next decade, was in search of soul. The Unitarianism I had grown up in had taught me tolerance, some critical thinking, a sense of social obligation and urgency, all good things—but, oddly, no vocabulary for the soul. I turned to poetry and felt the top of my head taken off by the image. I couldn't help memorizing these lines the first time I read them: "New ghost is that what you are / Standing on the stairs of water // No longer surprised // Hope and grief are still our wings / Why we cannot fly // What failure still keeps you / Among us the unfinished // The wheels go on praying." W. S. Merwin's *The Lice* taught me how language is the passageway to the ineffable, to that which surpasseth understanding. While Millay's sturdy and deftly veering pentameter could hold up her strong feeling, Merwin's slippery units of speech, with their indefinite beginnings and endings—that made reading like deciphering a chord written for piano, the notes sounding simultaneously, some overlapping while others fade away—had a way of tempting me into a realm beyond this realm, the roomless room of soul.

With Merwin—especially in his more recent poems—it's as if the pedal is down, the reverberations lasting, even dizzying. With Zbigniew Herbert, it's the opposite effect, clean lifts of the elbow, the next percussive stroke, the next, the next—the line breaks often do this—though the tones last, too, and overlap, and defy order. Herbert's "At the Gate of the Valley" has this mesmerizing effect, the calm voice leading the narrative on and on to the ultimate end as the players complain about their fates. It's less commanding than, say,

Milosz's "A Song on the End of the World," but I lean toward Herbert's accumulation and overflow. Even though I am a flutist, and doomed to play one note at a time, there are ways to make that note last in the air and in the mind to sing or collide with the next one, and even some ways to split the column of air into two notes at once. Somewhere in the very middle of an orchestra pit, my ears learned to hear the small song I was playing as part of the bigger song the rest of the orchestra was playing, and to hear that private and public sound in this moment as part of the ongoingness of the larger piece as it took place in time. So I enjoy the doubleness, the double entendres in a poet like Herbert. And if I want to hear lots of time happen in an instant, I go read some of Stein's *Tender Buttons* aloud. I let the sentences make the shape of a circle and I stand in the middle smiling. Stein, as much by my need for her to do this to me as by what might be her intentions, is like the echo chamber at St. Paul's Cathedral. If you climb up there needing to know something and whisper it to the wall, the dome will speak and speak.

But I was talking about soul. I read, for a time, writers who talked about God. To me, the word seemed like a sacrilege—to what, I'm not sure—but I knew I wanted to reclaim not the Word of God but the word *God*. I read Hopkins, and Dickinson, and Rumi. I read the Old Testament. I read Sexton again, the later books, and the Plath of "Berck-Plage" in which "This is the tongue of the dead man: remember, remember. / How far he is now, his actions // Around him like livingroom furniture, like a décor. / As the pallors gather—" and "the soul is a bride / In a still place. . . ." I don't know how it looks when an actor leads with the soul as he or she crosses a stage, but I know it when I see it. I feel it when I read it. I was aware of writing in a more expansive way, and my sentences got longer as I went. Instead of writing about terror, I was allowing writing to be terrifying. I needed the company of God, of gods. And then finally I needed to gather up my little gods and go.

I am walking across a stage although no one can see me. To me, it is a continuous relief that poetry can be written and read in private. No more sight-reading flute music in front of the teacher, no more standing in a strong wind wearing a wraparound dress, playing Mozart's Concerto in G for a grade-school audience. As I walk across the private stage of reading and writing, first one and then another part of me sets out. First, my heart. And then—my feet both on and off the ground—my soul. And then, somewhere in the middle of my life, a wind comes up, I think it is the wind of age, of people dying and being born around me, and I put my head down and try to lead with my brain. And so I rediscover a poet I had loved in my late teens when I tried, one word at a time, to translate her out of her native Polish through the German edition which was the only version I had. Wisława Szymborska. Her poem "The End and the Beginning" was another I turned to on September 11th: "After every war / someone has to tidy up." Pure thinking, this male province, is *her* province. She begins most of her poems with a conjecture and proceeds like an ant carrying, one by one, the grains of sugar to the nest, to build up a chain of thoughts and images. She loves the planet and our little species upon it. Instead of searching for god, I listen to her as if she is in the position of a god—not in terms of power, but perspective: I think there is a little planet just high enough above our little earth that she can reside there, or her poems can, and she can bring to us a species-view. While much recent poetry gets denser and denser, or leaves out the essentials from which we might construct an idea, a scene, a narrative, she carefully puts into place, plank by plank, idea by idea, the construction of her thinking, each plank bent just enough that the whole house tilts unexpectedly when it is done. She teaches me to be unabashed by thinking. She quotes Montaigne: "See how many ends this stick has." We can turn the stick over, and over, and over. Sometimes, as with Szymborska's work, reading is a slow forward motion, advancing by increments: "After every war / someone has to tidy up. / Things won't pick / themselves up, / after all." We can think about it and we can think about it some more. Sometimes, as with Lorca, reading is a sudden cohering, through one image: "Woodcutter. / Cut my shadow from me. / Free me from the torment / of seeing myself without fruit." Sometimes, as in Larry Levis' posthumous *Elegy*, one's reading seems to expand naturally until one small observation is transformed upon the large stage of myth, and no other world exists outside it. Sometimes, such large gestures are self-conscious and high-toned (Eliot: "In order to possess what you do not possess / You must go by the way of dispossession") and sometimes they are cut free from their moorings, adhering to stray images (Michael Palmer: "She asked / Have you lived for long in this odd house of air // but I could not tell whether she meant / this stone, or that one over there // beneath which we buried / the future of the past // its shawls and cups and tones . . ."). However it comes I am drawn to it. I am walking, now, my head bent low, my focus steady or unsteady, but walking, my head and heart and soul aswirl, walking until one day I become aware—as I began by being aware—of the footfall itself.

Which leads me to the body, the rhythms of the body. I have returned, of late, to sound itself, to the music- and reading-room where I began. I confess that if a poem does not engage my ear, I am not likely to go on reading it. I have a few favorite essays that talk outright about sound. Eliot's "The Music of Poetry"; a little essay by Jack Gilbert that appeared in *Ironwood* called "The Form of the

Invisible"; a book called *Music, the Brain, and Ecstasy* by Robert Jourdain that explains "how music captures our imagination"; and Frederick Turner and Ernst Poppel's "The Neural Lyre" in *Natural Classicism*, a piece whose observations about how the brain processes poetry are marvelously revealing, even if their conclusion—that the mind is best shaped to appreciate metrical poetry—is not one that I share. And I enjoy Jackson MacLow's sound piece "Is This Wool Hat My Hat": those six syllables, broken down, drawn out, quickened, slowed, orchestrated for four voices and spanning about four minutes, will warm up any audience's ears. It brings us back to the origins of poetry, what Donald Hall calls *milktongue*, the babbling start of it all. I'm drawn to the poems of Brigit Pegeen Kelly, which have this same effect on me, pulling me down into the rhythms of consciousness without self-consciousness, allowing chant to rise up inside the speaking voice, allowing the momentum to move both forward and backward, and using punctuation the way a musical composer uses musical symbols to notate just how a phrase should be heard. Kelly does it with the colon, as does A. R. Ammons. Etheridge Knight does it with the slash, or virgule. Dickinson, of course, with the dash. C. D. Wright with the period. We have twenty-six letters plus a lot of other musical symbols—punctuation marks—and I love the whole array of them. But that's another story...

...and I have come full circle, back to where I started in the music room. Listening, but this time, to poetry. Just now I am rereading *The Four Quartets* because I awoke with "Quick, said the bird, find them, find them" in my ear, and the bird would not leave all day and still has not left. We read for selfish reasons. Just now, I need to find that bird.

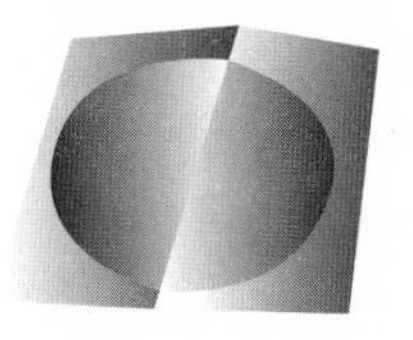

J. D. McCLATCHY

Required Reading

For years I lived in apartments too small for me to have a desk, so the bedroom was my study. Even now, with a proper desk at last, I still do most of my reading in bed. Perhaps for that reason I have made my bedroom into a sort of shrine. There in the pillowed, twilit gloom, a devotional halogen lamp casts a halo over the page propped on the duvet covering my crooked knees, and its light is reflected in dozens of glass frames—like ranks of votive candles—that line the walls around my bed. Behind each is a tutelary spirit. Over the years I've collected fetishes and set them around me—my lares and penates—to seep into my dreams as I sleep and stand as models while I work. In one frame I have a swatch of the Metropolitan Opera's original gold curtain; in another, a leaf from the Buddha's Bo tree in Ceylon; in another, a receipt, signed by Alexander Pope, for two guineas received from Mr. Craggs, "being the firft Payment to the Subfcription, for the Tranflation of Homer's Iliads; to be delivered, in Quires, to the Bearer hereof, in the manner fpecify'd in the Propofals"; in still another, two loops—one, snipped when she was a blonde girl, and the other, darker, cut after her death—of Emily Dickinson's hair. But most of the walls are covered with letters. Some were written by composers I especially admire: Ravel (an acidulous note to an editor), Stravinsky, Fauré, Rachmaninoff. My three heroes are directly over my head, their discipline and magnanimity a constant lesson: Lincoln, Verdi, and Proust. Actually, there are two pieces in Proust's hand. One is a postcard, and he's written on the front of it, across the sky in a scenic photograph. I'm fond of the fact that, as the writing extends down to the top of a distant mountain range, Proust's line of script follows the contours of the soft peaks. The other is a letter to someone who's asked him to contribute an essay to a book. Proust declines with a morbidly witty politeness, explaining that he has the worst and best reason to beg off: he hasn't long to live, and what can a dying man promise?

The other letters on the walls are by writers whose work has meant the world to me, as a reader and as a writer. There's Walt Whitman and Oscar Wilde, Ralph Waldo Emerson and Robert Frost, Colette and Mallarmé, Turgenev and Longfellow, Henry James and A. E. Housman, Cocteau and Auden, Marianne Moore and Louise Bogan. The list—and the frames—go on and on. One of my favorites, not least because it contains both sides of an exchange, is a fan letter to Wallace Stevens, along with his reply. The letter to Stevens is dated January 13, 1934, and is from one Anna Wirtz. (In his reply, Stevens has typed out her name and address. She lived in New Haven, so I checked an old city register in the Yale library and discovered her: a young widow working for the Post Office.) She had a question.

Dear Mr. Stevens:

May I take a little of your time to ask about your poem, "The Emperor of Ice Cream," appearing in *Fifty Poets*, edited by William Rose Benét? I am uncertain as to how to interpret the poem. Do you mean that so many things in life are ugly and disillusioning and that the only sure beauty is that of "concupiscent curds" of ice cream? You speak of so many imperfect things and then place ice cream as ruler over all.

The poem puzzles me and I crave your indulgence. Does the denseness of a 26-year-old mind make the request appear less ludicrous? I do trust so. In anticipation.

Sincerely yours,
(signed) Anna Wirtz.

Stevens replied, not on his office stationery, but in a note typed (and corrected) by himself, though with his office address typed in. His tone is seigneurial.

Dear Miss Wirtz:

Some time ago I made up my mind not to explain poems, because the meaning of a poem is merely one part of it.

Of course, I never meant that ice cream is, for good and all, the *summum bonum*. If the meaning of a poem is its essential characteristic, people would be putting themselves to a lot of trouble about nothing to set the meaning in a poetic form.

Very truly yours,
[scrawled] Wallace Stevens.

How I sympathize with Miss Wirtz! Her letter might have been my own. I was a dense eighteen-year-old when I first read "The Emperor of Ice Cream," and I didn't understand a word of it. Of course I was too arrogant to admit that, even to myself.

My copy of Stevens' *Collected Poems* is the Faber edition. I bought it in Oxford during the summer of 1966—now that I think of it, just a dozen years after it was first published. The price is still penciled onto the front endpaper: £2.50. I was in England then to study at The Shakespeare Institute in Stratford-upon-Avon, and to have made the fortuitous leap from Shakespeare to Stevens is to understand at once a crucial side of Stevens' rhetoric, its heady lusters and pulsing rhythm. I bought the book because of the poem that had scared Miss Wirtz and me.

A year after I bought the book, Richard Wilbur told an interviewer: "I'm sure that my enthusiasm for Stevens, circa 1948–52, has affected my own work, although I can't say just where. Of late I have found his work too undramatic, connoisseural, and inconclusively ruminative.... For all his stress on the *Ding an sich*, I find him too hothouse subjective right now." Wilbur's hesitations predict my own, but none of that was apparent in the first vertiginous rush of pleasure in Stevens' plush and gaudy metaphysics. My copy is cluttered with commentary. Allusions are tracked (next to the poem "Gubbinal," I've written a note: "Gubbins: a contemptuous name formerly given to inhabitants of a certain district in England, said to have been absolute savages"), references to a poem in Stevens' letters are cross-indexed, deleted stanzas restored, and reams of schoolboyish "interpretation" supplied (sample: "ego in relation with responsive ego transcends alien reality"—whatever *that* is supposed to mean). I had never read a book so intently. There were two results. First, I began to hear Stevens everywhere. Many evenings in grad school were spent—after dinner on a tray and an ill-rolled joint—reading aloud poems by Elizabeth Bishop or John Ashbery and listening for echoes of the old man. Also, the poems I wrote myself at that time now read like thudding parodies of the Stevensian sarabande—the slow, stately manner he had of turning his back on everything. It took some years to get that ringing out of my ears.

This was the same time, coincidentally, that I was befriended by Stevens' daughter Holly. The first time she invited me to dinner at her house, she'd cleared the table of our plates and glasses and served cups of coffee. As I raised mine to my lips, she casually remarked, "That's the cup Dad used every morning." Did my hand begin to tremble? That cup, suddenly transformed into the grail—would it have been a part of the scenery, among the peignoir's complacencies?

One of my teachers in college had once squired Holly Stevens around, and her father gave him a copy of his *Collected Poems* with this inscription: "Dear Elias: When I speak of the poem, or often when I speak of the poem, in this book, I mean not merely a literary form, but the brightest and most harmonious concept, or order, of life; and the references should be read with that in mind." The angelic orders of life. Though Stevens may sometimes seem like the longest distance between two points, how much more convincingly he sizes up and sings of those angelic orders than does, say, that plaster saint Rilke! Stevens' haughtiness was crucial, too, his measured authority. Perhaps fear should properly be a part of one's first serious literary encounter. How better get a taste for the sublime? Stevens was my Aladdin's lamp, and the auroras conjured from it first empowered my own imagination, and seem now in retrospect to glow with my own nostalgic gratitude.

There is one poet I esteem above all others. I read his work as the American scripture. Never has he failed to enthrall me. I quiver or weep as his lines direct me. He wrote not as Americans speak, but as they feel, as they wish to know themselves. He wrote this:

> Books are to be called for, and supplied, on the assumption that the process of reading is not a half sleep, but, in the highest sense, an exercise, a gymnast's struggle; that the reader is to do something for himself, must be on the alert, must himself or herself construct indeed the poem, argument, history, metaphysical essay—the text furnishing the hints, the clue, the start or framework. Not the book needs so much to be the complete thing, but the reader of the book does.

And he wrote this:

> *February 24th.* —A spell of fine soft weather. I wander about a good deal, sometimes at night under the moon. To-night took a long look at the President's house. The white portico—the palace-like, tall, round columns, spotless as snow—the walls also—the tender and soft moonlight, flooding the pale marble, and making peculiar faint languishing shades, not shadows—everywhere a soft transparent hazy, thin, blue moon-lace, hanging in the air—the brilliant and extra-plentiful clusters of gas, on and around the façade, columns, portico, &c.—everything so white, so marbly pure and dazzling, yet soft—the White House of future poems, and of dreams and dramas, there in the soft and copious moon—the gorgeous front, in the trees, under the lustrous flooding moon, full of reality, full of illusion—the forms of the trees, leafless, silent, in trunk and myriad-angles of branches, under the stars and sky—the White House of the

land, and of beauty and night—sentries at the gates, and by the portico, silent, pacing there in blue overcoats—stopping you not at all, but eyeing you with sharp eyes, whichever way you move.

Nabokov says somewhere that, for people like you and me, the greatest pleasure of the day is often the thought we carry around with us through the ordinary tasks and banal exchanges of our rounds—the thought of the book that awaits us on our bedside table at night. For me, as it happens, that book was at one time always *by* Nabokov. It was a case of bardolatry. I didn't mean to pester the man with my enthusiasms, but every year as a teenager I would send him a birthday card. (He shared his birthday, in fact as in the innermost chamber of my imagination, with Shakespeare.) Each was carefully addressed to him at the hotel in Montreux: I could picture him at his desk in the morning, opening the envelope.... I never had a single acknowledgment, and covered my wounded feelings by telling myself that, of course, the great novelist would only have been first bemused by and then contemptuous of my gushing. (Still, I'm told by a friend that my cards and letters to him are kept in the Nabokov archive at The New York Public Library. And I smugly grinned when I read Nina Berberova's description of him as a man who only extended two fingers to the world.)

No matter. Nabokov and I shared one thing in common—or rather, one thing other than our mutual admiration of Nabokov. We shared a passion for Proust. In one of the Cornell classes transcribed for Nabokov's *Lectures on Literature*, he writes of Proust, albeit for gum-chewing undergraduates of the 1950s: "The transmutation of sensation into sentiment, the ebb and tide of memory, waves of emotion such as desire, jealousy, and artistic euphoria—this is the material of the enormous and yet singularly light and translucid work."

He goes on to make a distinction between an "evocation" and a "description," in the sense that Proust offers us "a number of exquisitely chosen moments which are a sequence of illustrations, of images," as if the novel were a slide show. But of course Nabokov is a sophisticated reader and thereby immune to reduction. And he later goes on to isolate three especially distinctive elements of Proust's style which I recognize, thrill to, learned from. Myself, I've read *In Search of Lost Time* only three times, and can't claim Nabokov's intimacy. Still, I understand instantly his list:

> 1. A wealth of metaphorical imagery, layer upon layer of comparisons. It is through this prism that we view the beauty of Proust's work. For Proust the term *metaphor* is often used in a loose sense, as a synonym for the hybrid form, or for comparison in general, because for him the simile constantly grades into metaphor, and vice versa, with the metaphorical moment predominating.
>
> 2. A tendency to fill in and stretch out a sentence to its utmost breadth and length, to cram into the stocking of the sentence a miraculous number of clauses, parenthetic phrases, subordinate clauses, sub-subordinate clauses. Indeed, in verbal generosity he is a veritable Santa.
>
> 3. With older novelists there used to be a very definite distinction between the descriptive passage and the dialogue part: a passage of descriptive matter and then the conversation taking over, and so on. This of course is a

> method still used today in conventional literature, B-grade and C-grade literature that comes in bottles, and an ungraded literature that comes in pails. But Proust's conversations and his descriptions merge into one another, a new unity where flower and leaf and insect belong to one and the same blossoming tree.

But though it may be Proust-the-stylist one is first struck by, threading hesitantly through the maze of his rhetoric, that is not—and perhaps should not be—one's abiding initial impression. As an emotional bumpkin, I was first impressed by the heart's truths Proust had seemed to discover, like nuggets in his perforated pan. And those kinds of truths are often best found in fables and fairy tales, not in complicated realistic novels. Better Grimm than Dreiser? I've sometimes thought that Proust's famous opening sentence ought to be translated "Once upon a time I used to go to bed early." But Proust *is* a realist rather than a fabulist. My other favorite realist is Tolstoy. What I admire about both writers is this: there is not a single human emotion that they don't know and understand and sympathize with. And while I'm not especially drawn to the aristocratic circles he's obsessed with (there's too much of E. F. Benson's Tilling in Proust's Paris), I marvel at the precision with which they are drawn. "Profundity," said Paul Valéry, "is a hundred times easier than precision." Gesture, intonation, the cock of a head, the fit of a sash... no detail is overlooked, and each serves a moral purpose.

Part of Proust's realism is his rhetoric. The architecture of his sentences, the density of his metaphorical renderings—beside Proust, other novelists seem to skim. As a result, the great sections of the novel—the death of the narrator's grandmother, the dark underground caves of jealousy explored in *The Captive*, the final

Guermantes party with its pavane, now ghostly, now grotesque, on the effects of time—have a uniquely three-dimensional feel to them. One *sees* around to the hidden side of things. Poetry is written at the pace of dreams, while Proust's prose moves at the pace of life—strolling or darting or reversing, but constantly in motion, constantly revising itself.

I have myself written a poem about Proust, but not one in league with James Merrill's splendid "For Proust," published in his 1962 collection, *Water Street*. The poem is a richly dramatic and subtle enactment of Proust's own handling of time in the novel, the dissolves and dreamy montage. Having ventured into the world for a detail, a little phrase, to verify for his book, Proust returns to his apartment:

> Back where you came from, up the strait stair, past
> All understanding, bearing the whole past,
> Your eyes grown wide and dark, eyes of a Jew,
>
> You make for one dim room without contour
> And station yourself there, beyond the pale
> Of cough or of gardenia, erect, pale.
> What happened is becoming literature.
>
> Feverish in time, if you suspend the task,
> An old, old woman shuffling in to draw
> Curtains, will read a line or two, withdraw.
> The world will have put on a thin gold mask.

Merrill's technique here is admirable—from the internal couplet that shifts the meaning of the same word on to the final image that makes the dawn gleam like Agamemnon's death mask. That the image is itself drawn from Proust remains the final form of Merrill's tribute to his master. At the end of *Within a Budding Grove*, Françoise at Balbec comes in to open the narrator's curtains:

> And when Françoise removed the pins from the top of the window-frame, took down the cloths, and drew back the curtains, the summer day which she disclosed seemed as dead, as immemorial, as a sumptuous millenary mummy from which our old servant had done no more than cautiously unwind the linen wrappings before displaying it, embalmed in its vesture of gold.

How eerily the two writers mingle glamour and death, day and eternal darkness. Proust does not always inspire such brilliant echoes, but there is no attentive reader of his novel who does not return to his own life chastened, judged. And if that reader is himself a young writer, he will be haunted by a sentence near the end of the novel: "But excuses have no place in art and intentions count for nothing: at every moment the artist has to listen to his instinct, and it is this that makes art the most real of all things, the most austere school of life, the true last judgment."

Nearly four decades ago, when I first read Virgil (I was a college freshman and part of a small group selected to be that year's "Virgilian Academy," which would devote a year to the *Aeneid* and then, with an unmarked copy of the Oxford edition as our only companion, be publicly examined on our understanding of the poem by no less a master than Bernard Knox), I thought him an exotic, stiff with gold and purple (in Robert Lowell's phrase), fire-crested plumage and blood-clotted spear. The hero never emerged from the scenery—or was it the grammar? Years later, a novice teacher myself, explaining the poem's panorama but unconvinced of the truisms I'd outline on the blackboard, I insisted on the prerequisites of duty, the steep cost of both repressed passion and ruthless empire. This was as likely as not an echo of what I was at the same time complaining about to my psychiatrist. Both the poem and my life I saw then as an immense marble staircase with a narrow red runner rising toward an empty sky.

Nowadays, at last old enough to read the poem without the burden either of being deaf to its emotional appeal or of having to carry it on my shoulders from some burning classroom, it seems an altogether different work, at once smaller in scope and larger in resonance. Two strains have come to dominate. First, I watch it all—voyage or contest or battle, camp or palace—through a scrim, the *sfumato* effect of sadness. The sadness is neither grief nor weariness. It is psychological perspective and moral tone. Virgil wrote the consummate elegy of aftermath. Second—and in this he resembles no writer more than Proust—the *Aeneid* is a poem about memory, its intolerable system of weights and releases, the screech owl beating against the shield. Memory is fury and muse, and drives the poem's plot and characters. The poet's use of prophecy—"hindsight as foresight" in Auden's scolding phrase—is his shuttle. No earlier poem, and few later, pleated time so seamlessly. The past can force a civilization, or turn a heart inside out. In either case, only suffering is finally of use. Like his master Lucretius, Virgil saw love and war—Venus the mother of Aeneas, and Mars the father of Romulus—as the ancestors of Rome, as they are of memory itself, which both restores and festers. Just so is peace, whether in the lonely hearts of all the poem's heroes or in the realm of the Pax Augusta, an aftermath distilled from sadness and memory, if only sadness enshrined and memories projected.

And the style of it all? On the swags of syntactical and narrative brocade, the emotional pattern is stitched with a simple and subtle clarity. The half-light against which the poet's images flicker the more briefly and brilliantly dims until Dante and seems, after Leopardi and Montale, to be characteristically Italian. English's more garish and insistent maneuvers miss the cloudy linings of silvered words—though Robert Fitzgerald captures more than any other translator has, or probably could. The poem's symphonic organization, its harmonies and modulations, its swelling set-pieces and tender gestures, together define the lyrical epic. Pallas on his pyre, his head wrapped in Dido's gold-woven cloth, the trophies of war piled over the naked youth, and Aeneas's tight-lipped farewell . . . it is at such passages that the lines blur. Rarely has a public moment been rendered so intimately, nor a private moment so eloquently modeled into monumental sculpture.

There are two constants in the literary life. One, indulged more furtively than the other, is spite. Most writers think well of too few. Like the songs popular when we first fall in love, we esteem what we remember first inspiriting us, plus a pal or two. The rest is condescension. At the height of the Heian Era in Japan—by our reckoning, about 1000 A.D.—its two most renowned writers, both of them women, were Murasaki Shikibu, the author of what is rightly regarded as the first novel, *The Tale of Genji*, and Sei Shōnagon, whose *Pillow Book* is a diary famous for its detail, its frankness, and its elegance. We don't know that they ever met, but they certainly knew of one another. In her own diary, Lady Murasaki casts a sidelong glance at Sei Shōnagon, who had recently died. Its cattiness is emblematic of any writer's "candor."

> Sei Shōnagon, for instance, was dreadfully conceited. She thought herself so clever and littered her writings with Chinese characters; but if you examined them closely, they left a great deal to be desired. Those who think of themselves as being superior to everyone else in this way will inevitably suffer and come to a bad end, and people who have become so precious that they go out of their way to try and be sensitive in the most unpromising situations, trying to capture every moment of interest, however slight, are bound to look ridiculous and superficial. How can the future turn out well for them?

The other constant is misunderstanding. During the Heian Era, though Japan had cut off its contacts with China, it was still fashionable among the emperor's courtiers to display a taste for music played "in the Chinese manner"; it was a sign of her sophistication for a lady-in-waiting to recite a T'ang poem. The only problem was that everyone in Japan then thought that Po Chü-i was the immortal poet whose verses were to be swooned over. Though they were revered in China, Li Po and Tu Fu were overlooked by the Japanese cognoscenti as minor. Again, by our reckoning, and that of literary history, they had missed the true masters. Whenever I'm abroad and the subject of American poetry comes up, the name of Ezra Pound—they know nothing of Robert Frost or Wallace Stevens—is spoken in hushed tones as the supreme modernist, the source and guarantor of poetic ambition, the very model of a free verse held to be the essential American line. To my mind, Pound is our Po Chü-i.

Pound was a considerable influence, an eccentric critic, a minor poet, and a moral disaster. It didn't take long, even for an ill-read collegian, to realize that. I never got the point of William Carlos Williams—no *there* there—and Marianne Moore I found too whimsical. Of course, at that stage, it was T. S. Eliot who alone could slake my thirst for Great Modern Poetry. The margins of my copies of *The Waste Land* and *Four Quartets* were ascribble with head-scratchings and discoveries. I listened to recordings of Eliot drily reading, and made a pilgrimage to East Coker. And then, like other adolescent passions—that for Hemingway, for instance, or for cigarettes—it faded, until I could see that only "The Love Song of J. Alfred Prufrock" would last, in anthologies of light verse. So I moved on to greater poets, no less glamorous in their way but not pushed forward in school curricula: Yeats, Stevens, Crane. They *took*, in part, because they had to be got at privately. Then, finally, I turned to W. H. Auden. He saved my life. He was, as Edward Mendelson has rightly said, the first poet in English to have contained the twentieth century. And he remains any fledgling's best guide to what can and should be done with words.

I should have first been attracted to Auden's early poems, to their obliquity and spikiness, but I was oddly drawn to the garrulous late poems; I liked their tone, their having been written under the Stoic motto: hold on and hold off. But it was the work of the American Auden, the poems of the forties and fifties, that most exerted the sway I fell under, or tried breathlessly to rise to. They were the work of a writer who literally entertained ideas. Nietzsche, an Auden avatar, once defined maturity as the ability "to recover the seriousness one had as a child at play." He meant, I suppose, the quality of attention and of imagination—utterly free, utterly absorbed. For me, then and now, those poems brim with perfectly chosen details, with phrases that can upend a lifetime's complacencies, with further mysteries posing as fresh solutions.

My favorite poems? From the start, "The Shield of Achilles" and "In Praise of Limestone" have been touchstones. Among longer poems, I return most often to "Bucolics," "Horae Canonicae," and "Thanksgiving for a Habitat." None of these poems, though, do I find especially "useful" to me as a writer. What I have "taken" from Auden has been more general, or more technical. The occasional stanza scheme, a model for handling syllabics, that sort of thing. Most of all, the exhilarating example of his discursive mode; his sense that poems are not decorative, but diagnostic, not self-full effusions or mystical anecdotes, but practical investigations of the psyche and the culture. His *Collected Poems* hasn't been a hornbook so much as a pantheon—some cool vaulted marble temple I can stroll through, admiring the shrines, wondering at the shaft of light slowly circling through the giant hole at the top. He's a presence, a pressure, a model for the kind of poet to be, not just for a kind of poem to write. And because I consider him to be the greatest poet of his century—that is, mostly my century too—I am instinctively drawn to his formulations of experience. He looked under more rocks than any of his peers, and indulged an eccentric boldness of phrasing; with the exception of Proust, he was more honest about the heart's duplicities than anyone; and he used his capacious intelligence to create a wondrously kaleidoscopic mythology of modern life.

For myself, Auden was always a literary, not a personal model. I mean, I like a good martini, but I was never for a moment attracted to the slovenly, drug-addled, tyrannical, distracted elderly Auden of popular legend—except as a legend, rather like his iconic, Navajo-elder face. And I'm afraid I'm unworthy of the private Auden who was so considerate and generous, so disciplined and productive. But the way he construed the writer's life has been a model. Or at least a sanction. He only considered himself a "poet" when he was writing poems. There was nothing bardic about him. He was a man of letters for whom criticism, journalism, song lyrics, record jacket copy... anything went. He has led me to share his temperament, or at least his sense of the writer's pleasures and responsibilities.

Any true accounting for myself would probably be as thick as a Norton anthology. There were early passions—Marlowe, Donne, Keats, Whitman, Hopkins, Eliot—whom one might only adore, not presume to emulate. As a young reader, I wanted gods, not golden calves. Fortunately that changed. Other poets came along to glitter and prompt. The high-water marks, in approximate order, Roethke, Stevens, Crane, Lowell, Hecht, Merrill, Hollander... and, as I say, Auden. These were poets whose writing made me want to write. Their buckets drew up whatever muddy water was in the shallow well. Inevitably, in the process, the water is for a while bucket-shaped, at least until sloppily poured out. These poets were ledges on Parnassus. The point was never to ape a manner, or borrow singing robes many sizes too large. It was to learn what those poets argued with and how, how they lined their silver with cloud. Howard Nemerov, wisest of poets, knew the point was never to worry about having something to say. "Writing," he once observed, "means trying to find out what the nature of things has to say about what you think you have to say." Stevens, Whitman, Proust, Virgil, and Auden are, to my mind, "the nature of things." And each embodies a quality I find lacking in the writing of my contemporaries. Each of them moves across the clear sky like a giant, billowing, driving thunderhead, pinked and purpled, roiling and regal, the blue of habit peeking around its edges. What these writers have is *grandeur*.

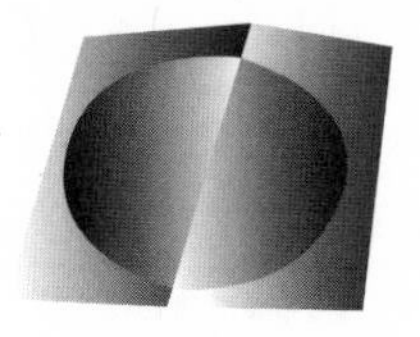

JACQUELINE OSHEROW

Reading Poetry

How explicit can you be about a daydream? That's what my most valued experiences of reading poetry have always been: a certain kind of anchored daydream. There I'll be, following along, in Xanadu, say, or Coole Park, or the third circle of Hell, and some ravishing combination of syllables—they don't even have to have behind them a very profound thought—sends me off in some previously unacknowledged internal direction. I have no idea precisely how it happens. But some piece of me momentarily expands; I become convinced, at least for that instant, that I know something I have never known before about what it's like to be alive on earth. Sometimes it's painful, sometimes it's exhilarating, but it's always—I'm talking, needless to say, about reading great poetry—utterly transforming.

Here: I'll tell a story. It was very early in my experience of genuinely attentive poetry reading, which is probably why I remember it so distinctly. I was a freshman in a Romantic Poetry course. A fairly diligent student, at least when it came to poetry, I generally did what the professor instructed us to do. And so, when he told us to read everything he assigned three times, I assiduously read everything three times. This particular evening my task was to read some poems by the quintessentially famous John Keats, whom I'd been meaning to read for some time. The poem in question was "Ode to a Nightingale." I believe we were meant to read a number of odes, but I can't remember reading any others. Nor can I honestly say that I remember anything at all about my first two readings of "Ode to a Nightingale." It was my homework, I guess, and I was doing it. The poem made no impression on me whatsoever. And then, suddenly, on the third reading, there it was:

> Fade far away, dissolve, and quite forget
> What thou among the leaves hast never known,
> The weariness, the fever, and the fret
> Here, where men sit and hear each other groan;
> Where palsy shakes a few, sad, last grey hairs,
> Where youth grows pale, and spectre-thin, and dies;
> Where but to think is to be full of sorrow
> And leaden-eyed despairs;
> Where Beauty cannot shine her lustrous eyes,
> Or new Love pine at them beyond tomorrow.

The stanza literally—I'm not exaggerating—made me swoon. I suddenly knew, momentarily and forever, that I was doomed, as a living, breathing human being, to infinite sorrow and loss. And I also knew, at the very same time, that I would not be thoroughly destroyed by this horrible reality: infinite sorrow and loss could be—indeed they had already been—if not redeemed, then at least exalted—through poetry. I had studied the history of physics and I was familiar with the medieval alchemists' quests to turn ordinary substances into gold. They had clearly gotten involved in the wrong discipline. Because here was a medium that really could take dross—or worse than dross, human pain—and turn it into something better, even, than gold. What this stanza made clear to me was that the world contained an intensity I had, quite simply, been unaware of—a searing combination of infinite beauty and infinite pain. I was, quite simply, overcome.

I think I read the stanza over and over again for the rest of the evening. Or maybe I called my friends up and read it to them. And, not surprisingly, I found I knew it by heart. I didn't have to learn it: I just knew it, because the words couldn't go any other way. So I've had that stanza of Keats in my life since that time and it has—believe it or not—if not mitigated stretches of intense pain, during which thought and sorrow really were interchangeable, at least provided a sort of exquisite container or outer limit for that pain, and made me know that I was not entirely isolated in its grasp.

It's an odd question to ask myself: what would pain be like without Keats? And truly—the answer to the question just brings up other moments in poetry: if there were no Keats in my head, I'd perhaps just sit and wait for the "formal feeling" that Emily Dickinson assures us comes "after great pain," for my nerves to "sit ceremonious, like Tombs." And I'm certainly not above begging God, along with Gerard Manley Hopkins, to "send my roots rain." If all else fails, there's always "how long, Oh Lord, how long?" Don't misunderstand me. I do not mean to suggest that any line of poetry, however great, can actually make the experience of personal pain less acute. But it can, perhaps, make it less amorphous.

Perhaps this is why I've kept my mouth shut about this for so many years. I actually do believe that with real poetry, everything that matters is at stake. I'm not interested in reading poetry for the sake of writing poetry, or even, for that matter, interpreting poetry, but rather for the sake of living my life. What I'm trying to express is that the store of poetry to which a lifetime of reading has given me access will actually widen or deepen or—who knows?—maybe even exalt the most unsuspecting waking moment. Take a line as seemingly simple and straightforward as "My cradled infant slumbers peacefully" in the midst of the "strange and extreme silentness" of "Frost at Midnight." There it is: the even breathing of a sleeping baby, all those lulling *l* sounds. How does Coleridge do it—a profound silence made even more silent by sound? I can't tell you how many times in the middle of the night, when I finally got a baby back to sleep, the resonance of that seemingly straightforward line in my head would make the newly quiet air in the now still room something like a thousand times more—to use Coleridge's own adjective—"sweet" to me. Not only was the peace more, to use another of his words, "extreme," it was also infused with that delirious sense of possibility which Coleridge experiences in the middle of the night with his own sleeping baby; I was also hearing—in that one line—my favorite phrases from the poem's final stanza: "heard only the trances of the blast," "the eavesdrop's fall," "quietly shining to the quiet moon." How did all of these sublime sounds get into the even breathing of my daughter's sleep?

I imagine that some readers of this essay will take pity on me. How sad it sounds—doesn't it?—from one point of view at least, that I can't seem to make the most of my life without someone else's words to give it back to me. All I can say is that I would be bereft without echoes in my ears, or, at the very least, impoverished. Perhaps my way of letting poems intensify my life is a cousin to that old theory—is it in vogue these days or not?—that words actually enable us to have consciousness of the phenomena they name: that we don't fully experience something until we have a word for it. What I'm suggesting is that the more refined or elaborate or concentrated the word, the more refined or elaborate or concentrated the experience. And, so, why wouldn't it follow that if we have a magical or sublime grouping of words, we'll be let into the secret magic or sublimity of what might otherwise have passed us by as an ordinary minute? How many minutes do we really have the energy or illumination to examine, to their fullest, on our own? And how many others will thoroughly elude us, while we're caught up in all our own finicky investigations?

Am I lazy? Perhaps I am. But I remain utterly delighted to let Mandelstam and Chaucer and Petrarch and King David do a little of my investigating for me. Actually, what most amazes me, now that I think of it, is that I don't just let them and their ilk do all of it. Why, when they've all clearly done it so brilliantly, am I so hellbent on doing a little of it on my own? This, too, I think, has something to do with the experience of reading poetry. It happens to me even now; I'll be reading—oh, who knows, anything at all, *Astrophel and Stella*, *Don Juan*, Akhmatova's *Requiem*—and I'll realize that I don't want to be just reading anymore, that I want to be part of the conversation. I'll really want to talk to these people, or, if not actually talk to them, at least enter into that heady space where a person might attempt—even for the benefit of no ear at all—to engage in that sort of expression. At times in my life, when, in poems, I've actually addressed great poets or the moon, or God, or any of a number of very, very questionable listeners, I actually believed—on some goofy poetic level—that I really could address them. Not that I thought they'd hear me—I'm not that goofy—but rather that this other realm of expression actually existed; imagine, if you will, an infinitely low-tech cyberspace, involving no machinery or phone lines or ethernet connections. Laugh if you like, but there *is* a realm of poetry in which you have access not merely across geography, but chronology and materiality and, if you're really cooking, language itself.

Something happens to a voice when it attempts to pitch itself across such impossible distances. It becomes, among other things, absurdly fearless; it honestly imagines that it might produce something worthwhile. It doesn't stop to wonder whether it dare actually say the things it says. It just presses forward, saying them. Later on, of course, you feel sheepish and full of doubts, but nonetheless you keep working on it, refining it, because there's something about it, even if it does make you nervous, that you just won't let yourself abandon. You know it isn't as good as the stuff that's moved you, but it is, at least, a little beyond you. Which is, you suddenly realize, all along, the very place you intended to go. And of course there's always the hope that it's better than you think it is, that someone else will read it, and then for some reason—maybe even because a teacher told her to—read it again. And then again. And before she realizes, she'll know it by heart. And a year or two later, she'll be walking down the street, or staring into space, or trying to put a baby to bed in the middle of the night, and suddenly a collection of syllables you yourself once put together will, with no warning, come back to her. . . .

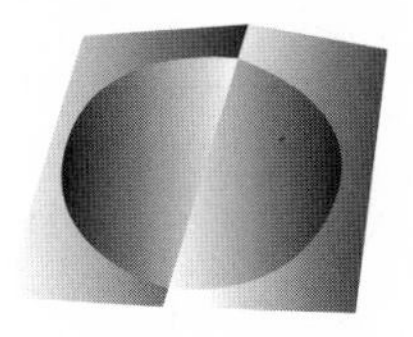

ALBERT GOLDBARTH

First Principle

In one of those strokes of serendipitous luck that thrive on lively browsing, I was reading in some astronomy journal of seven or eight years back about the guesses on whether our universe is boundaried (*yes*, and eventually it collapses; *no*, and it keeps expanding forever); and that same day I wound up discovering this in a supermarket tabloid: "Outrage! College S & M Club Funded By Taxpayers!" There's a photo above that article of two students sitting cross-legged over a spread of fetishy straps and a mini-ankle-fettered Barbie, the way that, somewhere else, two students might be applying themselves to the greenishly fuming vials of their chemistry lab.

It's a state university: public money. State Assemblyman John McEneny is quoted as saying, "There will be substantial [and then this *wonderful* phrasing] backlash from this, I guarantee it."

So do I. I understand some people will see this funky club as inappropriate to the image of, and extraneous to the mission of, an institution of higher education. Still, "university spokeswoman Lisa James Goldsberry" makes apt sense: "As long as they abide by the student guidelines, they're just another club as far as we're concerned." Our "founding fathers" boarding the *Mayflower* probably didn't seem any more unusual to their British Christian contemporaries than these few bondage apprentices seem to Assemblyman McEneny's supposedly wrathful constituency.

Boundaries: where, and why, do they get drawn? By whom, and who falls on which side of them? Collapse? Or expand?

This S & M club is one more interesting litmus test for "diversity." Will the members and supporters of the Students of Color Alliance, and the Campus-wide Special Olympics Club, and the Single Working Parents Association extend their organizational goodwill to their new, whip-wielding peers? And when, and to what extent, does consideration of "quality" supersede a university's commitment to "diversity," since of course the two are not the same and may, in a given arena, be at odds?

From here, a thousand other sticky questions pop their wormheads out of the opened can. If it breaks no city, state, or county laws, should a university campus accommodate meetings of a nudist club? And which is most "diverse" for the mission appropriate to a creative writing program: a poetry faculty of one black formalist poet and one white formalist poet? Or, for example, one white formalist poet and one white experimentalist poet? Or what does it mean for your local bookstore to celebrate "Banned Books Week," but not tolerate *Outlaw Biker* or *Lesbian Witch* on its periodicals shelves?

These kinds of very American questions, all of them coated with thorns and difficult adhesive, circle intriguingly about what is, I trust you understand by now, my own self-set First Principle: *Read Everything*.

Its breakdown specifics are few, but important. 1): I mean *everything*: the put-together instructions for a cheap toy from Taiwan; the whole of Dante. *Penthouse*, *Cosmo*, Lucretius's *On the Nature of Things*. *Vanity Fair* the novel AND the ooh-so-chi-chi magazine. *Both* invisible men. Tates: Allen; James. William Burroughs; Edgar Rice. The out-of-print and the in-your-face. The sacred; the slutty. Everything. (It *can't* be done. But it can't be stopped.) 2): You do this out of passion. You'd *pay* to do it: you *need* to do it: you aren't *complete* unless you do it. And you don't read out of obligation, you don't read to construct a "career." You *seek* it; you aren't "assigned" it. 3): If 2 is true for you (and it's something that of course can't be forced), then 1 takes care of itself. 4): There isn't any "canon." But there is, however, greatness—rarely, but really—and you can't be conned by fly-by-night tastes or political concerns into sanctioning substitutes for greatness. 5): You honor that greatness, and feel properly humble before it. (You always remember what it takes to write out *Bleak House* in full with a quill pen, sitting in formal clothes in a room and a time before electricity. Nobody *I* know could even *transcribe* it that way, much less create it.) 6): But you keep your standards; you don't feign rapt delight in encountering horseshit. 7): You're open, over time, to reconsidering what you mean by "greatness" and "horseshit." 8): Except there *isn't* "time"; or not, at least, in the realm of literary reading. All great writing is naturally contemporary with all great writing. 9): If it's available on paper—*real* paper, that turns, that's real pages, no e-paper, blip-paper, cyberpaper—*that's* the way you read it, and you'll go out of your way to do so. 10): You help shore up the structures of access and freedom that allow 1 through 9: you buy at bookstores; browse the local library resale shop; subscribe to magazines; and avidly support free speech rights, even (maybe *especially*) when you disagree with a certain opinion or lifestyle or vocabulary. 11): My favorite: go back to 1.

There are two things wrong here. All of the above seems *so* prescriptive, that its surface is in conflict with the spirit of its substance. And all of it (truly: every one of those eleven) is *so* obvious, I feel foolish for having written it down.

In Richard Wilbur's wonderful 1969 essay "Poetry and Happiness," one mentioned brand of this everything—what he calls "a primitive desire to lay claim to as much of the world as possible through uttering the names of things," and which we could more basically call cataloguing—is referred to as "a fundamental urge [that] turns up in all reaches of literature." And yet, as this poet rehearses his theme through calling up examples from other poets—Whitman, Hopkins, Roethke, and the gang—we certainly start inferring that a hunger, a *happy* hunger, for inclusiveness may stamp itself upon poetry with a frequency and an avidity that sets it apart from other genres.

This is, I know, an iffy argument; the standard lyric sonnet, range lavishly though it might, is a sparse, sparse thing in the shadow of Rabelais or of *Finnegans Wake*. Still, there's a sort of instinctual rightness to many of Wilbur's scattered assertions. "The poet is . . . moved to designate human life in all its fullness." "One perpetual task of the poet is to produce models of inclusive reaction." "Hart Crane said it was the great task of modern poetry to absorb." I'm reminded of an interview of Kenneth Koch I must have read twenty-five years ago, in an issue of *Field*. Talking about his long poem "Ko," he said he'd wanted to get every pleasure he knew of into its text, and so was disappointed the smell of the roller coaster at a Cincinnati amusement park—a "pied beauty" if ever there was one—got left out.

Not that I'm saying a poet whose scope of reading is wide must clutter her lines with welter, flotsam, bobbing kitchen sinks. The tersely sculptural work of Jack Gilbert, Linda Gregg, Lorine Niedecker, Harvey Shapiro, Louise Glück—five of endless possibilities—draws strength from strategies other than compilation. There's an allure to Bashō that's not to be found in *The Faerie Queene* or "Absalom and Achitophel."

And yet, and yet.... Dickinson's exquisitely balled-up poems, for all of their modest physical compass, signal to us that they exist inside of—*feed on*—a very large web of awarenesses. (A small poem isn't a synonym for the smallness of its maker's life.) Surely when, in the early days, she was submitting her poems to *Harper's*, she was *reading* the whole of those issues, all of their politics, arts reporting, gossip—and not submitting her work the way I sometimes see my students doing, mailing off to the journals of various marketplace lists without ever having read them out of sheer (and please allow this oxymoron) disinterested interest. I have a photograph of my old friend the poet David Clewell sitting reading a book on top of a pedestal that bears this plaque: When the Choice Is a Meal or a Book, I Can Go Hungry.

And I've seen his personal library, from its Shakespeare to its 1930s pamphlets of magic tricks and its tracts for flying saucer contact groups. If every title there indeed were a meal, his house would look like the fabled land where hams grow on trees, and cheeses bloom like dandelions, and rivers of rich cream slowly flow through hills of the purest chocolate.

Moments also come, I'd have to admit, when it feels foolish to try and steer a life through the dotcom waters of year 2003 by the compass of my First Principle. Sometimes these days, when a shipment of books arrives at the house ("I *ordered* these? *No* way. Oh...I remember, now"), I think of those rivalrous theories (something like a boxing match: *Cosmic Collapse versus Cosmic Expansion!*) with which I began this essay. I like rereading those serious, furious debates in which the universe was alternately squeezed in and then pulled out, like an accordion.

And I wish the universe better luck than Planet Albert currently has. There's no more room for expansion here, and each new book only sorely contracts the space that remains. There are days when it looks as if one more vintage paperback (where *can* my near-mint, lurid *Dante's Sinferno* go?) will fill the only vacancy left, and any book after that will need to be strapped to my Nissan's fender.

There are many books in the last few years—it seems to me more than ever—that celebrate just such bibliophilic sick pleasures as mine. I'm thinking, for example, of *A Gentle Madness* by Nicholas Basbanes, a wonderfully anecdotal, in-depth survey of book collecting (both sober and maniacal) over the centuries; and *The Book on the Bookshelf* by Henry Petroski, the history (by an engineer) of library shelving. Any linger in a bookstore will easily turn up further examples; often the cover art is an antique engraving or woodcut, or a photograph of spines of what are clearly old (used/rare/gilt-decorated) editions. You might think that it makes me happy—this sudden flurry of praise for the book. But the essence of a eulogy is also praise, and I'm afraid that's what the flurry is all about: swan songs from an industry that's e-booking its own product into oblivion. All of those Palm Pilots, waving good-bye.

It always happens, this sudden and last-minute fascinated focus on what's disappearing. Endangered animals; quilting bees; old-time burlesque; the pinball machine . . . they all have their books, from the days of their sun's setting. And now the book on the book (I mean, of course, the book on the real-deal paper, printed thing) is bringing that list to its close. A celebration of the book?—well, yes, it's that. But it's also a mourning. A *kaddish* industry.

Obviously I hope I'm wrong. But a lot—*a lot*—of money and fear and greed and techno-expertise is betting on the silicon chip and the screen; on dividing "authority" from the "author"; on having sidebars and MTV-image-barrage take over the work of the writerly word. And, face it: primacies dwindle away. The future *needs* to eat the present. There's no chronological version of being "vegan"; time gets gobbled up. "Sometimes these days, when a shipment of books arrives...," I said a few paragraphs back, but a "ship" is no part of my orders' delivery, any more than the flashing digital watches that my students wear move "clockwise."

I think it's my job to keep this seminal change from happening too swiftly. I think it's my job to steward a sanctuary for books. They're crammed; but, hey: at least they're here. I think it's your job, too. If this might be the age of the book's demise... well, demisery loves company. As Elton John says, "it's lonely out in space."

And speaking of rocket men.... In the early 1940s the pulp sci-fi adventure magazine *Captain Future* had its loyal fans. The eponymous space-zooming hero *did* go out to the universe's expanding rim, as if his superscience had conquered infinity itself. In the Winter 1944 issue, one reader wrote in: "I have an invalid father and an ailing mother to care for and it's up to me to look after everything, besides performing heavy manual labor on my railroad job. Without *Captain Future*, my life would be dreary, gloomy and lonely indeed."

But that letter appeared in the final issue. Not too long after, the pulps ALL were dead. We had entered a different future.

I'm not trying to suggest that reading a full run of those fine, flawed 1940s sci-fi escapist epics will help provide clear answers to the mess of questions I was listing earlier (Cap and his spaceship crew, so deft in dealing with outer space skullduggery, can only scratch their bubble-helmeted heads in consternation at the problem of the nudist club). But out of those zap-pow titles, and the thousands of Biblicopornocontempohistoricoscientificophilosophicofrivoloserioabsolutelyfantastico titles surrounding them, a scene I cherish does rise forth:

A great old-fashioned masted ship is finally landed, after months of voyaging. Its pilgrims row to shore: some actually kiss the shore in a sign of thanksgiving. Liberty! A new home! They feel blessed. And then they unpack their sacred objects: Ken in a tiny leather hood, Barbie in teensy handcuffs.

They have finally arrived in a place so large and commodious, it's one thing that holds *every* thing, equally. That's the "one" we find in "uni"-verse. Theoretically, in "uni"-versity, too.

I like to think it might also be a sweet and viable definition of any of my friends' bookshelves.

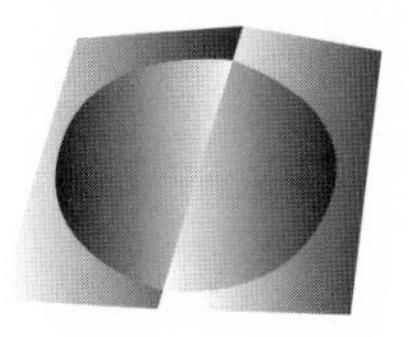

MARY RUEFLE

Someone Reading a Book Is a Sign of Order in the World

When I was forty-five years old, I woke up on an ordinary day, neither sunny nor overcast, in the middle of the year, and I could no longer read. It was at the beginning of one of those marvelous sentences that only Nabokov can write: "Mark felt a sort of delicious pity for the frankfurters. . . ." In my vain attempts I made out *felt hat, prey, the city of Frankfort*. But the words that existed so I might read them sailed away, and I was stranded on a quay while everything I loved was leaving. And then it was I who was leaving: a terror seized me and took me so high up in its talons that I was looking helplessly down on a tiny, unrecognizable city, a city I had loved and lived in but would never see again. I needed reading glasses, but before I knew that, I was far far away.

♦

The book I was reading I was rereading. Because some time before that terrible day I had reached a juncture in my reading life that is familiar to those who have been there: in the allotted time left to me on earth, should I read more and more new books, or should I cease with that vain consumption—vain because it is endless—and begin to reread those books which had given me the intensest pleasure in my past, books I had all but forgotten in their details, but loved in the shadows they cast over me, the moods created by the very thoughts of them. And there was curiosity, too, the curiosity of revisiting and remeeting. Some gigantic memory might strike me as being rather small in the flesh, or the altogether unremembered might strike me dead at a glance. It is not like returning to places; we don't find ourselves, in the fourth chapter of *Madame Bovary*, searching for the bakery that is no longer there. Our curiosity is always self-directed: have *I* changed? Do I still love the Makioko sister who has diarrhea on the train in the last sentence? *Is* that the last sentence? Was I too young when I read Proust?

I read Proust when I was in my twenties. I rationed that novel by reading one volume a year. I had a friend whose father was a man of letters, and he had said that once you read Proust there was no reason ever to read again, you had reached the end of reading, and as I was young and respected him enormously, I was afraid to finish that book, my incessant and increasing love for it was all wrapped up in this grotesque fear that my inner life was coming to an end before it had even begun. Which was correct. That's the cookie, isn't it? As for the larger statement—that once you read Proust there is no reason to read again—I found that, like most things, it was both true and untrue.

♦

Is there a right time to read each book? A point of developing consciousness that corresponds with perfect ripeness to a particular poet or novel? And if that is the case, how many times in our lives did we make the match? I heard someone say, at a party, that D. H. Lawrence should be read during one's late teens and early twenties. Since I was nearing thirty at the time, I made up my mind never to read him. And I never have. Connoisseurs of reading are very silly people. But as Thomas Merton said, one day you wake up and realize religion is ridiculous and that you will stick with it anyway. What love is ever any different?

There was one book I read not only at the right age, but on the right afternoon, in the right place, at the right angle. I read *The Waves* on an island, on a plotless day, when I was twenty-two years old, sitting on a terrace from which I could see in the distance the ocean, and the horizon where it met the sky and the changing light that played there as the sun climbed to its zenith and descended again while I thumbed the pages and my blood pressure washed up and down with the words. *The Waves* is not one of my favorite books. But my memory of reading it is. I was very silly when I was young. I have that to be thankful for.

I was very serious when I was in high school. I must have been, for my two memorable reading experiences from that time are very serious indeed. Both of them took place, of all places, in the classroom. Some English periods we were assigned to simply sit and read silently. We were reading *The Return of the Native* (or was it *The Mayor of Casterbridge?*), our silent minds on different pages. I was not in the classroom of course; I was in Wessex. And there came the inevitable Wessexian moment: a letter, *the* letter, *the one that would make everything okay*, in the act of being slipped under a closed door, got wedged under the carpet on the other side, where no one would see it. This was awful. What happened then I could not foresee: my arm threw the book as hard as it could across the quiet room. Mrs. Pacquette asked me to explain myself. All I could do was stammer that it was *awful, awful, awful.* She supposed I meant the book. I did not. I meant the thing that was going to happen in the book, because no one was going to read the letter. Therefore I was not going to read the book. In retrospect I see that even then I was engaged in the mirrored erotics of this compulsive activity, reading. Hardy grew up to be one of my beloveds, as did Kafka, to whom it happened next. "The Burrow" was in one of our textbooks. As the class sat reading silently, the silence seemed different. I was infuriated by my inability to understand what was happening in the story. What was happening? Deep inside myself I could not believe that anyone else was actually reading. I was convinced that a mistake had been made, that the printing plates—for I pictured them as such—had gotten smashed and all mixed up. There was a mistake. Was I the only one who noticed? Hadn't the teachers bothered to read the story? Their secret was out! There was a very special kind of attention that only I was able to pay to the story—it was absurd. And then I had a moment of doubt. *Who wrote this?* Perhaps *he* was the mistake, and not the story. I sat in the silent classroom and I heard all kinds of things—I heard the non-ticking clock tick, and the sweat beginning to form on my body, and the window glass was about to break into pieces. The pencil sharpener on the wall was salivating. I flipped to the back of the book where there were brief paragraphs about each of the authors, who they were, where they came from, what they wrote. Yes, I was certain now, the mistake was not in the story, but in its author. There was a mistake in the man. There had to be a mistake in the man because I was told where and when he wrote but not *why*. And of all the stories in our book, this was the one that remained starved and unfed unless I learned *why* he wrote it at all. I decided to hate the author. I decided to hate the author because he made me feel as if all my life I had been waiting for something to happen, and it was happening and it was not going to happen. It was many years before I understood that this was the secret labyrinth of reading, and there was a secret tunnel connecting it to my life.

I find nothing in my life that I can't find more of in books. With the exception of walking on the beach, in the snowy woods, and swimming underwater. That is one of the saddest journal entries I ever made when I was young.

Reading is hazardous. Here is a true story that proves it: a Chinese student, having read *The Scarlet Letter*, saw an American in China wearing a high-school letter jacket with the letter *A* on the front and said, *I know what that means.*

Hazardous even to the initiated: recently I was reading the notebooks of the Greek poet George Seferis (1900–1971). I was also reading, for the first and last time in my life, my own private journals, which I began writing when I was sixteen and ceased to write when I was forty. As is my habit, I was copying selected passages from the Seferis into a notebook. Later that evening I began reading a journal I kept twenty years ago. In it, I was reading the notebooks of the poet George Seferis (1900–1971) and had copied into the journal by hand my favorite passage, which was identical with the passage I had copied earlier in the day, believing completely that I had never encountered it before: *But to say what you want to say you must create another language and nourish it for years & years with what you have loved, with what you have lost, and with what you will never find again.*

> "Altogether, I think we ought to read only books that bite and sting us. If the book we are reading doesn't shake us awake like a blow to the skull, why bother reading it in the first place? So that it can make us happy, as you put it? Good God, we'd be just as happy if we had no books at all; books that make us happy we could, in a pinch, write ourselves. What we need are books that hit us like a most painful misfortune, like the death of someone we loved more than we love ourselves, that make us feel as though we had been banished to the woods, far away from any human presence, like a suicide. A book must be the ax for the frozen sea within us. That is what I believe." —Kafka in a letter, 1904

> "What kind of book would that dazzling human animal Consuelo sit down to read after she had finished wiping the blood off her hands and hidden once more her machete in the piano?" —Stevens in a letter, 1948

There was an anthology, a fat Bantam paperback with a glossy white cover (like the White Album) and something like an abstracted dove embossed on it, called *Modern European Poetry*, and it was mine, my joy and my solace when I was in high school; whatever problems I had with Hardy and Kafka in the classroom vanished in the solitude of my bedroom, which I shared with Rilke, Lorca, Montale, Éluard, Ritsos—everybody was in that book, I didn't have another book I loved half so much. I must have read it a hundred times, and then I grew up, and went out into the world, and promptly lost it.

◆

I've often thought in acting classes they should make the actors perform scenes in which they are simply reading. And I've wondered what subtle—or remarkable—differences there might be between the outward appearance of reading different books. Early Tolstoy versus late Tolstoy might be an advanced assignment . . . that kind of thing. Or would they all appear the same? The outward idleness, almost slumbering, that does nothing to convey the inner activity, whether it be reverie, shock, hilarity, confusion, grief. We don't often watch people very closely when they read, though there are many famous paintings of women reading (none that I know of of men) in which a kind of quiet eroticism takes place, like that of nursing. Of course, it is we who are being nursed by the books, and then I think of the reader asleep, the open book on his or her chest.

I don't know what my face conveyed while I was reading *The Seven Pillars of Wisdom* by T. E. Lawrence. It takes place in the desert and I read it in front of a woodstove during a four-day blizzard. I suppose it is very odd that I single this book out instead of, say, Lautréamont's *Les Chants de Maldoror*, an equally violent, anguished book, but I do. I've always defended *Pillars* as an unspeakable achievement in literature and disorder. In blood and displacement and an English lost in sand. Read only the first chapter and you will have read the human fate, "the implanted crookedness of things." I am exaggerating of course. Like a book.

There is a world which poets cannot seem to enter. It is the world everybody else lives in. And the only thing poets seem to have in common is their yearning to enter this world.

◆

For years I planned a theoretical course called "Footnotes." In it, the students would read a footnoted edition of a definitive text—I thought it might as well be *The Notebooks of Malte Laurids Brigge*—and proceed diligently to read every book mentioned in the footnotes (or the books by those authors mentioned) and in turn all those mentioned in the footnotes of the footnoted books, and so on and so on, stopping only when one was led back, by a footnote, to *The Notebooks of Malte Laurids Brigge*.

> "The burrow has probably protected me in more ways than I thought or dared to think while I was inside it. This fancy used to have such a hold over me that sometimes I have been seized by the childish desire never to return to the burrow again, but to settle down somewhere close to the entrance, to pass my life watching the entrance, and gloat perpetually upon the reflection—and in that find my happiness—how steadfast a protection my burrow would be if I were inside it."
>
> —Kafka, "The Burrow"

I had recently one of the most astonishing experiences of my reading life. On page 248 in *The Rings of Saturn*, W. G. Sebald is recounting his interviews with one Thomas Abrams, an English farmer who has been working on a model of the temple of Jerusalem—you know, gluing little bits of wood together—for twenty years, including the painstaking research required for historical accuracy. There are ducks on the farm and at one point Abrams says to Sebald, "I have always kept ducks, even as a child, and the colors of their plumage, in particular the dark green and snow white, seemed to me the only possible answer to the questions that are on my mind." It is an odd thing to say, but Sebald's book is a long walk of oddities.

I did not remember this passage in particular until later the same day when I was reading the dictionary, where I came upon the meaning of the word *speculum*: 1) an instrument inserted into a body passage for inspection; 2) an ancient mirror; 3) a medieval compendium of all knowledge; 4) a drawing showing the relative position of all the planets; and 5) a patch of color on the secondary wings of most ducks and some other birds. Did Sebald know that a compendium of all knowledge and the ducks' plumage were one and the same? Did Abrams? Or was I the only one for whom the duck passage made perfect, original sense? I sat in my chair, shocked. I am not a scholar, but for the imaginative reader there can be discoveries, connections between books, that explode the day and one's heart and the long years that have led to the moment. I am a writer, and the next step is inevitable: I used what had been revealed to me in my own writing.

We are all one question, and the best answer seems to be love—a connection between things. This arcane bit of knowledge is respoken every day into the ears of readers of great books, and also appears to perpetually slip under a carpet, utterly forgotten. In one sense, reading is a great waste of time. In another sense, it is a great extension of time, a way for one person to live a thousand and one lives in a single life span, to watch the great impersonal universe at work again and again, to watch the great personal psyche spar with it, to suffer affliction and weakness and injury, to die and watch those you love die, until the very dizziness of it all becomes a source of compassion for ourselves, and our language, which we alone created, and without which the letter that slipped under the door could never have been written, or, once in a thousand lives—is that too much to ask?—retrieved, and read. Did I mention supreme joy? That is why I read: I want everything to be okay. That's why I read when I was a lonely kid and that's why I read now that I'm a scared adult. It's a sincere desire, but a sincere desire always complicates things—the universe has a peculiar reaction to our sincere desires. Still, I believe the planet on the table, even when wounded and imperfect, fragmented and deprived, is worthy of being called whole. Our minds and the universe—what else is there? Margaret Mead described intellectuals as those who are bored when they don't have the chance to talk interestingly enough. Now a book will talk interestingly to you. George Steiner describes the intellectual as one who can't read without a pencil in her hand. One who wants to talk back to the book, not take notes but make them: one who might write "The giraffe speaks!" in the margin. In our marginal existence, what else is there but this voice within us, this great weirdness we are always leaning forward to listen to?

In the 2001 Kentucky Derby, which I watched live on television, Keats ran against Invisible Ink. There was no way I was going to miss this race. But I waited in vain for one of the sportscasters to mention that Keats was an English poet whose only surviving descendants must live in Kentucky, where his older brother had immigrated, remained healthy, and had children, and I waited in vain for someone to mention the poet's famous epitaph—*Here lies one whose name was writ in water*—and its curious connection to Invisible Ink. In all the network, that great kingdom of connection, what had been read or remembered? It was as sad as a horse's eye. Keats lost. Invisible Ink placed third, but had he been second, he would have showed.

Against the Grain. Nightwood. The Dead. Notes from Underground. Fathers and Sons. Eureka. The Living. The Marriage of Heaven and Hell. The Sun Also Rises. My Little Home. Venus in

Transit. The Wings of the Dove. The Journal of an Understanding Heart. Wuthering Heights. One Hundred Years of Solitude. Triste Tropiques. The Tale of Gengi. Black Sun. Deep Ocean Organisms Which Live Without Light. The Speeches of a Dictator. The Fundamentals of Farming. The Physics of Lift. A Complete History of Alchemy. Opera for Idiots. Letters from Elba. For Esmé With Love and Squalor. The Walk. The Physiology of Drowning. The Physician's Desk Reference. Bleak House. The Gospel According to Thomas. A Biography of Someone You've Never Heard Of. Forest Management. Black Lamb and Grey Falcon. Travels in Deserta Arabia. The Collected Works of Paul Valéry. A Book Written in A Language You Do Not Understand. Withdrawn. The Worst Journey In The World. The Greatest Story Ever Told. A Guide To Simple First Aid.

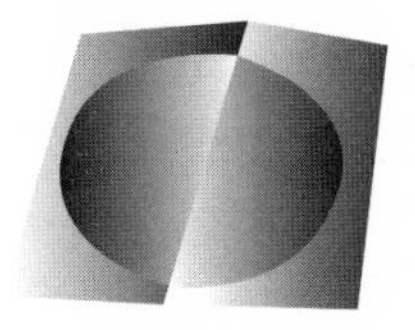

CARL PHILLIPS

Another and Another Before That: Some Thoughts on Reading

One way to look at reading: as the lifelong construction of a map by which to trace and plumb what it has ever meant to be in the world, and by which to gain perspective on that other, ongoing map—the one that marks our own passage through the world as we both find and make it.

If all we can ever know comes filtered through the lens of our own experience, and if we are readers, some part of our very selves will be the result of what we have read—this is obvious enough. Good writers not only have read widely and deeply, but they continue to do so—not in order to be better writers, but because for them the act of reading is as inseparable from living as writing is.

As for the fear that, by reading the great work that has come before, one's own original voice will either be influenced away from itself or overwhelmed into utter silence: an original voice can perhaps half-willingly be seduced; it is rarely mastered.

At the moment, I'm writing from a public library at one end of Cape Cod, very much like the library where I worked for three years of high school at the Cape's other end. It was there that, in the course of shelving books, I saw a book called *The Joy of Sex*; no sooner did I open the book than I dropped it, half in shock at a picture I'd seen, and half terrified I'd be seen by the head librarian and fired immediately, on the grounds of—what? Then I picked the book back up—

It was also in that library that I came across the selected poems of a man named Auden. I took the book from the shelf for how the name sounded—or I imagined it should—like "autumn." What brought me to check out the book were these lines to which it instantly fell open: "Lay your sleeping head, my love / human on my faithless arm. . . ."

I knew nothing about Auden's sexuality—and it would be almost twenty years before I entirely understood my own. But in "Lullaby" I first encountered what, for me, was then just as radical a notion: that love and faithlessness were not necessarily exclusive of one another, and that flaw did not always equal ruin. This can't have been the first time it occurred to me that "normal" was a vexed and relative term, and that there might be the possibility of another way to see almost anything; but this is one time I've not forgotten.

If it is true that what we read helps shape us, just as true is that our choices in reading are the result of our sensibility—teachers aside, who we are is a major force in shaping a personal canon. Back to *The Joy of Sex* and my encounter with Auden's poems: another person would never have picked up the former, simply because of the book's title; and Auden's poem might have bored a different teenage reader.

My father was a career Air Force man; this, for me, meant being raised to understand that for any situation in a life, there was a fixed—because correct—way to conduct oneself. The highly controlled environment of a military base only helps to reinforce this lesson, by removing from view any exceptions to established (again, "correct") rules. Sure, there are newspapers, but the only one that I recall seeing in our household, until my father retired, was the *Stars and Stripes*, a newspaper written and published by the military, and distributed weekly at bases around the world. It is possible to live on an Air Force base and never know that the Summer of Love is occurring outside it, that riots are brewing at a place called Stonewall. Possible, that is, unless you go to the library, where books seemed to have escaped the notice of military censors. I remember reading a book of ancient Greek poems in translation: there was Archilochus, saying he'd rather hide his shield behind a bush and run away from the fighting—and proud to say so. There was Sappho, a woman, speaking of her sexual desire for another woman—not only not afraid to say so, but apparently not even aware that she *should* be afraid.

A military upbringing also means constant travel—it seemed we moved every year, always in the middle of the school year, always therefore the awkwardness of trying to fit in, in the midst of things, both socially and academically. Whenever we moved, my books came with me, and I know that part of the role of reading became one of finding comfort: my world might have changed, but to reread *Tom Sawyer* or *The Call of the Wild* was to know the pleasures of stability, of being able to step back into a world that had given pleasure, and have my bearings—to know everyone already, as it were, in the room. A portable world to keep with me in the midst of traveling always—which is exactly what writing would become.

◆

Writing has always been for me an entirely private act—I don't share poems with other writers, I've no particular interest in having my work workshopped. Writing is one of the few spaces where I can be alone and not be questioned as to why or how I choose to be myself. Reading has also been that, from the start. I think it's true to say that, through childhood, the one thing I most looked forward to was being permitted to go upstairs to my room and read. Partly it was the privacy itself, but also the chance to see—in books—that it was in fact okay not to love baseball, a boy could lose his dog and cry about it, and often enough there was fantasy, to show that nothing could be called impossible. It turns out, of course, that there are some limits to possibility; but childhood seems the right time not to know this. Books confirm at the least anyone's right to dream.

In the course of reading, a taste gets shaped—for what appeals or doesn't. And a writer's aesthetic gets not so much shaped as informed. I've learned as much about writing from what I don't enjoy as from what I do. Even as joy is understandable finally only after its opposite, too, is known. Moreover, it is by extended acquaintance with both pleasure and pain that we begin to grasp the notion of degrees. And so it is with reading, whereby the self and the writing that comes from that self acquire both dimension and resonance, by the steady increase of which we win the right to exercise that lately suspect thing, authority. We *do* have the right to an opinion because it comes from more than ourselves, from a self that understands its own context within the history of being human, and within that of the literature by which we express being human.

To have read Homer's *Iliad* is not the same as having seen combat. That is, it would not be enough, only to read—that would be experiencing everything via another's experience. Equally, it would be inadequate to know the world only through one's own actual encounters with it. So, balance is important. It is hard to believe that Dickinson never came across the subject of death in her reading; and certainly she had seen more than her share of dying by the time she could say—and mean—"I like a look of agony."

Range is important. Often, young poets want most to know which poets they should be reading—and yet, any poet worth reading probably read everything that came to hand, out of that insatiable desire to know, that curiosity that makes us want to grapple with the irresolvable and/or memorable and transcribe it in lines.

What I most remember of deep winter, 1983, is that I read all of Milton's prose and poetry (in English, anyway) and—yes, from cover to cover—*The Joy of Cooking*. Some small part of a self is surely changed for having learned the best method for skinning a squirrel and having read the *Areopagitica* in roughly the same space of time.

Everything counts. I've no intention of canceling my subscription to *People* magazine any more than I'd stop getting *The New York Times* each morning.

I don't think there are any "shoulds" in the case of reading—that would lead to the usual thorniness of literary canons. Sure, I find it difficult to imagine writing—or indeed reading in an informed manner—without knowledge of classical mythology, say, or some grounding in the Old Testament; but another might say as much about the *Bhagavad-Gita*, which I have yet to read.

There is nothing wrong with asking for reading suggestions, so long as that request doesn't really mask a desire to have a sort of blueprint provided—an instinct which I fear writing programs tend to encourage, perhaps unintentionally: this notion that there is a "way," a structured means by which to become a writer, as if officially. As I say to my students, craft is teachable, vision is not. To read is to get a sense of the many ways in which vision has manifested itself in the past and continues to do so. We are wasting our time, though, if we believe that we shall thereby gain access to our own vision.

Also, asking what to read in order to be a good writer is rather like asking someone, "What should I do, in order to know life well?" The answer is obvious, to me at least: do all that you can do and care to do. Thankfully, there's no one model for any of this—it leaves the possibilities refreshingly, thrillingly wide open.

As far as I've been able to figure out, the truest—the most genuine, *authentic*—poem is the result of a consciousness articulating itself *as only that particular consciousness can*. Afterward, in the wake of that first making, there are the countless and usual "rules" to account for. That's where craft enters the picture. But the applications of craft must ultimately be governed by consciousness itself; each consciousness, over time (experience, again) incorporates those rules of craft—speaks to and away from the rules—in such a way as to produce on paper the authentic, the poem that is unique to that consciousness alone.

Those rules of which I speak are written down, but each time differently, in everything we read. The task of the writer, then, is hardly easy; but very clear.

Asked what I consider required reading for a writer, I can only say it depends, and is different for every writer. What I offer here is less a list of what to read than an idiosyncratic gathering of those writers who have had an influence on me as a writer and human being in general. This doesn't always have entirely to do with quality, but with timing and need on the reader's part. James White's *The Salt Ecstasies* is a lovely but uneven book—but, of contemporary poems, these were the first I read that spoke with disarming honesty about gay desire, desire generally, sex specifically. I myself had not come out yet, and had barely begun writing poems. White's was a crucial voice to encounter, for what it confirmed as possible—longing, homosexual longing, the expression of that longing in a poem. I think it's arguable that Dante's *Inferno* is better literature, but Dante couldn't have given me what White did.

As interesting, to me, as the writers we read is how we come to know of those writers in the first place. James White's book was in the bargain barn in back of a favorite bookstore in Falmouth, Massachusetts. White's book was a dollar, and poetry, and a strangely ordinary blue—and the title poem was stirring.

The poet Alan Dugan, after reading an early poem of mine, said: "If you haven't read Cavafy yet, you should." I did. And then read everything of Dugan's.

But when it comes to classical literature, I think I have to credit a book (yes, reading again!) that I bought through the Scholastic Book Club, with which most elementary schools were affiliated when I was growing up—the chance for every student in the class to order a book a month at a discounted rate. My parents agreed I could have the book on codes and code-breaking, which led to my spending a year inventing codes of my own. The following year, we were stationed in Germany; to me, German was a code, so it became the first foreign language I ever studied. A few years later, back in the States, I enrolled in a school where German wasn't offered—but there was room, still, for one more student in the beginning Latin course.

Thus began an interest in classical literature that would lead to my getting a degree in Classics and teaching Latin for almost ten years.

And thus, while I wasn't thinking about it, began the development of a sensibility and aesthetic that would end up marking as uniquely mine the poems I would, years away, start writing.

Greek lyric—Mimnermus, Alcman, Alcaeus, Anacreon, and particularly Sappho and Archilochus: I continue to admire the ability of those poets to waste no time in locating the precise point of human vulnerability, and to sing that vulnerability into a great openness. Though many of their poems are short because of manuscript damage and loss over time—that is, not because of a deliberately fragmented style—a single surviving line in many instances can resonate more than do many entire poems; and I think it is from these chance fragments that I learned about the effects of a purposeful fragmentation, as well about brevity and the crucial element of the actual placement of words in a line or in a series of lines. For the same reasons, the choruses of Greek tragedy have also been significant for me—choruses whose relentless winging toward a truth that is unbearable and yet—borne upon flawless meter and rhythm—is unable to be turned away from, is all prefigured in Greek lyric. The choruses are usually complete, so there's less of the brevity of Greek lyric, but there is a similar exactness and a fuller, more measured music.

I am also drawn to and no doubt influenced by the hieratic and vatic qualities of poetry in ancient times, the way in which poetry and the petition and vow of prayer become one. At the same time, there's a mix of familiarity and awe when it comes to the poet's relationship to divinity. Sappho, in addressing Aphrodite, can essentially wonder why the goddess won't give her an even break when it comes to loss and heartache—and yet the poet never loses sight of the superiority of the goddess; she knows that, without the gods, poets would be nothing.

Mary Barnard's translation of Sappho has its inaccuracies—it also has its charms. For Greek lyric more widely, an exciting translation is Guy Davenport's *Seven Greeks*.

From Pindar's *Odes* (the Lattimore translation captures the right muscularity) I learned much about the possibilities of syntax. But more from the prose of Cicero, Tacitus, and Sallust. In the case of Cicero, not only are individual sentences models for how syntax can be manipulated to snare and win permanently one's listener, but it's a great pleasure to read an entire speech for its overall structure—and this is a level on which Cicero can be easily enjoyed in translation: the syntax isn't always easily translated, but the structure is. It was with Cicero that I came to understand how stylized and regimented rhetoric once was—I admire the way in which words evinced an athleticism then that seems less in evidence today.

Between the verblessness of many of their sentences and the asyndeton out of the blue, after some lengthily unfolding sentence has been eloquently, precisely laid before us—these effects in the Roman prose stylists convince me that I learned most from them about the possibilities for surprise in syntax and, by extension, a great deal about the psychology of line break as well.

Frequently, more lessons from prose than from poetry. In many ways, the sentence—the poetic line, as well—is for me a bow astrain; the poem is the arrow whose flight depends so heavily on the bow—and of course on the fletcher's hand behind it. Essential fletchers: Henry James, especially of *The Golden Bowl*; Proust; Virginia Woolf, especially *The Waves*, especially *To the Lighthouse*; George Eliot, who shows how syntax can be made to bear a great weight of intellect without becoming less fluid; Marguerite Yourcenar's *Memoirs of Hadrian*, for how the graces of syntax and sentence structure seem to graph or mirror the grace of memory itself.

The Old Testament (especially Isaiah, Proverbs, and Psalms).

Oh—and the Apocrypha.

Everything by M. F. K. Fisher, but especially the four or five early books published together as *The Art of Eating*. Not for nothing did Auden—who wasn't bad, himself, though I'd easily prefer Fisher—consider her the best prose stylist writing in English.

More poetry, less ancient: Hopkins is near if not at the top of the list—but not just the poems, the sermons and other prose as well. Everything is there in his work—the concern with syntax and rhythm, the classical training, the nexus of sacred and profane, in the later sonnets especially. The conviction wrought of a vision wrung from agony.

The seventeenth-century English poets in general, but Herbert and Donne in particular. Of the former, all of *The Temple*, of course, but also the prose work *A Priest to the Temple*. Of Donne, the *Holy Sonnets*, but also *Sermons on the Psalms and Gospels* and *Devotions upon Emergent Occasions*.

Two essential volumes to which I continue to turn are Williams' *English Renaissance Poetry* and *Poetry of Meditation* by Martz.

Berryman's "Eleven Addresses to Our Lord" in *Love and Fame*.

Yes, I traveled everywhere, for a time, with Plath's *Ariel* in my backpack.

O'Hara—for the dialogue-influenced delivery, the unabashedness of emotion, the sudden poignancy. "Meditations in an Emergency."

"To the Harbormaster." "Music." "Having a Coke with You." "You are Gorgeous and I'm Coming."

For similar reasons, all of James Schuyler's poems—the following a particular favorite:

Suddenly

it's night and Tom
comes in and says,
"It's pouring buckets
out," his blond hair
diamond-dusted with
raindrop fragments.

Everything by Li Po and Tu Fu, but especially those poems in a collection called *Bright Moon, Perching Bird*, translated by Seaton and Cryer. Also persuasive is Young's *Five T'ang Poets*. The old translations of Arthur Waley may or may not be the most accurate—I can't claim to know the poems in the original—but as with Barnard's Sappho, they are charming, and I believe the spirit of the original remains intact.

The wonderful, eerie verbal landscapes of Reverdy—whom I discovered via Frank O'Hara, who mentions buying the poems of Reverdy in his own poem "A Step Away from Them."

A story about my copy of a book I mentioned earlier—Williams' *English Renaissance Poetry*. It was given to me by one of my teachers, Robert Pinsky, who urged me to read the poems included by Fulke Greville. Once I opened the book, I found it had been the copy of Frank Bidart when *he* was a student. Something seems to be getting said here about reading, writing, and how the communion between the two makes possible the continuation of literary tradition.

◆

Five favorite contemporary books that seem to me oddly neglected but from which I continue to learn: Pamela Alexander's *Navigable Waterways*, Linda Gregg's *Too Bright to See*, Peter Klappert's *Lugging Vegetables to Nantucket*, Laura Jensen's *Bad Boats*, and Martha Collins' *The Arrangement of Space*. Pushed to say what I've learned from each, I'd say—respectively: how experiment becomes invention; that sacrifice is most persuasively enacted on the page when brief and with the swiftness of mercy; that play and comedy need not compromise depth of feeling; how to go on sheer nerve because there is no other; about sequencing, that the arrangement of the words is as important as the words themselves.

From Robert Hayden's poetry, I learned that the only obligation of the poet is to write honestly, from that part of identity that is the essence of self past race, sexuality, gender. Which is to say that I see such aspects of identity as simultaneously crucial to and incidental to our individual versions of being human. In Hayden's work, I find everywhere the particular and what transcends it intertwined. Hence, a poem like "Middle Passage" is as much an examination of a moment in racial history as of national history and of the kind of brutality that marks human history more generally. The father in "Those Winter Sundays" is any father, and he is the particular, African-American father who seeks to offer all he can to his sometimes less-than-appreciative son: love, hard generosity, an example both of endurance and of responsibility. What is the color of any of these?

Everything by Jarrell, but especially *The Woman at the Washington Zoo* and *The Lost World*; I've learned so much from him about how syntax and structure can variously enact, mirror, and prefigure psychic crisis.

Also a book he wrote for children—which I still read—called *The Bat Poet*. It says as much about being a bat as about being a poet—there *are* similarities.

And his prose, reminding of a time when reviews were written with unflinching honesty and unabashed intelligence. Integrity, crossed with taste.

H. D. Again, the vatic, the hieratic. A conviction that victory comes in many forms, and that the vision that is poetry is one of them—as she says in *Hermetic Definition*, "where there is Olympia, Delphi is not far." She also understood that all literature is influence, that tradition means a handing down: "the torch was lit from another before you, / and another and another before that. . . ."

The emperor Marcus Aurelius wrote his *Meditations* in the midst of watching his empire get steadily eroded by barbarians. He turns away to the interior of the self not as escapism but as a means of understanding how a self is made: via experience, community (in which friends and foes are equally instructive), and—yes—reading. A kind of guide for the shaping of character, and for the ways in which—to be shaped—we must take advantage of even the least inviting lessons—for instance, those afforded by the example of an empire in shambles. He intended what he wrote to serve as guidance for one of his heirs. His writings have proven to be worthwhile guidance for many heirs since—myself among them.

At one point in the *Meditations*, Marcus Aurelius writes about the body as a corpse, and its life a back and forth one of being carried, and the soul its doomed and small courier. He is more or less quoting, though he doesn't say so, someone else with whom he assumes his reader will be familiar. It was the second century A. D., when to be a reader at all, let alone a writer, was to have read as much as was available. Why should this be any different now? Time, as they always said it would, has passed, and there's considerably more to read than there was back in the second century. But my point is not that we should have read everything. Maybe folly figures somewhere in all of this. If we are genuine readers and writers, we should see squarely the impossibility of reading everything there is to read—and yet, impossibly, we should want to *try*.

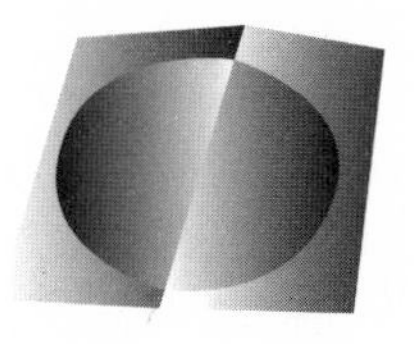

EDWARD HIRSCH

One Life, One Writing: The Middle Generation

It's probably futile to try to speak about them dispassionately, these initiating poems—these first presences—who lodged in me long before I ever understood what they asked of us, these core writers whose work launched so many of us into poetry, who delivered us to our own enchantments, our own imaginative lives. I stumbled across Jarrell's *The Lost World* at about the same time that I discovered Bishop's *Questions of Travel* and Lowell's *For the Union Dead* and Schwartz's *Summer Knowledge*. Soon I had also given myself over to the linguistic richness—the splendid oddities—of Roethke's "The Lost Son" and Berryman's "Homage to Mistress Bradstreet." I used to walk around reciting lines from these poems to myself, daydreaming them, so that they all started to fuse together in my mind. Somehow the farmer who stripped down to a blind wish in

Jarrell's "Field and Forest" merged with the man who decided to become a witch doctor—a *sacaca*—and who went down under the river in Bishop's "The Riverman." Somehow the watchful, feverish writer in Lowell's "Night Sweat" combined with the nameless speaker surveying the shadows in his room in the middle of the night, smoking at the window, in Schwartz's "In the Naked Bed, in Plato's Cave." I still love the invocation to the animals, the primal creatures, at the beginning of Roethke's "The Lost Son." I'm moved by the Blakean suggestion that all that lives is holy. It's an invocation to the Muse, a cry for divine help, that takes us down to the earth. And I still link it to that affecting moment in Berryman's "Homage to Mistress Bradstreet" when the twentieth-century poet declares to the seventeenth-century one, "We are on each other's hands / who care. Both of our worlds unhanded us." Berryman's lines are a statement of lyric interdependency, a recognition that the dramatic poet does not have his meaning unto himself. His need calls out, and he turns for help to a poet from the past. All these poems are in some sense about the urgent necessity—and the cost—of vision. They get down into our bodies, our deep minds. They speak to—*they are*—enchantments that put off the practical world, that estrange us from the familiar and signal the presence of something in us that is deep and demonic, something wild and unruly, irrational, imaginative. We followed these voices into the silken river—the blind wish, the night mind—and ended up giving our lives to the visionary realms they inaugurated.

> *It is like what we imagine knowledge to be:*
> *dark, salt, clear, moving, utterly free. . . .*
> (Elizabeth Bishop, "At the Fishhouses")

It's the dark poetic knowledge—mesmerizing, mobile, free—that we sought from them. It's the human clarities they brought back from the deep. And it's the intensities they proposed, the excitement with which we pored over their poems and took them into ourselves. I remember the wild fervor and exaltation with which I first encountered the vehement, flamboyant, exclamatory lines—"I want the old rage, the lash of primordial milk" (Roethke, "The Lost Son"), and "You know what I was, / You see what I am: change me, change me!" (Jarrell, "The Woman at the Washington Zoo")—and at times almost shouted them aloud:

> You could cut the brackish winds with a knife
> Here in Nantucket, and cast up the time
> When the Lord God formed man from the sea's slime
> And breathed into his face the breath of life,
> And blue-lung'd combers lumbered to the kill.
> The Lord survives the rainbow of His will.
>
> (Lowell, "The Quaker Graveyard in Nantucket")

We imbibed these apocalyptic poems like sacred texts, as if they could teach us the secret of poetry itself. They were the strangely American portals through which some of us passed into poetry—the signs under which we walked—and their fluencies had come to set up house inside us, their rhythms circulating in our blood.

Sometimes when I am lying in bed at night with my eyes closed, the phrases start to come back to me, a little jumbled, out of order, almost like a dream, with a dream's utter indelibility. It's as if the words have come welling up from the unconscious, like the answers to a riddle. At these moments the lines seem to have come from a single cauldron, like the audible formulations of the darkness, instructions from the deep:

Often I am permitted to return to a meadow
as if it were a given property of the mind
that certain bounds hold against chaos,

that is a place of first permission,
everlasting omen of what is.

(Robert Duncan)

They were the voices of first permission, and their poems point to the eternal unfolding of what exists, everlasting omen of transformation. Each of these poets adapted an utterance, inscribed an indelibility. So original is their contribution, so distinctive their achievement, that it takes an effort of will to recall how seriously they struggled with feelings of belatedness, with the anxiety that everything had already been accomplished. It's true that after the titanic achievement of the great modernists who were very much at their peak when these writers began, after the impersonal heroism—the heroic impersonality—of modernism itself, their work seems quickened by losses, freshened by warmth, scaled down to human size. They were highly personal writers. They may have begun under the scrupulous and austere sign of New Criticism, but, ironically, they ended up using their ironic sensibilities to bring a messy humanity, a harsh luminosity, a well of tenderness, back into poetry. To do so they had to walk out from under the living shadows, the Jamesian greatcoats, the smothering grandiloquence. They are like Yeats at the turn of the century. Everyone got down off their stilts. They found more enterprise in walking naked.

The radical impulse to self-exposure is, perhaps paradoxically, one reason these poets were so liberated by the dramatic monologue, which they mastered and deployed in order to probe a selfhood. ("I am obliged to perform in complete darkness / operations of great delicacy / on my self," Berryman's alter ego Henry announces in *The Dream Songs*.) It allowed them to act as anonymous shape-shifters, to conceal secrets inside their exclamatory revelations.

The quest for identity is a key subject for these poets, who had so much anxiety about the nature of the self, and so much faith in its metamorphosis. They are tireless and self-renewing. It's worth recalling the seven dramatic monologues in *The Mills of the Kavanaughs* which stand between Robert Lowell's early work and the so-called confessional poems of *Life Studies* which give the carefully fostered impression that the reader is breaking through into life and getting the literal or actual Robert Lowell, whereas in truth we are getting a canny and dynamic invention, a supposed person, a created figure, a made man. Lowell may have removed the mask—as M. L. Rosenthal first suggested—but he replaced it with another one. He never spoke "unequivocally" as himself, but he did draw radically—shockingly—from a secret well of feeling and experience, a hidden world which he exposed to the glare. He refigured and refashioned his raw and wounded self into a series of brash and layered self-portraits, colorful exposures crafted into an artistic fable, a cracked family album. It's a move from painting to photography. It's telling that Lowell followed *Life Studies* with his book "of versions and free translations," *Imitations*. He resurrected and expanded, perhaps unrecognizably, Dryden's notion of "imitation" in order to give himself a greater range of voice, or voices, turning for inspiration to the whole compass of European poets from Sappho to Pasternak. He took a startling and controversial license with his sources; the book that resulted doesn't seem to me a collection of translations so much as a work of mergers and acquisitions, a book of possessions, a series of dramatic monologues animated by one far-reaching voice displacing and distilling itself into the voice of other poets—Rimbaud, say, or Rilke—and inhabiting the body of other poems.

The dramatic monologue provided a strategy—a space—for self-projection and metamorphosis. I think, for example, of the brilliant way in which John Berryman learned to administer pronouns, at first in "The Ball Poem" and then in "Homage to Mistress Bradstreet" and culminating in *The Dream Songs*, wherein he created a purposefully sliding boundary line between himself and the character of Henry. ("There ought to be a law against Henry. / Mr. Bones: There is.") It's altogether remarkable how Randall Jarrell thrust himself so fully into the role of a woman in the splendid triad of poems strung across his work: "The Face," "The Woman at the Washington Zoo," and "Next Day." Each of these women stands both as herself and as a sort of Everywoman. The double standing makes these figures exceptional. Or so it seems. "This is what happens to everyone," the woman declares in "The Face": "At first you get bigger, you know more, / Then something goes wrong." Jarrell's poems unnervingly pursue the moment when something invisibly turns and goes awry, when the naked self radically breaks down its last defenses. Their wit belies their fury. I find myself reeling a little at the shocking recognition in the last two stanzas of "Next Day."

> And yet I'm afraid, as I was at the funeral
> I went to yesterday.
> My friend's cold made-up face, granite among its flowers,
> Her undressed, operated-on, dressed body
> Were my face and body.
> As I think of her, I hear her telling me

How young I seem; I *am* exceptional;
I think of all I have.
But really no one is exceptional,
No one has anything. I'm anybody,
I stand beside my grave
Confused with my life, that is commonplace and solitary.

This is the American vernacular pressured to a Rilkean pitch. The ruthlessness of insight, the startling truthfulness, the depth of ordinary courage it takes for the speaker to recognize herself in her dead friend, *as* her dead friend, to confront her own bewildering and commonplace fate, seems heroic to me. The poetic technique operates in such a seamless and unassuming way that it's easy to overlook: I'm thinking of how the rhetorical argument relentlessly pushes the voice to its heart-rending conclusion, as in a Shakespeare sonnet ("And yet"; "But really"), and of the shapely, symmetrical six-word progression of triple adjectives in the fourth line ("Her *undressed*, *operated-on*, *dressed* body") that Lowell also made one of his signatures ("your old-fashioned tirade," he writes in "Man and Wife," "*loving*, *rapid*, *merciless*—breaks like the Atlantic Ocean on my head"). The rhymes in the last stanza of "Next Day" act as a ghostly haunting of sounds; I hear the identical rhyme on the word "exceptional" (a word refuting itself), the irrefutable connection of "have" and "grave," the off-rhyme on the words "any*body*" and "solit*ary*" that drives home the unbearable truth. It's characteristic of Jarrell, as it was of Bishop, to put his technique in the service of an ordinary woman's voice. No wonder he loved Hardy. It seems to me that Jarrell's poems are not authentic or convincing because he learned about and understood female experience per se, but because he credited himself with "a semifeminine mind" and he mined it to project himself into another skin, another body, another self. He used all the imagination and technique available to him to propel himself across a divide.

Jarrell was especially drawn to the dramatic monologue from early on because he was seeking a register that left room for uncertainties and doubts, for stuttering hesitancies and bewilderments. He sought a poetry, as David Kalstone once put it, "that accommodated more of the human voice and its contradictions." Yet in an acute essay on Jarrell's work in his book *Modern Poetry after Modernism*, James Longenbach also points out how little Jarrell actually had to do to turn "The Face" from a self-portrait into a fictive dramatic monologue from an unnamed woman's point of view. He simply changed the word "handsome" to "beautiful" in the first line ("Not good any more, not beautiful—") and added an epigraph from *Der Rosenkavalier* ("Die alte Frau, die alte Marschallin!") and, presto!, someone else was speaking. Wisdom is learning what to overlook, as William James said quotably, and so it may be unwise to point out that there's an uncanny continuity of voices between the housewife who speaks in "Next Day" and the man himself who shows up in "A Man Meets a Woman in the Street." And why shouldn't there be? Sometimes, "We can't tell our life / from our wish."

For a little while, forget:
The world's selves cure that short disease, myself. . . .
(Jarrell, "Children Selecting Books in a Library")

I find in these American poets a deep sympathy, an attentive regard, an overwhelming and overwhelmed reverence for all living things, but especially for whatever is wounded or broken, flawed, vulnerable, lost. They are seduced, enabled, and traumatized by sympathy. They are bedeviled and determined by it. They are its broken masters. "But I identify myself, as always, / With something that there's something wrong with, / With something human," Jarrell put it eloquently in "The One Who Was Different." This defines a sensibility—it locates poetry on a human scale (Jarrell, like Bishop, was always emphatic about this)—and it bespeaks the empathic imagination. The epigraph from *The Tempest* that Berryman chose for *Recovery* speaks to the nature—the character—of that imagination. Miranda says, "Oh! I have suffered / With those that I saw suffer."

This passionate involvement and deep identification with the sufferings of others, this apparently simple commitment to the humanly flawed, this way of weighing things on a subjective human scale, is radically different from the impersonal and objective standard set forth in the Pound era, by the Eliot generation. Such a credo, a textual project, carries a radically different politics, a democratic ethos, and speaks up against authoritarianism. They did not fear social contagion, or edit out their semifeminine minds, or embrace reactionary politics, group hatreds. Who among the previous generation, except perhaps William Carlos Williams, could have written a poem such as Jarrell's "Say Good-bye to Big Daddy," an elegy for Big Daddy Lipscomb, the Baltimore Colts defensive tackle and a mountain of a man who died of a heroin overdose and who once said, as Jarrell quotes him, "I've been scared / Most of my life. You wouldn't think so to look at me. / It gets so bad I cry myself to sleep—"? Jarrell's *Complete Poems* is like a Quaker Meeting House for those who have something wrong with them, who feel misallied: sick children, teenage girls, boyish soldiers bewildered at being sacrificed, sad office workers, aging suburban housewives. I think of all the misallied and misshapen creatures in Bishop's work, from "The Man Moth," which she wrote in 1936, to "Pink Dog" ("O never have I seen a dog so bare!"), which she completed not long before her death in 1979. I think of Lowell's many poems of social outrage and public engagement—from his early Catholic radicalism and apocalyptic antiwar poems ("I was a fire-breathing Catholic C.O., / and made my manic statement, / telling off the state and president," he famously summarized in *Life Studies*) to the humane northern engagements of *For the Union Dead* ("Pity the monsters!," "Florence") to his improvisatory *History* sonnets, such as his memorial poem to Martin Luther King, Jr. ("Two Walls"), his elegy for Robert Kennedy ("For Robert Kennedy 1925–68"), and his dedicatory poem, "For Eugene McCarthy," which praises McCarthy for being "coldly willing / to smash the ball past those who bought the park." Lowell could be stagy, but he used that stage to speak up on behalf of the disenfranchised. Who among the previous generation would ever have proclaimed, as Rukeyser did at the peak of the Nazi genocide, "To be a Jew in the twentieth century / Is to be offered a gift" ("Letter to the Front"), or written with such sympathetic intelligence as Berryman about *The Diary of Anne Frank*, or praised freedom as eloquently as Robert Hayden in his sonnet "Frederick Douglass," which speaks of liberty as "this beautiful / and terrible thing, needful to man as air, / usable as earth"? I suspect many contemporary poets, readers, and critics are continuing to read and respond to the mid-century difference from modernism, without always defining it, and thus find themselves turning for company to a more approachable and vulnerable group of democratic masters.

There was something broken in each of these poets, I suppose, something that could not be mended—was there ever a generation of poets more prone to alcoholism, more stormed and afflicted by mental illness, more devastated by suicide? "I'm cross with god who has wrecked this generation," Berryman declared accusingly in one of *The Dream Songs*, a work which magnetizes the deaths of his contemporaries at every point, like iron filaments. And yet one of the things that strikes me about these poets, in retrospect, in this fresh century, is how actively, how acutely they managed to transfigure extreme suffering into a body of work characterized by "wit, pathos, and brilliance of intelligence" (to employ on a larger scale the words that Robert Lowell used to describe Randall Jarrell). They are personal, playful, learned, heartbreaking.

We are grabbed by these poets into art. "I'm sure that writing isn't a craft," Robert Lowell told an interviewer, almost offhandedly: "It must come from some deep impulse, deep inspiration." "We asked to be obsessed by writing, / and we were," Lowell also recollected in his elegy "For John Berryman." The poem, written after reading the last *Dream Song*, has a retrospective shine. It speaks to an intention—almost a prayer really—that had been transformed into lifetimes of work.

"You need to read good poetry with an attitude that is a mixture of sharp intelligence and of willing emotional empathy, at once penetrating and generous." Jarrell's witty, fierce, enthusiastic, and passionate devotion to poetry set the gold standard for his generation and, perhaps, for the one to follow. We ought to bring it back as a standard of measure. I discovered this aspect of Jarrell's influence and character in the first book of criticism I ever bought on my own, the elegiac collection *Randall Jarrell, 1914–1965*, edited by his friends Robert Lowell, Peter Taylor, and Robert Penn Warren. I paid $2.45 for the Noonday paperback in 1968, my freshman year in college, and it paid me back with an affectionate, insightful, and teeming group portrait that instilled in me the sense, which I have never quite shaken, of what a literary life could be, how it might be conducted. I pored over the photographs, too—Jarrell with Delmore Schwartz, Jarrell with an engraving by Dürer, Jarrell teaching poetry with great animation and evident joy (now there was a novel idea: teaching poetry!). I was particularly struck by John Berryman's elegy, "Opus Posthumous #13," with its bewildering title, its overwhelming nostalgia, and its tenderhearted, nearly unbearable longing for a final reunion:

> In the chambers of the end we'll meet again
> I will say Randall, he'll say Pussycat
> and all will be as before
> whenas we sought, among the beloved faces,
> eminence and were dissatisfied with that
> and needed more.

I noted, too, that in a review of *Poetry and the Age*, a book which I went out and found the next day, Berryman had praised Jarrell's criticism because "it sounds always like a human being talking to somebody." The idea was so simple it seemed—and still seems—revolutionary. And he added: "But what really matters in Jarrell are a rare attention, devotion to and respect for poetry." This rhymed for me with Lowell's observation that Jarrell's essays "have the raciness and artistic gaiety of his own hypnotic voice."

I've always adored the wise enthusiasm in Jarrell's essays, especially his encomiums, his pieces of praise (for Whitman, for Frost, for Moore, for Williams, for the early Lowell, for the late Stevens). "Eulogy was the glory of Randall's criticism," Lowell said memorably: "Eulogies that not only impressed readers with his own enthusiasms, but which also, time and again, changed and improved opinions and values. He left many reputations permanently altered and exalted."

This may be the place to add that I've felt for some time Jarrell's deadly negative and at times cruel reviews have been overvalued and badly misused as a model by many contemporary poets. So, too, I hope that we'll permanently retire Helen Vendler's over-quoted formulation that Jarrell "put his genius into his criticism and his talent into his poetry." It's clever but untrue, and it sets up a needless dichotomy between Jarrell's poetry and his criticism, which are both, after all, part of one project, one practice. *One Life, One Writing!* What matters in both Jarrell's poems and essays are his canny intelligence and uncanny insights, his deep reserves of tenderness, his acute emotional enthusiasm and presence, his reverent humanity. Why has postmodern criticism almost entirely passed him by? ("I feel like the first men who read Wordsworth," he writes in "The One Who Was Different," "It's so simple I can't understand it.")

"Poetry is a terminal activity, taking place out near the end of things, where the poet's soul addresses one other soul only, never mind when. And it aims—never mind *either* communication or expression—at the reformation of the poet, as prayer does" (John Berryman). It's characteristic of Berryman to compare poetry to prayer. What he said about Jarrell applies equally to himself, for he showed his own "rare attention, devotion to, and respect for poetry." Among the dozens of possible instances and examples, I would summon up that moment when Berryman testifies to how radically he was affected by the comprehensive air of majesty—the sublime assurance—that emanated from a review by R. P. Blackmur which first appeared in *Poetry* magazine. Blackmur's statement is highly revealing, but so is the characteristic intensity of Berryman's response. His poem "Olympus" quotes, lineates, and extends one of Blackmur's keynote sentences across two quatrains so that the prose commentary is transformed into a singular piece of poetry itself.

> "The art of poetry
> is amply distinguished from the manufacture of verse
> by the animating presence in the poetry
> of a fresh idiom: language
>
> so twisted & posed in a form
> that it not only expresses the matter in hand
> but adds to the stock of available reality."
> I was never altogether the same man after *that*.

Poetry is for Blackmur both expressive and generative and, in retrospect, it seems almost as if he was invoking and magically summoning up the radically twisted and utterly fresh idiom of *The Dream Songs*.

Ever since I first discovered it in *Opening the Hand*, I've liked W. S. Merwin's poem, called simply "Berryman," in which he recalls his teacher's astonishing advice:

> he suggested I pray to the Muse
> get down on my knees and pray
> right there in the corner and he
> said he meant it literally

Berryman deeply understood, as his advice suggests, that in the writing of poetry there is always something outside the dispensation of the will, something dependent upon luck or grace. And he was humble before that force, that knowledge. He wanted to instill such humility in his protégé. Merwin also recollects Berryman's passionate vehemence, his utterly authentic, highly physical, even bodily, mental engagement, with poetry:

> his lips and the bones of his long fingers trembled
> with the vehemence of his view about poetry
>
> he said the great presence
> that permitted everything and transmuted it
> in poetry was passion
> passion was genius and he praised movement and invention

One feels, reading Merwin's poem, say, or Philip Levine's evocative memoir, "Mine Own John Berryman," or James Merrill's preternaturally clever poem for Elizabeth Bishop, "The Victor Dog," or Allen Grossman's acute essay on Lowell in *The Long Schoolroom*, that the lesson was not lost on the generation that followed.

> *When they meet me they say:*
> *You haven't changed.*
> *I want to say: you haven't looked.*
> (Jarrell, "The Face")

> *—and looked and looked our infant sight away.*
> (Bishop, "Over 2,000 Illustrations
> and a Complete Concordance")

I want to take a moment to praise Elizabeth Bishop's vision as well as her eyesight. She did look with great forthrightness at the way things changed, and she described the world with a scrupulous, variegated, almost offhanded virtuosity that has been justly praised. Jarrell set the terms when he reviewed her first book and said, "All her poems have written underneath, *I have seen it.*" But I would also say at this late date that there's a strong element of anxiety and at times even desperation that gives Bishop's descriptive hold on the world so much of its tenacious force. "Surely there is an element of mortal panic and fear underlying all works of art?" she asked rhetorically in her memoir about Marianne Moore, "Efforts of Affection." Surely there's more than an element of such mortal panic and fear—there's a deep almost oceanic undertow—in most of Bishop's characteristic poems. I've always loved her letter about Darwin that reveals so much about the nature of her project:

> There is no "split." Dreams, works of art (some), glimpses of the always-more-successful surrealism of everyday life, unexpected moments of empathy (is it?) catch a peripheral vision of whatever it is one can never really see full-face but that seems enormously important. I can't believe we are wholly irrational (and I do admire Darwin!). But reading Darwin, one admires the beautiful solid case being built up out of his endless heroic observations, almost unconscious or automatic—and then comes a sudden relaxation, a forgetful phrase, and one feels the strangeness of his undertaking, sees the lonely young man, his eyes fixed on facts and minute details, sinking or sliding giddily off into the unknown. What one seems to want in art, in experiencing it, is the same thing that is necessary for its creation, a self-forgetful, perfectly useless concentration.
>
> (*Elizabeth Bishop and Her Art*)

Bishop, too, represented herself in her poems as a supposed person, a supposed observer on whom nothing is lost. It was not just in her life but also in her work that she carried on what James Merrill so acutely called her "instinctive, modest, lifelong impersonation of an ordinary woman." As it did for her contemporaries, the dramatic monologue gave her a space both for revealing and concealing herself, for escape and transfiguration. "I envy the mind hiding in her words," Mary McCarthy readily admitted, "like an 'I' counting up to a hundred waiting to be found." I can't help but think of the Giant Snail who says, "Draw back. Withdrawal is always best" ("Rainy Season; Sub-Tropics") and of the numerous animal masquerades that move so hauntingly through her work.

I've always been fascinated by the poem "The Riverman," perhaps because it's such an unusual, even unlikely poem for Bishop to have written since it doesn't present itself or pose as a lyric of description—as so many of her most typical poems seem to do. It doesn't build up the beautiful solid case—or even appear to—before taking off for the unknown interior, the sacred spaces. That's one reason Bishop herself was so discomfited by the poem, which uses the story of shamanic initiation to probe her own deep-reaching expressive powers and commitments. She hadn't been to the Amazon yet when she wrote the poem, and so here at least one would have to revise Jarrell's formulation to read, *I have envisioned it.* Charles Wagley's book, *Amazon Town*, which lent the poem so many of its authentic details, may have helped her to escape the literal—her literalist—self. A triggering Amazonian voice and folkloric subject matter opened her up to charges of primitivism, but also freed her to relinquish the claims of the ordinary social world in order to write—to embrace—an extreme poem of vision.

◆

Yet really we had the same life,
the generic one
our generation offered.
(Lowell, "For John Berryman")

At times I see them almost as one organism, an entity alive in all its parts, an Ovidian myth. Most of them were born in the second decade of the twentieth century. They began in the Depression, constellated after the violent years of World War II, marked the mid-to-late forties with their breakthrough collections, the first and second books that trumpeted their arrival: Delmore Schwartz, *Genesis: Book One* (1943); Randall Jarrell, *Little Friend, Little Friend* (1945); Elizabeth Bishop, *North and South* (1946); Robert Lowell, *Lord Weary's Castle* (1946); John Berryman, *The Dispossessed* (1948); Theodore Roethke, *The Lost Son and Other Poems* (1948). Weldon Kees's initial collection, *The Last Man* (1943) belongs here, and so does Robert Duncan's first book, *Heavenly City, Earthly City* (1947). They endured what Lowell labeled "the tranquilized *Fifties*" ("These are the tranquilized *Fifties*, / and I am forty. Ought I to regret my seedtime?"), and circulated America's social problems in their bloodstreams. Their personal lives swam away from them, swam back. "I have been thinking much about you all summer," Lowell wrote to Berryman in 1959,

> and how we have gone through the same troubles, visiting the bottom of the world. I have wanted to stretch out a hand, and tell you that I have been there, too, and how it all lightens and life swims back . . .

One thinks of the constellation of key middle works: Lowell's *Life Studies* (1959) and Jarrell's *The Woman at the Washington Zoo* (1960), Berryman's *77 Dream Songs* (1964) and Bishop's *Questions of Travel* (1965). All through the sixties and early seventies, their devotion to poetry remained intense and irrepressible, exalted, even as they instigated divorces and suffered breakdowns, and competed with each other, often unhealthily, like kids playing King of the Mountain, and won prizes, and lost them, and protested the Vietnam War, and lit up classrooms, and changed as the country changed—prying themselves open, breaking into blossom—and immeasurably deepened their achievements. I suppose that most of them felt they had made messes of their lives. All of them had to contend with what Berryman called the true subject of *Homage to Mistress Bradstreet*: "The almost insuperable difficulty of writing high verse at all in a land that cared and cares so little for it." And yet they registered a poetry that is quicksilver, luminous, and enduring. Each of us will have a favorite moment in overall bodies of work of continuous distinction—some of mine are early Lowell, middle Berryman, late Jarrell. Each of us can supply a somewhat different list of names and books. But I would have us stop pitting them against each other and instead celebrate an inclusive, creative moment in American poetry, a ferment, a generation who worked under the stimulus of each other. I would celebrate the muddy vibrancy and dynamism of their excitement, the materialism—the odd extravagance—of their achievement.

"The glories of the world struck me, made me aria, once," Henry sings out in *Dream Song* #26: "—What happen then, Mr. Bones? / if be you cares to say." Everyone remembers their failings, their malaises, their manias—a critical industry has practically been built up around them, but not everyone seems to remember the transfiguring power of poetry in their lives. I would also have us recall how in 1946 Delmore Schwartz told Robert Lowell, "Let Joyce and Freud, / the Masters of Joy, / be our guests here" ("To Delmore Schwartz"). Joy, too, was invited to the table. It did sit and eat. "Find yourself / a little spectrum of exact / terms of joy, some of them / archaic, but all useful," William Meredith recalls in his poem "What I Remember the Writers Telling Me When I Was Young." "Nourish beginnings," Muriel Rukeyser instructs us in her poem "Elegy in Joy": "The blessing is in the seed." Everyone remembers that glorious moment in Bishop's poem "The Moose" when the giant animal—a figure of matriarchal grandeur—looms up out of the woods and a group of people on a night bus experience together a precious moment of childish wonder and pleasure:

> Taking her time,
> she looks the bus over,
> grand, otherworldly.
> Why, why do we feel
> (we all feel) this sweet
> sensation of joy?

Bishop's poem acknowledges with a sweet and rare insistence (*we all feel*, she repeats) a communal sensation of joy, a shared recognition of the mysterious sublimity of the nonhuman world.

Reading Bishop's poem, I feel akin to the speaker in Theodore Roethke's poem "I Cry, Love! Love!" who declares, like some mad magisterial governor, "I proclaim once more a condition of joy." I remember, too, how in his piece "Open Letter," Roethke announced:

"None the less, in spite of all the muck and welter, the dark, the *dreck* of these poems, I count myself among the happy poets." I feel almost like saying this about an entire tormented generation. One learns from these poets of tragic joy that no one escapes from overwhelming pain, that everyone suffers, perhaps inordinately, but that poetry itself is a joyous and even redemptive calling—a saving grace, a noble enterprise, a sacred passion.

> *Those blessèd structures, plot and rhyme—*
> *why are they no help to me now. . . ?*
> (Lowell, "Epilogue")

> *Will I ever write properly, with passion & exactness*
> *of the damned strange demeanours of my flagrant heart?*
> (Berryman, "Monkhood")

The art of last things—memorial, humane, translucent. Art going on nerve, on raw courage. Art trying desperately to transcend itself, to go beyond art. There is something helpless—and triumphant—about their final books, completed achievements: Jarrell's *The Lost World* (1965), Bishop's *Geography III* (1976), Lowell's *Day by Day* (1977), Roethke's *The Far Field* (1964), Berryman's *Love and Fame* (1971) and *Delusions, Etc.* (1972) These books are now inscribed in our literature. They are the late Shakespeare of postwar American poetry.

Perhaps they wanted "to make / something imagined, not recalled," as Lowell put it in "Epilogue," but in truth their houses were haunted by ghostly memories, and the ghosts were strong, at times invincible. One thinks of Berryman's resignations ("Age, and the deaths, and the ghosts") and the haunted understandings he is desperately trying to displace by projecting them—weakly foisting them off—onto Henry:

I won't mention the dreams I won't repeat
sweating and shaking: something's gotta give:
up for good at five.
("Henry by Night")

And there's Lowell's sense of helplessness before his own demonic memories. He is tethered to the past, whiplashed by what he has done, by what he finds himself writing:

But sometimes everything I write
with the threadbare art of my eye
seems a snapshot,
lurid, rapid, garish, grouped,
heightened from life,
yet paralyzed by fact.
All's misalliance.
Yet why not say what happened?
("Epilogue")

This is the poetry of final changes, last revisions, letters of resignation, leave-takings. Art pared down to what is essential, art created at the edge of a void where language is unmade. So many final changes, resignations, accountings, so many lost worlds. The elegies they tried to avoid ("I used to want to live / to avoid your elegy," Lowell confesses in "For John Berryman") and ended up writing for each other, such as "Glimmerings," the group of ten dream songs—"one solid block of Agony"—that Berryman inscribed for Schwartz ("This world is gradually becoming a place / where I do not care to be any more. Can Delmore die?"). There's Berryman on Jarrell ("Let Randall rest, whom your self-torturing / cannot restore one instant's good to, rest"), on Thomas ("O down a many few, old friend"), on Roethke ("The Garden Master's gone"). There's Meredith on Lowell ("The message you brought back again and again / from the dark brink had the glitter of truth"), on Berryman ("Friends making off ahead of time / on their own, I call that willful, John / but that's no judgment, only argument / such as we've had before"). There's Lowell on Jarrell, Bishop on Lowell, Swenson on Bishop, until it all starts to seem like a mournful procession, a sad vanishing, a terrifying regress. . . .

And yet there's also so much nobility in their ritual poems, their naked suffering. We are contacted and humanized by these poems, these books, we are made more present by these oddly American deaths. It's the end of the line, the end of all the lines. So many of their own edgy last poems speak to a final transformation. Here is Proust in plain American, Jarrell's three-part terza rima masterpiece, "The Lost World," and its splendid epilogue, "Thinking of the Lost World" ("I hold in my own hands, in happiness, / Nothing: the nothing for which there's no reward"). Here are the nine poems of Bishop's last book, including her masterly villanelle, "One Art," which comes to terms with a universe of loss, and her Stevensian seashore lyric, "The End of March," and her scrupulous reconstruction of her own engendered identity, the poem that reels her back to the brink of self-consciousness, the dizzying recognitions of "In the Waiting Room" ("But I felt: you are an *I*, / you are an *Elizabeth*, / you are one of *them*"). Here are Lowell's last Odyssean voyages ("Ulysses and Circe," "Homecoming," "Last Walk?") and his final poems of praise ("Shadow," "Thanks-Offering for Recovery") and his Orphic dream ("Shifting Colors") and his ferociously self-accusing "Epilogue," which prays for the grace of accuracy ("We are poor passing facts, / warned by that to give / each figure in the photograph / his living name"). And here are Berryman's "Eleven Addresses to the Lord," and his stoically suicidal "Henry's Understanding," and his jubilant "King David Dances" ("all the black same I dance my blue head off!"). These poems have the driving sincerity, the magisterial grandeur of prayer.

We learned from them a world of knowing. Peace, then, to the makers. Time itself should pause to reckon and savor what they created. Here was what Bishop called "Life and the memory of it so compressed / they've turned into each other" ("Poem"), here was the postwar Imagination's daily claim. "Really I began the day / Not with a man's wish: 'May this day be different,' " Randall Jarrell confesses at the end of "A Man Meets a Woman in the Street." "But with the birds' wish: 'May this day / Be the same day, the day of my life.' "

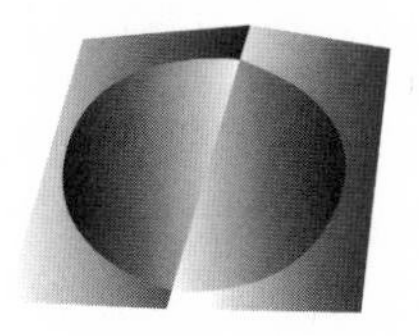

EAVAN BOLAND

Shadow Life

I.

If I believed that a poet had a single reading life—one only, one truly—then this would have been an easy piece to write. But I don't. And it wasn't. Instead, I believe there are two; that one may be the shadow of the other. It is the other one, the shadow-life, which I have chosen to write about here. And that—to my surprise—has involved me in more complication and more reflection than I expected.

But let me for a moment imagine that there had been just one. What would this piece, I ask myself, have been like in that case? How would I have written it? Which details would I have chosen to portray? Which ones would I have left out? How would I have represented this part of the poet's journey?

To start with, of course, everything would have looked solid and clear to me. I would have had a simple task: to make a program of remembrance, a catalog of illuminations. I would have merely been required to list and interpret the poems and the books which had led me to my own poetry and, even more, to my own sense of being a poet. I could have made a saint's calendar of first lines, and last stanzas. I would have pointed out this sonnet, that sestina, that strange but clever ending, and immediately I would have cleared the way. Essentially, I would have chosen poems and poetry books as if they were hours on a sundial. I could have marked them out to catch the light and record my life: my adolescence, my early adulthood, my first publication, my belief—from beginning to end—in the connection between the life of poetry and the reading life.

And of course—in describing this connection in more detail—I would have made a lexicon of objects and events. I would have turned remembrance, as we all do, into a narrative of self-discovery: the bookshelf that held that first book, for example. The dust jacket with rosy paper and one sharp tear at the bottom. The old sofa on which I sat reading, and reading. First turning the pages, then not turning them. The way I halted at a single page. A single poem. How the windowsill rattled with cold air and the winter daylight. And then, as twilight came, just cold air. How darkness plucked at the page, and pestered those lines. How I got up and turned on the lamp. How those words looked surrounded by their new, electric hinterland. How I prepared to reread lines I would remember for the rest of my life.

And even that is not enough. The physical recollection would have been only one aspect of it. To celebrate that ideal and single reading life—and after all, many poets both have it and want to celebrate it—I would also have sought a grander representation for the kind of reader I could have been. I would have wanted more than the personal and local narrative. I would have wanted something with more sweep and substance; less personal, more fitting. An emblematic narrative, in fact. Nothing less. If, that is, that single, uncomplicated reading life had really existed.

What would I have chosen? What quest out of the past of poetry would have seemed to me best fitted to represent such an illumination; such a series of discoveries? Even now—and even though I am not writing about this life—I know what it would have been. It would have been a walk. A predawn walk, in fact. It would have been William Hazlitt's journey in the bitter, small hours of January in that year.

William Hazlitt was the son of a minister, and lived his childhood in the tiny town of Wem, in Shropshire, within sight of the Welsh border. There in the dark, wintry hours before dawn in January 1798, he got up and prepared himself for a journey. He was twenty years of age. On the edge of "the cold, raw, comfortless dawn," as he later described it, he turned west toward Shrewbury, the county town of Shropshire. He walked along, skirting the Welsh mountains—"their blue tops seen through the wintry branches." And what did he see when he got to Shropshire?

He saw Coleridge. Samuel Taylor Coleridge. He saw a confident, willful young man who believed ardently and utterly in the life of poetry and in himself as a poet. He found a poet, a reader of poetry—and, what's more, in his own mundane neighborhood—speaking in the defiant and luminous tones of poetry and authority. And so as Hazlitt turned for home, after that meeting, everything was different. He turned back on the same road. He navigated the same decade of miles. But this time it was all changed. As he wrote later—*a sound was in my ears as of a Siren's song*. And again: *I was stunned, startled with it, as from deep sleep*. The morning was no longer cold. The air was no longer bitter. He had seen the witness of poetry in his time.

"That my understanding also did not remain dumb and brutish, or at length found a language to express itself, I owe to Coleridge."

Here surely is the narrative of the ideal reading life: The doubt. The effort. The solitary journey. The discovery. The confirmation which lasts forever. And the discovery that this confirmation can exist in exactly the same surroundings which before—before the window crackled with winter air, before the book lay open under the lamp—had seemed so dull and oppressive.

Hazlitt's journey to find Coleridge—and his finding of himself instead—remains one of the beautiful fables of the canon. It became the substance of his own headlong essay, "My First Acquaintance with Poets," published in *The Liberal* in 1823. But as well as representing a powerful self-discovery, it also serves as an image for everything that the reading life should be: its promise, its reward. As he walks back he knows he has found in Coleridge the confirmation of his hopes: that poetry lives, that it will always live. Hearing him talk, hearing him mix poetry and rhetoric, has proved that. And then comes the long, enchanted walk home when "the cold dank drops of dew, that hung half-melted on the beard of the thistle, had something genial and refreshing in them."

And that, surely, is how the poet reads in that ideal, singular reading life. With the hope of such a meeting, such a confirmation. That I have not chosen that life to write about here is simply a testament to my belief that we are shaped as poets not by the ideal, but by the real. And the real, in my case, requires a portion of autobiography:

II.

I was the fifth child of larger-than-life and willful parents. I was born in Ireland, and even now my parents seem to me perfectly Irish, completely of their time and place. They were eloquent and expressive. They waved their friends off after a late-night party, standing in doorways, framed by noise and laughter, blue cigarette smoke, whiskey kisses. Their life seemed to have happened in their words, before it ever got to their actions. I was their last child.

But we did not stay in Ireland. We moved, when I was six, to London. It was seven years after the end of the Second World War. This was not the city of the cosmopolitan adventure. That would come later. Nor was it the city of style and empire. That had come earlier. It was a city of debris and survival: of ruined buildings and spaces in a state of repair. Of red buses. Of strange vowels. For my parents—large of soul and eloquent and adaptable—it was a place to manage. For me it was a place to be lost in.

I disliked my school. I disliked my journey there. I missed the green spaces and freedom of Dublin. I resisted the new speech, the new vowels. I was not quick at school, not especially interested in my English classes. My memories of Dublin began to fade. But my feelings for this new environment were no more affectionate.

At home I was struggling, too. My sisters and brothers were in boarding school in Dublin. Only one sister was with me. I felt the cutting-off of family life and associated it with the gray, melancholy streets and the urban shadows. And had things remained like that, then I would not be writing this.

Instead, something else happened. Two things, in fact. I inherited an old set of children's encyclopedias which had belonged to my older siblings. And I began to deal with the strange city, the new dispossession, by looking for its opposite in language. That is, of course, a hindsight, a more sophisticated later perception. At the time I simply stumbled through this new and awkward world. But later, as I looked back, I understood that here—strange as it may seem—was the start of an encounter in reading poetry which would influence me for the rest of my life.

The encyclopedias were large and blocky, with crimson covers. They were illustrated with glossy, magazine-type illustrations. Such photographs as they had, on the other hand, were dark and yellowish-gray. There were chapters on almost everything. The text talked down in the mode of a lofty, impatient, and erudite governess. There were sections on history, photographic essays on machines, chapters on the growth of ideas, chapters on the growth of empire. And sandwiched between all of this, at various intervals, were sections of poetry. Strangely chosen, with small blurbs of explanation above them. Almost invariably, they were about England.

There were other subjects, to be sure. There were occasional nursery rhymes illustrated with dull yellow boys tumbling down a flowered margin. Or an oversized pink egg sitting on a wall. There were also good poems, if you trawled for them. William Blake. Alexander Pope. Extracts from Shakespeare and Chaucer. Even Dryden and Marvell. But always at the back of the section, densely packed on the page, were the poems of England—its countryside, its history, its pastoral and decorative peace, its court and its empire. Unerringly, over and over again, I went to the poems in this part of the section. It became a ritual. A comforting ritual at that. At the end of the day when I had felt at a loss—in a strange school, in a strange city, among strange-sounding voices—they were always there, as if waiting for me alone.

By and large, these were short poems, written in one or two stanzas, but sometimes they were longer. Mostly they were from the nineteenth century, and by far the larger number were from the last sixty years of the century. They were the lyrics of a self-confident imperial consensus. They were often musical and snappy, showing their origins in drawing-room songs or the Book of Common Prayer.

They might also be defiant, bombastic, and confident. Above all, they were England-makers. They were nation-builders. They wrote of belonging. Of pride in belonging.

Breathes there a man with soul so dead. Over and over again I returned to that line. The soul. Its breath. Its life. Outside the window a fog curled and yellowed into an English night. Not my country. Not my literature. Not even, had I understood it then, the language I should have spoken. In fact, had I known, I was only reading this poem because I had lost my own language through colony and dispossession, through the very powers of entitlement it celebrated.

But irony was a long way off. The result of estrangement is often not a new strength, so much as an intense empathy and longing for what you are excluded from. I was tired of being different. I knew nothing of history or colony. I wanted this grandiose diction, this expansive sentiment. *Breathes there a man with soul so dead.* This was possession indeed and it was possession I was interested in. *Who never to himself has said.* These were the songs of a world where no one doubted their place, no one doubted their entitlements. This was the world I gazed at, as through a sweet-shop window, every day in north London, in Finchley, in the anti-Irish, upscale day school I had been sent to. Where the teachers scolded when I used the wrong phrase or the syntax that marked me as an outsider. *You're not in Ireland now*, one teacher said to me briskly.

When the day ended I would take two buses home. I would stare sullenly out the windows at the bomb-pocked city, the gray and early twilight. I would go to my house, have my tea, and do my homework. And sometime later, in my own room at last, I would take down the dark, crimson-covered books all over again. I would read the triumph of the lines: *This is my own, my native land.*

The simple truth was that those poems came from a moment

when poetry—whatever its values—had reunited two of its old functions: to delight and instruct. The late-Victorian poets of empire, from high to low, from Tennyson and Arnold to Francis William Bourdillon, made their language serve their moment. They lived in the harsh light of prosperity and expansion. They lived in the myth of steel, cotton, lumber, coal. Their cities were machines of prosperities. Their armies and cadres of civil servants were staining the map with deeper and deeper shades of coral. These poems—from "The Charge of the Light Brigade" to the patriotic quatrain—broke language into refrain and made refrain a message of certainty and uplift. Half-hymn, half-song, and all imperial lyric, these poems would be swept away at the end of the century. But for me—too young to understand their values and ready to yield to their music—they promised that language could heal loss and restore identity. *This is my own, my native land.*

But it wasn't. And it would never be. So what exactly was I accomplishing with this strange, early series of choices? Why was I, an Irish child, turning to these poems of empire? And what do I mean now by suggesting this strange, lost taste as a reading life for a poet?

I was reading these poems, after all, not for the truth they brought, but for the delusion they offered. There was nothing considered about it. There was nothing self-educating about it. Instead, there was something darker and more interesting. A wish, a longing, a hunger to put the ambiguities of life into something simpler. To bang the confusion of those days against hard, ringing musical lines, the way I hit the steel triangle in the school orchestra. To hear certainties vibrating out of language, hanging in the air, singing themselves out into a different, more composed silence. We say that the reading of poetry shapes a life. In fact, the life shapes what poetry we can see, what poetry we can bear. This article is about the poetry I could bear when I was young. Not so much the individual poems—they are not so important here—as the fact that I wanted poetry to tell me lies. I wanted it to fib and giggle and evade. And it did, it did. And so this piece is the opposite of a description of the usual: it is not about truth and poetry and the first reading encounter. It is about the first encounter, and reading poetry, and deception. And it is also about the love I found and kept and still have for the one language which took the time, all the time, to pretend to me, and to agree with me.

In actual terms, something simple and human had happened to me: I was a child. I had no sophisticated power of reasoning. I had, as I've said already, grown tired of not belonging; of being powerless in a place. And so I turned instinctively to this medium where power and place were restored to one another. To these short, forceful lyrics of empire. To these cadences which promised me over and over again that moment of ease and illusion and location. To "The Charge of the Light Brigade." To the "Night with a Thousand Eyes." To my own, my native land.

In strict and literal terms, there was not a word of truth in these poems for me. When I finished the poems—some of which I now knew by heart—nothing changed about my present circumstances. I was not less Irish. I was not less displaced. The fog outside the window was still as thick, as yellow, and as ominous. The streets were as inhospitable. My present remained unaltered when I put the poem down.

But I had changed my future. I had learned forever the power of poetry to restore and console and persuade. I had assisted, in some slight way, in the magic of that power. And for that inch, and by that atom, I was less powerless. And by that small amount—if only for believing ardently in what the poem did while I read it—I had been part of a transformation.

I had also infinitely complicated my sense of a reading life. I had, after all, not found truth. In fact, the opposite. I had found a truth of language which did not represent a truth of fact. And that, in many ways, constitutes a quicksand. And even later in my life, when I read with a consciousness of poetry, and with a consciousness of being a poet, I still was troubled by my sense of illusion, deceit, music—that skewed view of the world which made my first encounter with the form.

But now, from a distance, I see something different. I see the large, old books again. But the perspective has shifted. Those marvelous pages, which were once sinuous and willful, which appeared to have a life of their own, always alive and always consuming themselves like firelight, are inert. The covers look like what they are: just covers. I see the room, the windows, the yellow seep of the fog at the windowsill. I see the child still there, in the same place after all these years, and still reading. And I realize now that the encounter with poetry is never pure, but always human. And therefore in that moment, because of that participation—a moment which became deeply implicated in my sense of all poetry—I see myself taking my first steps toward walking a part of the way home with Hazlitt on an enchanted morning.

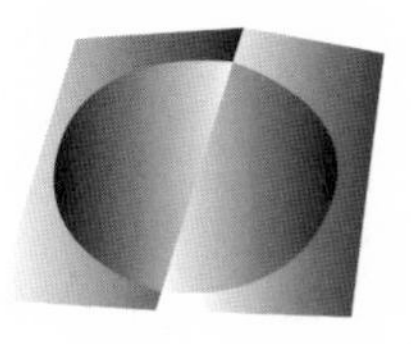

STANLEY PLUMLY

Reading Autumn

1

I guess I'm thinking of two or three poems, maybe more, and of the planet on the table of which they are a small part. In the northern hemisphere of this planet the season would have to be, for me, autumn—all of it, both at the beginning and the ending of the harvest, both a little before and a little after. It would be an autumn you could follow from the American Northwest to the Middle West, down to the Mid-Atlantic and up through the Great Lakes and Pennsylvania, then the Adirondacks and New England, over to England and Europe, a season of "Indian-summer-sun," as Hart Crane puts it, "On trees that seem dancing," a season of spilled apples and rows of shocks of grain, a season of brick-dry air in which sound begins to carry the way it will in winter, a season of blown leaves, early frost, early dark, the evening season, the slow sunset season, "the human season," as Keats once called it.

A "Season of mists and mellow fruitfulness," Keats also called it. A season in which autumn is an interior experience. "I stand by a low fire," Theodore Roethke writes, "Counting the wisps of flame, and I watch how / Light shifts upon the wall. / I bid stillness be still. / I see, in evening air, / How slowly dark comes down on what we do." Keats himself preferred, he'd once said, the warmth of "a stubble plain . . . to the chilly green of spring," meaning the fire-sweep of the scythe at harvest. He meant, too, those evenings Roethke is alluding to, of the mind's getting lost in the leaves of the flames of a good working fire. "I should like a bit of fire to night—one likes a bit of fire—How glorious the Blacksmiths' shops look now—I stood to night before one till I was very nearly listing for one. Yes I should like a bit of fire—at a distance about 4 feet 'not quite hob nob'—as wordsworth says."

The corner of the autumn landscape Keats is speaking of and from is Winchester, the cathedral town southwest of London, in Hampshire, in 1819, and just north of the port city of Southhampton and the Isle of Wight, two other places prominent in the seasonal life of Keats. Aside from his first years in Finsbury and school years in Enfield, Keats has never really had a home. Orphaned early, itinerant always, renting rooms with his brothers and later leasing space with or from his friends, he has seemed to be searching. The crucial criterion for where he might be at any given time is whether or not he can write there—whether the climate, the beauty, the proximity, the society and/or solitude of a place suit him, inspire him. And whether or not he can afford it. Winchester, on almost all accounts, for this late summer beginning autumn, is more or less perfect.

2

"This Winchester is a fine place," Keats writes to Fanny Brawne in mid-August. "A beautiful Cathedral and many other ancient buildings in the Environs." Not only is his room large enough for him to "promenade at my pleasure," he has the advantage of "the convenience of a Library," in a university setting "surrounded by fresh-looking country.... Tolerably good and cheap Lodgings," too. By mid-September he is writing his brother George (who is in America by now) that his "promenade" has extended throughout the town and into the open countryside. "I take a walk every day for an hour before dinner and this is generally my walk—I go out at the back gate across one street, into the Cathedral yard, which is always interesting; then I pass under the trees along a paved path, pass the beautiful front of the Cathedral, turn left under a stone door way—then I am on the other side of the building—which leaving behind I pass on through two college-like squares ... garnished with grass and shaded with trees...."

This little map of early nineteenth-century Winchester (out of Jane Austen) is only a moment in a long, emotionally up and down journal letter (September 17–27) intended to remind George of the sweetness of Mother England and the special civilizing way an English town yields to country, warm "in the way that some pictures look warm." "I pass through one of the old city gates and there you are in one College-Street through which I pass and at the end thereof crossing some meadows and at last a country alley of gardens I arrive ... at the foundation of Saint Cross, which is a very interesting old place, both for its tower and alms-square.... Then I pass across St. Cross meadows till you come to the most beautifully clear river—now this is only one mile of my walk."

In addition to this pastoral interlude, this involved and involving letter amounts to nothing less than an autobiography of the complexity and uncertainties of this time in Keats's life—he has eighteen months to live. The letter ranges from complaints about his literary standing ("My name with the literary fashionables is vulgar—I am a weaver boy to them") to anxieties concerning his love life ("A Man in love cuts the sorriest figure in the world") to what he has been reading ("lately Burton's *Anatomy of Melancholy*") to remembering the summer before's walking tour of Scotland ("The finest thing is Fingal's cave") to reporting on his health ("I have got rid of my haunting sore throat") to speculating on the nature of physical change ("Our bodies every seven years are completely fresh-materialed.... We are like the relict garments of a Saint") to realizing that, even in so short a career so far, his writing has become "more thoughtful and quiet" ("I want to compose without...fever").

3

The letter also includes—in fact, begins with—an apology from Keats that all he could extract from their guardian, Richard Abbey, is a promise to send George more money as soon as possible, which is a month and more prospect in the ocean-going mails. George is bankrupt. Keats receives this news on September 10th and immediately interrupts his Winchester idyll to return to London in order to try to raise funds. He has no money of his own and is himself "in fear of the Winchester jail" for debt, so the manipulative Abbey is his only option. His five desultory days in London are themselves a separate story. He returns to Winchester on the 15th exhausted, having ridden again, as is his habit, on the outside of the coach. It's cheaper, if chillier. If the town-and-country walks he's been taking up until now have sharpened his appetite, the Winchester walks after he gets back from his mission to help George will soften the emotional edges. Writing letters, especially long ones, is a kind of walking as well.

Keats's letters generally have for him a therapeutic function, as the ten-day journal letter to George suggests. Filled with speculation, distraction, worry, complaints, theory, discourse, frustration, fear, loneliness, luminosity, great beauty—the letters stand as the world out of which the poems gain fuller life. The week he's writing George he's also writing four of his closest friends. To Charles Brown, his confidant and collaborator, he confesses that "It is quite time I should set myself doing something, and live no longer upon hopes. I have never exerted myself. I am getting into an idle-minded, vicious way of life, almost content to live upon others." He asks Charles Dilke, his close Hampstead neighbor, to help him find "any place tolerably comfitable" when he moves back into central London and gets "employment in some of our elegant Periodical works." To Richard Woodhouse, his best literary benefactor, he states flatly that "I am all in a Mess here—embowell'd in Winchester." He also rues the fact that "things won't leave me *alone*." He encloses in his Woodhouse letter a lyric, an ode, he's written just two days earlier. And to John Hamilton Reynolds, his colleague-poet, he adds that "To night I am all in a mist; I scarcely know what's what—But you knowing my unsteady and vagarish disposition, will guess that all this turmoil will be settled by tomorrow morning."

Settled is the word, in a state of settlement, in a state of contemplation, resolution. "How beautiful the season is now—How fine the air. A temperate sharpness about it. Really, without joking. Chaste weather—Dian skies—I never lik'd stubble fields so much as now—Aye better than the chilly green of spring. Somehow a stubble plain looks warm—in the same way that some pictures look warm—this struck me so much in my Sunday's walk that I composed upon it."

The Sunday Keats is speaking of is the 19th of September, a day in the midst—let alone the mist—of days of his heavy correspondence. This comment to Reynolds is matched by the poem, the "composition," he encloses in his letter to Woodhouse. In addition to *settled*, another word that covers Keats's clarity of purpose as well as serenity of means in the middle of the whirl of his personal and familial pressures is *composed*. You could argue that the walks themselves, his Winchester walks, aid and abet the poet's ability—his "negative capability"—to separate himself from his troubles long enough to write as if they didn't exist. You could even argue that the letters, like the walks, have a cathartic effect until the effect wears off. I would argue, though, that the season itself, the arrival of autumn, the idea of autumn, is very much at the heart of the *calm* Keats needs to compose—so much so that *calm* itself becomes part of the subject.

4

Calm, in "To Autumn," translates into those warm and temperate values Keats values in his description of his walks. The "stubble plain" evokes the happy result of the autumn harvest, the gathering and garnering of the grain, and recognition of "the maturing sun" that fills "all fruit with ripeness to the core." Mists and mellowness, warmth and temperateness, sweetness and ripeness constitute the images here, along with the grain-gold and rosy hue of "the soft-dying day."

To Autumn

I

Season of mists and mellow fruitfulness,
Close bosom-friend of the maturing sun;

Conspiring with him how to load and bless
With fruit the vines that round the thatch-eves run;
To bend with apples the moss'd cottage-trees,
And fill all fruit with ripeness to the core;
To swell the gourd, and plump the hazel shells
With a sweet kernel; to set budding more,
And still more, later flowers for the bees,
Until they think warm days will never cease,
For summer has o'er-brimm'd their clammy cells.

II

Who hath not seen thee oft amid thy store?
Sometimes whoever seeks abroad may find
Thee sitting careless on a granary floor,
Thy hair soft-lifted by the winnowing wind;
Or on a half-reap'd furrow sound asleep,
Drows'd with the fume of poppies, while thy hook
Spares the next swath and all its twinèd flowers:
And sometimes like a gleaner thou dost keep
Steady thy laden head across a brook;
Or by a cyder-press, with patient look,
Thou watchest the last oozings hours by hours.

III

Where are the songs of spring? Ay, where are they?
Think not of them, thou hast thy music, too, —
While barrèd clouds bloom the soft-dying day,
And touch the stubble-plains with rosy hue;
Then in a wailful choir the small gnats mourn

Among the river sallows, borne aloft
Or sinking as the light wind lives or dies;
And full-grown lambs loud bleat from hilly bourn;
Hedge-crickets sing; and now with treble soft
The red-breast whistles from a garden-croft;
And gathering swallows twitter in the skies.

Enough has been written about this great ode—and the spring odes, too, for that matter—to fill the granary, the cyder-press, and more. The poem may be entitled "To Autumn," but it's actually looking toward autumn from the edge and ending of summer, a late summer "o'er-brimm'd." It was written on summer's last weekend and acknowledges "That full draught" that is "the parent of my theme," as Keats puts it in the other notable work concurrent with the autumnal ode, "The Fall of Hyperion," which is an improved and updated revision of the failed epic *Hyperion*, from the year before. Keats writes and retouches "To Autumn" in a couple of sittings; "The Fall of Hyperion" is written into the remains of a brilliant fragment of five hundred plus lines. Both poems, however, represent Keats in his newer, cleaner, "Grecian mode." He had said in his journal letter to George that "Some think I have lost that poetic ardour and fire 'tis said I once had—the fact is perhaps I have: But instead of that I hope I shall substitute a more thoughtful and quiet power.... I want to compose without this fever." The walks in the "Environs" of Winchester have helped him achieve that quieter power, and the season has softened the fire, though the sad truth is that Keats is at one with autumn in the worst way as well. The September after this Winchester September he will be on a boat headed for Italy, to die, and, apparently, to disappear.

5

Because it so perfectly embodies the voice of its speaker without directly referencing the speaker—except as an implied interpreter/interrogator—"To Autumn" is often lauded as Keats's purest poem of resolution, standing, to quote Walter Jackson Bate, "transparent before its subject." Aileen Ward, Keats's other important American biographer, writes that the "poet himself is completely lost in his images, and the images are presented as meaning simply themselves: Keats's richest utterance is the barest metaphor." The union of structure and texture in the poem is indeed unsurpassed: the way in which the rhythm of a day's harvest pastoral painting is created, in triptych, before us, following its fulsome "hours by hours" from the dew-starred morning to the drowsy noon to the resonance of the "sinking light" of sunset; and the way in which the painting's perspective enlarges, stanza by stanza, from the cottage and "cottage trees" to the low-lying fields and hills to the softly animated "skies" themselves. So inevitable is the scene—or more precisely, scenes—it is as if the poem itself were speaking into a mirror in the still, calm voice of the gathered harvest.

But it is this tone—the vocal tone, the color tone, the imaginative tone—that interests me about this great poem. Its autumnal tone, if you will. We think of the concept of the correlative in terms of establishing a direct connection between self, speaker, subject, whatever, and the object, the image, the evoked event. "To Autumn" instead correlates self and image "event" indirectly, since the voice of the speaker and the voice of the poem, in this case, are indistinguishable, as if there were no speaker in the usual sense, but rather, synesthetically, an eye that hears what it sees—an eye instead of an "I." The collective correlative of the exhausted goddess, the spilled store of gathered grain, the half-reaped furrow, the swollen gourd, the fume of poppies, the wailful choir of gnats, rendered in terms of mourning, soft-dying, and ripeness to the core—all these details and many more and the attitude brought to bear on their moment derive from a process, a sequence, of witness and surrender, acceptance and reconciliation. No wonder the poem feels tragic, no wonder it seems to arrive so completely at resolution. Its cornucopia runs over.

"Negative capability," the famous phrase Keats has conjured a couple of years before "To Autumn," might serve as an insight of the ideal perspective from which to view the vision of the poem. And perhaps all successful correlatives are negatively capable, like electric wiring. But I find its application here too much from-the-neck-up and not enough from-the-heart-down. Feeling is what we are talking about, the intelligence translated through the senses and the senses understood and translated through the eyes. If we think about the whirl of emotional, financial, personal, and mortal issues surrounding Keats at the time, it seems amazing that he could write poetry at all, let alone compose with mastering composure. One school of thought, certainly, is that writing, regardless, is a form of escape, based on the assumption that poetry in particular is fantasy. On the other hand, Stevens tells us that if poetry is a supreme fiction that makes it an ultimate reality. Eliot draws the distinction between the mind suffering and the mind creating, though he never says how, exactly, this is achieved—he seems to offer the distinction as a definition of the true artist.

Keats's brother George is off in alien America, broke, with a young family, and desperate; Keats himself is penniless and jobless, despite bravura plans and hopes; Keats's love life is an oxymoron; and in the wake of his brother Tom's consumptive death less than a year earlier, Keats is aware he is ill with similar symptoms. There is a connection, I believe, between Keats's personal problems in his last full September in England and the "impersonal" art of this last complete great poem. As a symbolist, Keats has been, in his best work, "impersonal" from the beginning; that is what most distances him from the narrative impulse in Wordsworth and the conversation poems of Coleridge, and what distinguishes him from the didacticism of Shelley: the sense that a poem is a transformative act invested in the object, that the subject of the poem is the object brought wholly into its own free space. The emotion comes to life from the empathic contract with the object and is made vital by the separation from yet identification with the object. The spring odes may be written with more "fever" than a maturing Keats would find interesting, but the dynamics of his relationship to his material are essentially the same. The spring odes may make more of an announcement of their respective speakers while "To Autumn" makes its speaker into a kind of announcer fond of rhetorical questions, but the presence of the poet is the same. The difference between the spring odes and the autumnal ode is tone and the degree to which the writing is divested of anything not immediately and perfectly in the picture.

6

If negative capability has real artistic function—as opposed to being a critical apparatus—it connotes the ability to both separate from and identify with something or someone all at once. Its tensile strength is in direct proportion to the difficulty in exacting art from circumstance. "To Autumn" may seem more impersonal when in fact its quiet power and subtle tension come from the difficulty Keats must have had in entering the imaginative space of the poem without projecting his personal, the world-won't-leave-me-alone troubles. His daily Winchester walks must have helped. But sitting down to write the poem is another matter. Keats must have entered some sort of circle of light, autumnal light; the tension within the space must have been tremendous, enhanced, if possible, by the very problems that defeat lesser writers. The muscle of our being reacts in much the same way: first the resistance, then the relaxation, and the greater the one the greater the other. That tension, in my opinion, underwrites the strength of the rich syntactical intensity, even imagistic and rhythmic density, of the poem. That tension underscores the tone that some readers have found tragic and some readers have found sublime. That tension attenuates by extending the feeling of delayed gratification of closure before the held moment of the "gathering swallows" at twilight.

Can a lyric of thirty-three lines achieve such spaciousness? It's hard not to retro-read Keats's own impending tragedy into this luminous poem. Such a reading, however, substitutes the first-person pronoun for the painter's profound eye. Yet if you think of the poem as a painting only in the sunset hues of, say, a Claude or Poussin, with the backup detail of a harvest scene in a Gainsborough, you focus some of the stillness and solidity as well as the dramatic "blocking" but miss the dimensions of what the poem displaces: you miss the resonance of its widening voice ("thy music too"); you miss the size of its subversion of or separation from an implied narrative; and you miss its "patient" symbolist progression within an eternal autumn. You miss, in a word, what a great painting effects more than any other form: the illusion of simultaneity, in which, in this instance, the heaven of autumn—its mists, its ripeness, its harvest, its drowsiness, and its warmth—is realized as a whole, self-contained, is represented as one "gathering" picture at the very verge of breaking, falling, ending, darkening. The near-burst suspension of things is at the heart of the poem's tacit tension, the way the filled vessel of what has been acknowledged, reaped, and gathered travels beyond the particulars and is lifted, in total, to another level. The feeling of sublimity, right from the start, has to do with this impression of the poem traveling out of its rich, drowsing, melancholy body—no, that's wrong—this impression of the poem as having already traveled, at the outset, from one body into another embodiment is what lifts it, is what gives the poem its deeply spiritual tone.

7

Something about the season helps. The accumulating scene of "To Autumn" is a working landscape whose pastoralism itself is interrogated, and the muted nature, the "mellow fruitfulness" of its world, should not mitigate the rigor of what the "ripeness" means: it means work, and like the pattern of the day and the length of the season it has a rhythm of cutting and gathering and garnering, of which the exquisite near-exhaustion of the scene is the consequence. This is not about fever, therefore; it's about reflection, of thinking, as Keats often did on his walks, in front of a blacksmith's fire. The reader feels the exhaustion as well, that sense we have of receivership, of that "greeting of the spirit" Keats once spoke of. When we meditate we invariably sit or stand in front of a visible or invisible fire, a low fire like a setting sun in its grain-gold autumnal shades. We leave behind, in that moment, the litter of our dailiness; we may even throw it into the fire. We are calm, and if not yet, we'll get there. It's a held moment, a moment of suspension, and if we're lucky it's a moment that allows us to see what otherwise would have been obscure. In its luminous, and illuminating, twilight, autumn is the human season. To me, the most brilliant aspect of "To Autumn" is that nothing in it exists, save for its "music," without the human, yet the complete sublimation of the human hand in the poem is what gives it its sublimity. The harvesters are gone, we are the harvest, we are the fire.

And even if the haystacks and granary cribs and apple stores are only the half of it, nature, in its "leafy ruin," its "golden grove unleaving," sustains its own involuntary harvest, a harvest perhaps all the more powerful because, like "the soft-dying day," it acts on us rather than the other way around. It keeps its own clock and rhythm. The intimate sublime of the changing leaf surpasses us and thus compels us. In his "Autumn" section of *The Seasons*, James Thomson envisions the pastoral and natural worlds as undifferentiated "Woods, fields, orchards, all around"—this "desolated prospect," he says, "thrills the soul." The thrill is in the discovery of desolation, in the impact of the idea of ruins, in the inspiration we find in absences, and in the connection we make between the abundance of the tree of life and, in the same long sentence, its slow stripping away—"bare ruined choirs." If autumn's twilight tree weren't so beautiful, winter really might be unbearable, "When yellow leaves, or none, or few, do hang / Upon those boughs which shake against the cold." That may be part of the warmth Keats finds in the "stubble-plains"—the humanity of the harvest as opposed to the neutrality of naked trees. Yet at the end of the day it's all one, the winnowing season up against the cold winds, wall to wall.

8

That hard edge, though, tends to be attenuated in October and November, extended in time to the extent that autumn often seems the longest season, the season of farewell, departure, memory, resonance, the piecemeal ruin of what is passing, so that when winter finally arrives it slams the door. Before that, autumn is like watching a slow, lovely fire go out, in a room filled with comfort and a window still open, "A Quietness distilled."

1540

As imperceptibly as Grief
The Summer lapsed away—
Too imperceptible at last
To seem like Perfidy—
A Quietness distilled
As Twilight long begun,
Or Nature spending with herself
Sequestered Afternoon—
The Dusk drew earlier in—
The Morning foreign shone—
A courteous, yet harrowing Grace,
As Guest, that would be gone—
And thus, without a Wing
Or service of a Keel
Our Summer made her light escape
Into the Beautiful.

This concentrated, autumnal ode by Emily Dickinson is as pure a poem as she ever wrote—pure in its imaginative terms, pure in its sublimation of the "fever" that sometimes pushes her work, pure in the tone it "distills." Her best poems, regardless of apparent subject, were written during the Civil War, a distant but audible trumpet in Western Massachusetts. This poem comes at the end of that period, in 1865, compared with 258 ("There's a certain Slant of light"), 280 ("I felt a Funeral, in my Brain"), 341 ("After great pain"), 465 ("I heard a Fly buzz"), and her longest lyric, 640 ("I cannot live with You"), all circa 1860–62. And although none of these poems seems remotely related to the war and its consequences, it cannot be possible that the tragedy in the air in most of the rest of the country did not drift north to remote Amherst, and did not only influence the unacknowledged source of grief in this period of her work but helped create a space, postwar, in which to reconcile. Poem #1540 may be about the natural seasonal cycle *cum* autumn, but more to the point is the autumnal tone that builds from its "Grief" to its "light escape / Into the Beautiful," its sense of grace. The linking of language from beginning to end—from "lapsed away" to "imperceptible" to "Quietness distilled" to "Twilight long begun" to "Sequestered afternoon" to "Dusk" to "Harrowing Grace"—is itself a plot, in increments, of linguistic and imaginative reconciliation.

Written in the autumnal year of the First World War, 1917, W. B. Yeats's "The Wild Swans at Coole" also reconciles with change and the future—"when I awake some day / To find they have flown away." The quietness distilled here is defined as stillness, as both adjective and adverb, just as the stillness itself is defined by the breaking of it by the alternate paddling and wheeling "in great broken rings" of the swans' "clamorous wings." Images of stillness and references to "still" as continuance ("Unwearied still") appear in four of the poem's five stanzas; they help organize the silence, the mirror calm of sky and water, against which the swans "drift" and fly and within which the speaker sees and hears more deeply. The trees, says the speaker, are in their autumn beauty; naturally, it's twilight, "October twilight"; the paths are dry, the water "brimming . . . among the stones"; and the swans, "those brilliant creatures," are "Mysterious, beautiful," all fifty-nine of them. Counting is the speaker's way of paying attention, and of measuring the mortality implicit in the scene. Leaf by falling leaf, it seems, he is aware. Melancholy may enhance the tone of the experience of what the speaker is listening to and looking at, but clarity, a certain bell-clarity ("the bell-beat of their wings above my head"), underwrites the heart of the poem and warms the elegance of its distances. The speaker realizes that like the leaves and the swans he too is interchangeable. The counting goes on, regardless of who's counting, just as the longing so given to the season is eternal.

9

My heart aches, "my heart is sore," says a lovelorn Yeats. Autumn will make a ruin of the heart, but it will also fill it. It's off the subject to suggest some of the intersections meeting in "The Wild Swans at Coole," including the off-stage presence (no pun intended) of Maud Gonne, the precursor presence of symbolic swans, the allusive presence of war (Yeats will go on to make it central to his work), and the aesthetic presence of the Celtic Twilight (symbolist mist). But one thing for sure, Yeats, like Dickinson and Keats, *sees* and by his own eyes is inspired, scene and setting, while autumn is a place to come to, not so much to escape war and personal conflict but to put them in perspective, the perspective of a larger, transcendent rhythm, removed in time from time. Robert Frost's "After Apple-Picking" is written at the beginning of the First World War, and at the beginning of modernism, but these events seem worlds away from the ambivalence, exhaustion, and, in the end, emptiness blessing Frost's poem. Frost is as much an existentialist as the next modernist, "overtired / Of the great harvest I myself desired." Nor is his autumnal insight any less ambiguous, since

> I cannot rub the strangeness from my sight
> I got from looking through a pane of glass
> I skimmed this morning from the drinking trough
> And held against the world of hoary grass.

The early announcement in the poem that the speaker is "done with apple-picking now" serves to intensify what this postharvest state of being amounts to: a body burdened by its own desire, filled, and desiring to be empty. It's the in-between of these desires that makes him, like Keats's Ceres, so drowsy and dreamy. The keenness in the air of the season is here turned in on itself—sleep, or, better, sleepiness becomes the twilight vision, the dream vision, through which Frost's speaker can see: the harvest's excess is also its emptiness, and both states are as undesirable as desired . . . "oozings hours by hours."

The Dickinson in Frost not only feels the ache of the "instep arch" from standing hours on the ladder but knows the potential pleasure, the excess, of the fantasized "ten thousand fruit to touch / Cherish in hand, lift down, and not let fall." Yet the fruit will fall, regardless, picked or not. The vision of the cup "o'er-brimm'd" is completed by the reality of the cup spilled. The richness of the harvest season becomes its ruin—its warm "stubble-plains," its "bare ruined choirs" of the orchard. To drowse, to see in an altered state that includes, at once, the richness as well as the ruin is to reconcile with the season after apple-picking, winter. Autumn's leaner, winter-edge, on the December side of "To Autumn," maintains this tone but with sharper focus and a change of light. Late autumn is about the value that endings give to things.

10

"Is there an imagination that sits enthroned / As grim as it is benevolent, the just / And the unjust, which in the midst of summer stops / To imagine winter?" Stevens asks this question in the midst of "The Auroras of Autumn." It's asked in the typically abstract language of the senior Stevens, but it means to address the palpable nature of what autumn is: transition, contradiction, resolution, the opposite of "breeding / Lilacs out of the dead land." It's a rhetorical question, since the strength of the imagination is to imagine winter in summer—i.e., Autumn—and the greater the tensile strength in the polar separation of the seasons, the greater the negative strength the more sublime. Hence the great summer-in-winter meditation, Walt Whitman's great late autumnal ode, "Crossing Brooklyn Ferry," written in December, while the light is still white gold before it turns to snow. The negative capability here applies to setting as much as season. Imagine the scene of the harvest as a harbor and the "tall masts of Mannahatta" as the trees, backed up by the "beautiful hills of Brooklyn" and the emerging skyline of Manhattan. Imagine the honey-white light of a December evening and ferry crossing of the East River, "the sun half an hour high," sparkling in the air and dazzling on the water. Imagine the travelers themselves—those crossing the river now and those who have crossed it and will in the future—as part of the harvest, part of the change and renewal, upon whom "the dark patches fall."

No poem in American poetry, perhaps any poetry, more movingly articulates the "impalpable sustenance" of disintegration of self in terms of all of that which is not self than this hundred and thirty-two line contemplation. For Keats, it's as if the self disappears a priori into the poem; for Dickinson the self is the interrogator and mortal witness; for Frost the self is the dreamer, between waking and sleeping, fulfillment and loss. For Whitman, though, the self is in process, *in medias res*, in both space and time, river and crossing, and whose realization is only possible through the "dumb, beautiful ministers" of the urban natural world he has envisioned. For Whitman, the city, "mast-hemm'd" Manhattan, is nature, and the medium of passage is light, late autumnal, penultimate light, and life-bearing water, "the float forever held in solution," and each of these—light and water inseparable—is manifested in detail throughout the poem—in the "scallop-edg'd waves of flood-tide" to the "fine spokes of light, from the shape of my head, or any one's head, in the sunlit water."

Again and again, detail by accruing and returning detail, Whitman comes back to the "eternal float of solution," water as light, light as water, in order to demonstrate the ritual imaginative dissolution required to join that "which none else is more lasting," which is a harvest of all that is palpable in the poem, including ships and seagulls, buildings and hillsides, ferry and passengers, past, present, and future, all of them, great or small, furnishing their parts toward the impalpable, which Whitman calls the soul. The suggestion is that the fullness of being that autumn represents and the corresponding emptiness (dissolution) it simultaneously creates are not only cyclical, seasonal, but predictable, thus eternal, a kind of afterlife to spring's rebirth of life. Light and water are ancient symbols for these passages, but by reinventing them in an urban pastoral Whitman gives added dimension to the sublime. "Crossing Brooklyn Ferry" is a crucial act of imagination, whose substance draws its sustenance from the time of the year and the angle of the early December light on the East River, facing away from arrival and against the setting sun.

11

Exactly to the Sunday one year after he writes "To Autumn," Keats makes his own crossing, entering what he calls his "posthumous existence," his autumnal afterlife. Along with a friend, and now fellow-traveler, Joseph Severn, Keats is on a small brig, the *Maria Crowther*, heading down the Thames for Gravesend to the open sea and then to Italy. It's September 19, 1820, with the prospect of a warmer winter climate seen as a possible remedy for what ails him, which is a subject of some conjecture. Clearly he is ill, and has been in degrees of declension for a long time—certainly since the first near-fatal hemorrhaging the February before. Because of storm delays, rough seas, indifferent food, crowded conditions, and further bouts of hemorrhaging, plus a ten-day quarantine once they reach the many "mast-hemm'd" Bay of Naples, the voyage—if such a clumsy crossing can be called a voyage—is excruciating, leaving Keats to wonder why he's left England in the first place, if only to die so far away. It will be Keats's twenty-fifth birthday, October 31, before passengers and crew again touch land.

Keats's and Severn's destination is Rome, the Eternal—if you will—City. It's a hundred and forty miles north along the Mediterranean coast from Naples. In too many ways the journey by small, slow, hard-bottomed carriage over a rutted road will reprise their painful three-week sea-journey. The ride in the vettura and the overnights in the "villainously coarse and unpalatable" accommodations, however, will be in dramatic contrast to the nature—both human and otherwise—they encounter on their sixteen-miles-a-day passage, a passage that for Keats becomes a descent. The coastal road means stopping at such places as Terracina, Mesa, Torre de' Tre Ponti, Velletri, and Albano; it means moving in and out of sight of the sea, among lush hills of olive trees and Lombardy poplars and stone pines. November rains have visited the coast in the week right before they've started, so that now, suddenly, the weather has improved to the point that blue skies, blue views, and warmer temperatures have taken over. "The pure air," Severn will note later, "was exhilarating," and at the walking pace of the speed at which they're traveling, they have plenty of time to breathe and drink in that atmosphere. Pale Keats is managing as best he can, in the bob-and-weave of the ride. To give him more room Severn decides early on to amble beside the carriage.

Severn is a young painter. The subtext of his companionship of Keats is that the art community in Rome may advance his artistic career by supporting his chances for a Royal Academy traveling fellowship. But that is in the future. Right now it's his painter's eye that helps to bring the slow trip north to life. Two or three sights dominate Severn's memory when, many years later, he writes his memoirs. One is the giant aqueducts, the great land bridges for water, that the ancient Romans have engineered, just as they engineered the well-worn road they are traveling. The aqueducts give the effect of ruins, of great twilight structures lost between worlds; if Severn had thought for a moment he might have linked their fragmentary look to certain scenes of desolation in Keats's *Hyperion* poems, where old Saturn sits like broken statuary awaiting the change of gods. There are even, intermittently, leftover gibbets for the crucifixion of thieves, though their status as ruins is somewhat compromised by the ragged bones of bodies still adorning a few of them. Then there is the example, as they approach the Campagna, of the cardinal, in full regalia, who along with the aid of his footmen is shooting out of the sky songbirds. "He had an owl tied loosely to a stick," Severn writes, "and a small looking-glass . . . annexed to move about with the owl, the light of which attracted numerous birds. The whole merit of this sport seemed to be in not shooting the owl. Two footmen in livery kept loading the fowling-pieces for the cardinal, and it was astonishing the great number of birds he killed."

Such sights serve an ironic texture, completely exotic to these two bright young Englishmen. The looming stone bridges over land, the hanging crosses, the Catholic clergyman, himself dressed in and named for the color of a bird yet shooting them for sport—these human parts have an otherworldly, grotesque, transitional feel to them, alien—at least to an outsider—to the Italian arcadian autumnal landscape. To Keats, whose consumption has severely weakened him and given him the look of his "palely loitering" knight-at-arms, such strangely real yet surreal encounters must reinforce how far from home he is. As if he has entered a demi-mortal world. On the other hand, the freshening sea wind and new November warmth have brought the wildflowers back, of which, Severn says, there is a "profusion." He doesn't say which wildflowers, though at that time of the year yarrow, Queen Anne's lace, and tansy would be popular, and maybe hawkweed and goldenrod, all off-whites and yellows. And for fresh color, if they are near the sea or among the marshes, an occasional marsh rose. The Campagna, too, trying to redeem its reputation for evil air (*mal'aria*), produces flowers. Perhaps if Severn had stayed with Keats in the carriage he would have enjoyed the profusion as an observer. But since he is walking, and wanting to cheer his friend, he decides to pick some of the flowers and to fill "the little carriage." Severn reports that Keats "never tired of these . . . they gave him a singular and almost fantastic pleasure that was at times almost akin to a strange joy."

12

He picks a lot and for several days, placing and replacing his bouquets around the ailing poet until the vettura is "literally filled . . . with flowers." Though no one mentions the obvious—including the biographers—by the time they reach the outskirts of Rome, Keats is in his funeral carriage. From this moment on the story is, in the words of one commentator, "a masterpiece of disintegration," culminating, in three excruciating months, in Keats's death. They enter Rome through the Lateran Gate, pass the Colosseum—yet another autumnal ruin—head north for a mile or so and arrive at the Piazza di Spagna in the late afternoon in the middle of November. Keats's Roman doctor, a Scotsman by the name of James Clark, who, like many in the English colony, lives on the Piazza, has found rooms for them a bird's walk away at number 26. Suffice it to say that if too many of the images from Keats's life, particularly near the end, become emblems of foreshadowing, such as the flowers he arrives in Rome surrounded by, then the famous little room to which he becomes confined and in which he dies, will more and more resemble his living tomb. He must have become fairly familiar with the "festoons of Roses" adorning his ceiling, for example, enough so that at one late point he tells Severn that he can already feel the flowers growing over him. Even books and letters he will not open begin to take on the autumnal odor "of mortality."

Winter in Rome is a twilit season, a kind of crepuscular, chill fall. There are rains and there is morning fog and in the evening an almost invisible mist. But in between, on the best days, the soft gold light brings out the texture in the travertine stone and the old color in the rosso Romano and yellow ocher buildings. Autumnal colors, fading tones. On those rare days when they do get out, in late December, early January, when the air still has some warmth in it, Keats and Severn "stroll on the Pincio . . . particularly because it was sheltered from the north wind." Keats also occasionally rides, but "at a snail's pace," with Severn matching stride by walking shoulder to shoulder with the horse. Once the companion, Severn is now the nurse, ever conscious of the weather that seems to be sustaining his friend, weather that can be "warm like summer" or "lovely . . . like the Italian spring in winter." Keats, for his part, must be thinking he's entered an afterlife for sure, a place in beautiful mid-light between nothingness and the palpable something whole life is. Outside, in "the balmy air," the bits and pieces of Rome he manages to see must seem imaginary, like a floating Arcadia, while inside, in the half-dark, staring at the painted roses on his ceiling, Rome must feel like a mausoleum, a space—as he writes in *Hyperion*—that "where the dead leaf fell, there it did rest."

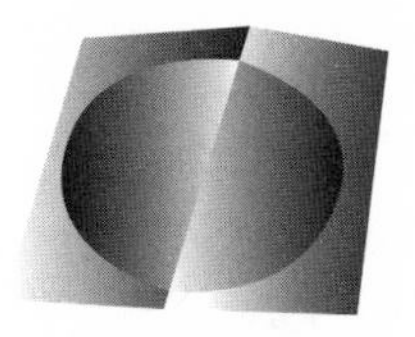

J. ALLYN ROSSER

Caveat Lector

The question of what to read is so crucial, so personal, so staggeringly impactful for a writer, so potentially oppressive, so equally potentially liberating, that one can only presume to offer recommendations with a disclaimer, such as: "In this case, consult yourself; you are your own best guide."

But you really ought to listen to me first.

Doing What You're Told

Let me guess: you are reading this essay for the same reason I used to eat cooked carrots in my college dining hall. I hated cooked carrots for most of my life. But then I *chose* to eat cooked carrots when I was no longer under the parental roof, far from cooked-carrot pressure—I dumped double helpings on my plate, grimacing, whenever I felt guilty for not studying hard enough. You may be thinking that the poetry you have been reading and enjoying—not to mention the novels you have surreptitiously devoured over the past three months while Marvell, Tennyson, and Stevens languished untouched on your shelf—must now be relinquished in favor of a beta-carotene-rich canon decreed by others. You plan to read many essays like this one and to glean therefrom the most frequently recommended texts, and you will dedicate yourself to ingesting those pages, no matter how distasteful they turn out to be. Now you're going to pay your dues, suffer properly.

Well, I can tell you from my experience that this is the wrong way to go about keeping your love of poetry alive. I can tell you that the nutrients I might have absorbed from choking down a third of a serving of overcooked carrots were nothing compared to the healthful benefits I'd have derived from any number of fruits and vegetables that I loved and therefore would actually have finished entire portions of.

Read what you want to at least sixty percent of the time.

It would be felicitous, of course, if you discovered that Keats or Milton were your natural fixation, since then you could feel dirty and virtuous all at once, indulging yourself with the literary equivalent of royal jelly, reserved in bee colonies for the queen or the queen pupa.

More often it will be a "lesser" poet, roughly contemporary, who grabs you by the lapels and won't let go. One who writes about the things you are experiencing and whose lexicon and style approximate the way you think and speak. Or you are fascinated by the otherness of a writer, the exotic environment, atmosphere, language. (I once went on a three-month Charles Bukowski binge; still recovering.) You know this poetry is not considered "great" by your teachers, or by critics you've been persuaded know more than you do. It's possible they do. But they don't know what you need right *now*. That charged-up, pulse-racing attention you can give to the literature you most love now will teach you more about how to write well than the texts you sigh listlessly over, checking your watch and seeing if the mail has come or the tea water is boiling yet. Am I saying, "Don't bother to read Dante, Wordsworth, Robert Penn Warren"? No. But I would like you to treat your reading as if it were a party, and crash it. Do not let yourself be introduced to any writer. Find a way to bump into one. Be creative, be random, casual in your approach. Read his last volume first; sneak up on her from behind. Don't tell yourself you have to go home with him. Don't expect to recognize your soul mate within an hour of meeting her.

Perhaps the party metaphor isn't working for you: you're shy, you don't drink, don't dance well, you're feeling bloated tonight. Let's say you really would like a list, a list of writers to read and take seriously, a list of writers you wouldn't naturally be drawn to in your meanderings at the bookstore. You want your goddamn carrots and you want them now. You want to draw up a cozy, customized syllabus for your progress toward becoming a well-read, not-too-eclectically influenced poet. And let's say you're mortal. You have limited waking hours during a limited number of years to devote to reading. Therefore the selections must be judicious—respected work that has been recommended to you by someone respectable. You do not want to be filling your head with crap, and there is a whole lot of that to contend with in the library. The syllabus must not be overwhelming—the shelves you assign yourself must not be so numerous that you'll despair before you've even bought a bulb for your new reading lamp.

Where to start? One of your writing teachers insists that what turned her on to poetry was Spenser's *The Faerie Queene*, and has urged you to read that first. Don't listen to her. Do not ever believe what a writer tells you. She is not in the business of sharing or recording facts. She probably started writing in the first place because the facts always struck her as inadequate, or as distortions themselves.

Forgive her: she may not actually remember what first illuminated the poetry chamber of her heart; she knows not whether she's repressing it because she'd be faintly embarrassed to admit that Walter de la Mare was the first poet she grew to love. De la Who? Or she may merely be fantasizing: what would her own education have been like if she'd been advised to start with Spenser? It's sort of fun to tell people what to do and then watch to see what happens when they do it. This is one reason she became a teacher. Another reason is that she really does love Spenser, and teaching gives her an excuse to read him again. For a twenty-first-century person who has not already digested good chunks of Chaucer, Shakespeare, and Milton, however, Spenser will not go down easily.

Another of your mentors swears by Swinburne; another adores Dante; another exhorts you to memorize all of Hopkins before you dare sharpen your own pencil. Some writers will tell you the Bible is their main influence (in writing but not in living—which right there should make you suspicious); some will insist that Proust has been seminal to their evolution, when almost invariably they have not finished more than one translated volume of Proust's work. Wallace Stevens claimed that he never read contemporary poetry, so as to avoid contamination of style. Well, this is an absolute crock, as anyone who has read his letters (and book reviews) can tell you. Read what you like, read what makes you stand up every now and then, pacing and exclaiming, gesticulating and pulling at your hair. But save some time for the things you've been told to read.

The Rating Game—Anthologies

When making decisions about what to read, you must primarily consult yourself the way you do in a relationship, since you are intellectually mating with any author you read intently. This is part of the reason you can't just dutifully read a list of works that has been handed off to you. "There, see that guy in the corner by the poster of James Dean, nursing his Glenfiddich? Go over there, be seduced by him. I know he's your type. And after him there's the flashy number in white cutoffs, be seduced by her, too; and don't neglect the dark-haired sultry one filching maraschino cherries from the bar." You're probably not in the mood for the bar scene, either.

So if it's got to be your choice, how do you choose? You already know most of the candidates, since they're listed in all the Big Anthologies, tamely bio'd and lined up chronologically, sometimes even by school. Oh sure, there are plenty of names missing that should be there. And you're absolutely right, there's the problem with trends, and with anthology chestnuts, everywhere you look the same ten poems by Dickinson, the same ten by Auden, the same ten by William Carlos Williams. And what have they done this time with Robinson Jeffers? Where is Josephine Jacobsen, for crying out loud? I'm with you: anthologies stink. They stink of conservatism, if they don't stink of a similarly smug claim of being the most experimentally inclined collection, the most "cutting edge," the most contemporarily "out there." But so what if anthologies exclude, so what if they misrepresent, so what if they only offer the safe, inoffensive stuff, so what if they are more worried about giving the historically underrepresented a boost than about quality? Don't we need them to get a sampling of writers we would ordinarily never get to? Yes! *Mais oui!* Don't you want to find out what the writers in Ghana are doing these days?

I own many many many anthologies and I love drifting through them when I want to read but feel unfocused (far too often the case). But there is a grave danger: if you treat the anthology as your principal guide to the authors represented in them, you may prematurely dismiss a poet whose other works might well serve as the tributary leading to your new vision, or your as-yet-embryonic voice. The danger of an anthology, as with anything else, lies in how you use it. If you believe the editors have miraculously managed to select the five or ten or even twenty poems that are the most representative of the poet in question, and you don't care for those poems, how can you possibly expect yourself, a reasonable, sane pleasure-seeker, to seek out more work by that poet; to try a whole book by her or him?

Read your anthologies. Read your friends' anthologies. Read anthologies left on park benches. But beware. If you are unlucky enough to read all of the Larkin selections and none of them is "Aubade," you may overlook the poem you most need from him. Give the anthology poets you initially labeled Losers second and third chances. Try to read a whole book by a poet, hell, go for two, before dismissing her or him.

Recently I was in a bookstore (the kind you hardly ever buy books in because they're choking out the independent bookstores, but they make good coffee and allow you to browse all day in their better-than-average poetry section), thumbing through yet another brand-new expensive-smelling anthology, and was smirking over how predictable its contents were—so much laziness and looking-over-the-shoulder, unimaginative repackaging—when I halted at Dante Gabriel Rossetti's "The Woodspurge." Of course I had read it a hundred times before, hadn't I? Yet its moves felt unfamiliar. It seemed kind of good. I read it very softly out loud to myself (vague paranoia and/or awareness of the man at the next table twitching with irritation over his latté) two times through. It was good. All this time I had let Rossetti fall to the wayside of my reading path, probably due to some bad choices made by an editor of Pre-Raphaelite poetry. Or to my listlessness when I had finally dragged myself through the sonnet cycle "The House of Life" and "Sister Helen" all the way to "The Woodspurge" in the Rossetti section of whatever book, beaten down by the florid drama of many of his other poems, beaten into uncomprehending glassiness. What caught my interest this time? The breathless use of repetition in the first stanza?

> The wind flapped loose, the wind was still,
> Shaken out dead from tree and hill:
> I had walked on at the wind's will, —
> I sat now, for the wind was still.

The way the word *wind* dominates the stanza and persona equally? The trope of wind as an old dusty rag that swats repulsively when it blows, lies there as if ready for the trash heap when it ceases? The prosodic variations that feel absolutely allied to the plodding exhaustion expressed in the lines? There is the determinedly wooden simplicity of the lexicon, enhancing that sense of stunned lostness Rossetti is getting at. The *aaaa* rhyme scheme, which is unusual because it is practically impossible to pull off without sounding like a nursery rhyme. The way you feel buffeted, shoved at, by the spondees "walked on" and "wind's will," followed by the dumped-down feeling of "I sat now." The echo of line one's "the wind was still" at the end of the quatrain reinforcing the atmosphere's deadness with even greater force because the "ill" rhyme (the persona is ill, no question there) clangs its immutable, unchangeable, obstinate syllable down finally in its full original morpheme so that we viscerally can feel the fixed, rigged, forget-it-pal hopelessness of his circumstances.

Shall I stop here? I don't want to talk about how well this poem is orchestrated—I really do want to talk about you—but look at those entirely forgivable syntactical inversions in stanza two, given that the persona has literally been through an upheaval, emotional and now physical as well:

Between my knees my forehead was, —
My lips, drawn in, said not Alas!
My hair was over in the grass,
My naked ears heard the day pass.

Rossetti is careful to point out that there is no breast-beating here. You don't say *Alas*, or anything else for that matter, when you're really down and out. His life is over; man, even his hair is over. The lifelessness of this speaker is dramatized by his hair hanging down, mingling with the grass—as if his corpse had sprouted from six feet under?—by his near-fetal pose, his return to unaccommodated "naked" being, stripped of normal consciousness. You know what it's like, this kind of grief: you don't really process anything. You're completely withdrawn. Even your lips are "drawn in"; your self simply shuts down in psycho-emotional coma. Now we move into the third stanza, where he stares zombielike before him:

My eyes, wide open, had the run
Of some ten weeds to fix upon;
Among those few, out of the sun,
The woodspurge flowered, three cups in one.

The positioning of "wide open" in the line seems almost an afterthought, offered as descriptive rather than active (they were wide open through no agency of his own; that's just how they were, and how they were going to remain). In my former Rossetti-resistant stance, I'd have widened my own eyes a little in exasperation, translating: O, I am miserable and here comes yon goode olde nature to solace me! But the poem has somehow caught me off guard. I trust him now. I keep reading.

From perfect grief there need not be
Wisdom or even memory:
One thing then learnt remains to me, —
The woodspurge has a cup of three.

That's it. None of his overbearing symbolism, his overblown, fanciful, infelicitously choked prolixities (e.g., "Life's foam-fretted feet"), none of what I'd come to expect from Rossetti. You can accuse the poem, I suppose, of a kind of sentimentality, the sort I allude to above. But I think that's a misreading. The poem does not exalt nature, does not even pat it on the head. What it does, and I think marvelously, is hand over this grieving experience intact, unbrooded-upon, disjoined from any kind of analytic or moralizing angle, disengaged from one's customary responses to the world. For an entire day the man stared at a single spot, which happened to be a weed. At the time he didn't fully assimilate the weed as such; it simply provided a kind of emotional black hole. There is a certain casualness of expression here, particularly in stanza three: it's as if he needs to bring you to the spot and describe it faithfully in order to tell you how he felt, the way your friend wants you to see where she grew up, the exact house ("It used to be green") to help you understand who she is. "The Woodspurge" conveys the absolute futility of this condition. Grief has no practical function: it doesn't make you strong; it doesn't teach you anything; it doesn't help to resolve the problem. Is this a revelation? I think (though many would argue that grief does make you strong, despite the fact that it quite often proves lethal) that we all know this deep down, have known it—but we're always being fed that Pollyanna cant about its redemptive virtues: the bright side of grief! In revisiting his own grief, Rossetti's speaker grasps at nothing. Just this image, which means nothing. The time spent in the state of grief has yielded an insignificant and entirely impersonal observation. Nothing, really, at all. We are asked to perceive, to feel, its hollowness.

There are many moving poems about grief, but very few have made me feel so certain that the author is remembering it as it was. Dickinson does it devastatingly in several poems ("There is a pain – so utter –"; "I felt a Funeral, in my Brain"); Ben Jonson does it in "On the Death of My First Son"; Bishop does it, astonishingly, in "One Art"; yes, I have a short-list, and Rossetti is suddenly there on it. That last line, "The woodspurge has a cup of three," blows me away with its resigned, wooden shrug, its self-appalled matter-of-factness.

Here lies the value of the anthology—even the kind that contains poems your other anthologies contain. An anthology can recontextualize a poem whose effect you've listlessly mummified, the way spiders wrap their victims, for a later reading you may never get to. Anthologies let you make the rounds of your mummies, and in the right mood you can unsnap your judgment, unwrap and reexamine them and be surprised. Another advantage: you can poke desultorily through an anthology without feeling guilty, whereas you know, don't you, it's a sin to do that with an individual poet's book. So read, read anthologies, but do not trust them.

Whole Books

On the other hand, if you never settle down with whole books you'll miss the very fine poems that were too fine—too subtle or heart-wrenchingly understated or too strange—to make the editors' top ten, if in fact the editors have read those very fine poems with more than a cursory scan. One of my favorite Frost poems has never, to my knowledge, been in an anthology; in fact, I don't think it makes the cut of any Frost "selected." The poem is a sonnet called "Meeting and Passing." It appears just before "Hyla Brook" and "The Oven

Bird" in his 1916 volume, *Mountain Interval*, so you could say it faces some fierce competition rather directly. When I discovered the poem I was on a Frost kick; I needed the feel of his career, the whole arc, and was planning to read all the books seriatim. I wish I could say I got through them all during that month, but I don't think so. I'm sure I had a very good excuse at the time. Never mind, never mind. The point is, I read the poem and was surprised by the numbness, the in-your-face dullness, of the last two lines:

> Afterward I went past what you had passed
> Before we met, and you what I had passed.

Clunk-a-clunk-clunk. Here again (as in the first stanza of "The Woodspurge") we see the use of the identical word for the rhyme, this time for the crescendo of the final couplet, if you could call that a *crescendo*. But I was onto Frost. He had deliberately wiped the lines clean of any possible inherent interest. In fact the interest is precisely in their lack of interest. The first quatrain of the sonnet more than prepares us for such a closure:

> As I went down the hill along the wall
> There was a gate I had leaned at for the view
> And had just turned from when I first saw you
> As you came up the hill. We met. But all
> We did that day was mingle great and small
> Footprints in summer dust as if we drew
> The figure of our being less than two
> But more than one as yet. Your parasol
> Pointed the decimal off with one deep thrust.
> And all the time we talked you seemed to see

> Something down there to smile at in the dust.
> (Oh, it was without prejudice to me!)
> Afterward I went past what you had passed
> Before we met, and you what I had passed.

A person who was not already passionate about Frost's poetry would be more than happy to pass this poem without a backward look. But because I had been reading so deeply in his work, I was attuned, I was primed for his slyness, whereas a mere "poking around" in his books would have left me baffled and bored by this deceptively bleached-looking little dustbath.

The encounter of the two young people in this poem is charged with significance: it marks a turning point in their relationship, which is about to become more intimate ("being less than two / But more than one as yet"). Because there usually is no way to convey the amazing incredible power and blazing importance of such a moment to one who is not party to the relationship, Frost decides to play his restraint card. The words seem to efface themselves even as they appear. He really pushes it, going so far as to use the word *past* within the final couplet to double down on the *passed/passed* rhyme, numbing the reader further. He will make the encounter—at least his initial and closing descriptions of it—so mind-numbingly bland that the reader is startled, and, if she hasn't fallen asleep, she will begin actively to search for significance. Of course it's in there. Frost lets the earthshaking quality of the meeting creep up on us just as it takes time to register on the personae in the poem. The second two quatrains do spice it up—he couldn't hold our attention otherwise, could he?—but then he fully relapses into that flattened-out language in the closing couplet. He must. Because everything has changed as a result of this meeting, the old boring words are, for the speaker, pulsating with magic and beauty; he cannot see how dull they are. The reader cannot immediately understand this because all she has to go on is the outwardly dull statement and the dusty, flat language; the reader is so mystified and struck by that flatness (now contrasting with the "spicier" two quatrains) that she must "enter" the speaker in order to feel anything at all, and when she does she sees, as if experiencing the change with him, that everything he now passes has become infused with the recent presence and witness of the beloved, and vice versa. So the same old same old they pass every day now begins to reverberate with enchantment and mystery. I do not think I *would* be moved if the language itself were not so superficially unmoving.

Had I not forced myself to read Frost's whole (almost) oeuvre, I wouldn't have this poem in my arsenal. What arsenal? The weaponry a poet needs to fight off that cloying sense of nothing-new, the sense of everybody flapping their lips and who cares, the sense of glut you get when you've been reading too many bad books. . . .

Shakespeare

Should you read and reread the sonnets (how many will give one a passing grade in well-readness?) and the most famous plays? Should you read *Cymbeline*? *Timon of Athens*? I've never read either, and I'm not proud of it. (Give me credit for *Coriolanus*.) But I have read *King Lear* and *Hamlet* and a dozen others more than once. This is because I am a slow reader. I have to be selective! I have felt more urgently drawn to the better-known plays because they're so obviously great and because references to them are rife in the literature that I read, and I hate being excluded from the world the mind I'm mating with has been soaked in. I would wager that Milton read every last pica of Shakespeare. But he went blind, didn't he? Maybe he overdid the reading thing. Moreover, he didn't also have William Wordsworth,

Derek Walcott, Alfred Tennyson, C. D. Wright, *American Poetry Review*, Jorie Graham, *People* magazine, and T. S. Eliot on his plate, did he? He could afford to read *Cymbeline*.

Milton and His Ilk

Should you read *Paradise Lost*? Yes. Forget everything I said back there; read the whole thing. You will learn everything there is to learn about meter by reading it. You may want to read Paul Fussell's *Poetic Meter and Poetic Form* also if you still have questions.

The Canterbury Tales? Yes.

Dante? Do it.

Homer? Well, you could read him or you could walk around the rest of your life with one hand tied behind your back.

Proust? *Swann's Way*, then decide about the rest. You'll know if you need more.

Beckett? Until I read Beckett's prose trilogy (*Molloy*, *Malone Dies*, *The Unnameable*) I couldn't comprehend Ashbery. Perhaps comprehend is not the word; twig, get, enjoy. How are they connected, you ask? How can I tell you until you've read the trilogy? The fact is, Ashbery himself has never read Beckett's prose. He told me this. I was shocked, dismayed; I was sorry for him. Those who influenced Ashbery may have read and been influenced by Beckett. Is this significant? Maybe not one bit.

I even told Mr. Ashbery to read the stuff, but did he do it? Ask him, if you're not too busy reading *Timon of Athens*, and get back to me. The point is, reading Beckett and loving Beckett and laughing my pants off over Beckett opened up some dormant synapses that expanded my appreciation of a worldview, a vista, an angle, that gave me a port to Ashbery as a bonus. You will never know how your reading will help you until you've done the reading.

How about Henry James? You're a poet, you believe in brevity. So do you read *The Ambassadors* and roll your eyes, then the first third of *The Golden Bowl*, and then quit? Well, let's see. What happens to you when you read James? Does he make you want to shatter expensive crockery, or does he chime with a way of thinking about the world that is already mapped into your creative chromosomes, that makes you want to write in a new clause-rich labyrinthine psychological minefield kind of territory you had never known was more you than the fragmented, disjointed things you've been writing because that's what your reading has heretofore trained you to value? I'd be willing to bet C. K. Williams has read plenty of James. Check with him, if you're not too preoccupied with the *Iliad*. Let me know.

Here's What You Do

Read what makes you want to keep reading. Read what you're addicted to. Suck the juice out of that while it still tastes so good. Next year it could turn your stomach, but by that time you'll have drawn from it what you need to keep going. Sometimes it's the bad poetry that will encourage you; sometimes the good stuff will make you feel small, smaller, smallest. Thackeray once threw down Dickens' *Dombey & Son* in despair: how to keep writing with such competition in the world? Push past all of that. Sixty percent of the time, read what you like to read. Okay, take seventy. But save thirty percent for what you've heard of, what you suspect you should at least have a passing acquaintance with, what might just, after all that procrastination and resistance, change your life.

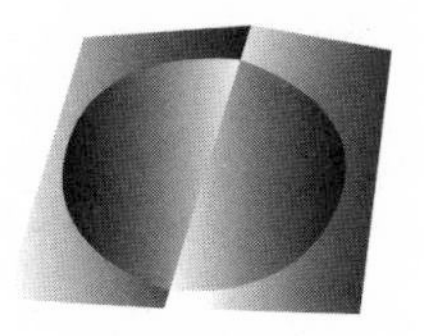

MARVIN BELL

Prosody & Reciprocity (On Reading)

Part 1: Why Read?

Learning to write is a simple process: read something, then write something; read something else, then write something else. And show in your writing what you have read.

You do not learn from work like yours as much as you learn from work unlike yours.

In 1976 I went to live in Spain with a single book of poetry, *Spring & All* by William Carlos Williams. One book can be enough if you intend to read it as people used to read and reread the few books they owned.

•

Reading as a writer is not the same as reading as a nonwriter. A writer, reading as a writer, absorbs the sounds, rhythms, feel, mind, even the look of the text. A writer reads on the edge of his or her chair. A writer goes slowly and doubles back. Part of the poetic encounter is a quality you experience when you pay special attention to language. After all, poems are not the process but the result. To be seriously influenced by reading, you must try to feel how the very words of the poem came about. You must be willing to lose yourself in the reading and perhaps be changed by it.

Why such an apprenticeship? Why master classes? No matter how good you are in your hometown, at some point you have got to play with the best. If your child is really that talented on the violin, he or she needs a world-class teacher. It's not for nothing that the best athletes head for those coaches, schools, and playgrounds where the other hotshots have gone. Louis Armstrong and Miles Davis didn't become great trumpeters by stepping on the football field with the high-school band. You want to be a carpenter, you've got to apprentice yourself to a good one. You want to be a tailor, it helps to know at least one person who can make a suit.

The way things are, we can't always move across the country to the great coach or master artist. But in literature it's different. One can hang out with the best, day and night. They are all at hand, in the library and the bookstore.

Part 2: Apologia

I cannot be sure which poets others should read first. That is an individual matter that depends on such intangibles as timing and temperament. In practice, I suggest books based on both a person's writing and his or her background. I believe a woman's reading should include women writers, a Latino's should include Latino writers, an Asian-American should read other Asian-Americans, etc. Literature has both technical and cultural components.

One doesn't teach vision any more than one teaches genius. One only tries to help a writer locate his or her individuality. Deep inside, people are wired differently, one from another. Poetic genius lies in tapping into one's special wiring. It's groovy to claim that good poetry is heartfelt expression and can do without talk of technique. The facts suggest the opposite: that poems that do not exhibit an interest in language and form have a short life span.

But what of Ezra Pound's quotation from, he says, De Quincey or Coleridge (he is himself not sure which) to the effect that, "The character of a great poet is everywhere present yet nowhere visible as a distinct excitement." Doesn't that suggest that an individual voice can be overly prized? Yes, it does, but research shows that even those poetic voices that seem most located in the center of our experience, emotionally and linguistically, have come by way of an amalgam of strong, unique voices. They too made a new blend from strong flavors.

Experience suggests that it is helpful, if not crucial, for young poets interested in achieving an individual voice to have read poetry of past centuries, to have lingered over many of the significant modern poets, and to have absorbed the work of some of the more distinctive of one's immediate predecessors.

◆

For me, that last category meant an unusually rich generation of poets who created strong individual voices. Their individuality was considered a great achievement. The unique tone of voice was what lyric poetry was all about. The Imagist credo had said that a new cadence was a new idea, and the sine qua non of poetic modernism was that the poem should give visible indications of listening to itself as it went. If every poem was in some sense a graph of the mind, modernism meant being able to witness the graph come into being.

The poets in the generation ahead of mine explored new cadences with a self-awareness that was not so self-conscious about language as to lead to reductive artifice. They still wrote of the world. They sought a language that matched what was inside them to what was outside. They were not inhibited by the imperfect and impure nature of referential language. Some may think that it was a more innocent or simpler time for poets. Whether or not that was the case, the time made for an explosion of individual poetic voices. Moreover, they gathered influences from other cultures and other poetries and hastened the day when American poetry would become a more integral part of world poetry. For all these reasons, they remain a useful range of influence on young poets.

Part 3: About the List

The list of poetry books that follows was originally compiled in the mid-1990s—on request and with some reluctance—to describe a range of American poets from midcentury whose writing had been crucially instructive to young poets. It was intended as an aid to understanding the creation of contemporary styles of free verse in

English in the United States. These books represent a flowering of individual voices that began in the 1950s and continued for at least two decades. They confirm that, beyond the simple matter of a rhythmic pattern, free verse is neither a form nor an absence of form but a method for finding new forms.

The list below comes with many qualifications. It is not intended to be comprehensive of English language poetry of the time. It omits the British and their former colonies. It makes no attempt to include all individualistic methods, particularly those at the stylistic or conceptual extremes (though many of the books on this list were considered ground-breaking). It does not attempt to represent poets whose poetic individuality was not primarily that of tone of voice or poetic form (what might be termed "literary values") but was rooted instead in content specific to gender, ethnicity, or sexual identity (what might be termed "cultural values").

Nor is the list meant to be authoritative. It is in no way intended to suggest a canon. For one thing, it lacks the multicultural dimension that enriches American poetry. The list's author has a long roster of favorites that goes well beyond this list.

Nonetheless, reading a fair share of these books along with the great mommies and daddies of modernism should give the reader a fair sense of the period when our forebears developed individual voices so strong that they would make free verse the prevalent style of the age. These books were at the center of American poetry and were for me a good place to begin. If you intend to climb a tree, you don't start by grabbing the thinnest branches first.

◆

These poets went to school on formalism and modernism—especially that of Eliot, Williams, Pound, and Stevens—then diverged from the formalism of their early writing. Many attributed their conversion to the work of poets writing in Spanish (Lorca, Neruda, Vallejo . . .), Portuguese (Andrade . . .), or German (Rilke, Trakl . . .); Snyder bowed to ancient Chinese poetry; Bly swept up Spanish poetry together with the Chinese; James Wright took in Chinese verse along with German and Spanish poetries; Koch, O'Hara, and Ashbery were the comedic geniuses of improvisation with roots in the art world of abstract expressionism and ears in French poetry (Rimbaud, Valéry, Baudelaire, Mallarmé . . .); Ginsberg, a scholar of holy scripts, recaptured Biblical verse (as had Whitman and Smart before him). As always, originality came from close reading and a mix of influences.

The list groups, very roughly, poets with sympathetic aesthetics. Where more than one book is listed for a poet, it is advisable to read them in order. In many cases, the books listed have by now been subsumed in a *Selected*, *Collected*, or *Complete Poems* by the poet. The individual volume is usually a better choice than a *Selected*.

No judgment is implied by the number of books listed for each poet. The books listed are simply those in which one can see the beginnings of an individual voice and witness that voice gaining strength through increased definition. Often a young writer learns more from a poet's second, third, or fourth book than from later books because it is in the best of the earlier books (often not the first) that one can still see the scaffolding.

The list below emphasizes the individualities of free verse but is not meant to suggest that free verse is superior to formalist verse.

Hardly. A brief listing of a few of the poets of the time who remained primarily committed to formalism, and who were as much a part of the scene as the others and no less important to American poetry, appears at the bottom.

Now to those big mommies and daddies of modernism in American poetry. My list would begin with Whitman and Dickinson, followed by William Carlos Williams, T. S. Eliot, Ezra Pound, Wallace Stevens, Hart Crane, Robert Frost, Dylan Thomas, E. E. Cummings, Marianne Moore, and the Englishman W. H. Auden. In the case of the overwhelmingly prolific Williams, I would begin with the two-volume *Collected Poems of William Carlos Williams*, edited by A. Walton Litz and Christopher MacGowan, and *Imaginations*, edited by Webster Schott. For the others, I suggest beginning with the earlier books in their *Collected* or *Complete Poems*.

Finally, a few words about the poets of my generation and later. There is no one way to write and there is no right way to write. Skip the party, avoid the crowd. Find your favorites yourself.

Part 4: The List

A. R. Ammons: *Tape for the Turn of the Year*
Robert Bly: *Silence in the Snowy Fields*; *The Light Around the Body*
James Dickey: *Drowning with Others*; *Helmets*; *Buckdancer's Choice*
Alan Dugan: *Poems* (first collection)
Richard Hugo: *The Lady in Kicking Horse Reservoir*
Galway Kinnell: *Flower Herding at Mount Monadnock*; *Body Rags*;
    The Book of Nightmares
Philip Levine: *Not This Pig*; *They Feed They Lion*

John Logan: *Ghosts of the Heart*; *Spring of the Thief*; *The Zigzag Walk*
W. S. Merwin: *The Moving Target*; *The Lice*
Sylvia Plath: *Ariel*
Adrienne Rich: *Diving into the Wreck*
Anne Sexton: *All My Pretty Ones*; *Live or Die*
Louis Simpson: *At the End of the Open Road*
William Stafford: *West of Your City*; *Traveling Through the Dark*; *The Rescued Year*; *Allegiances* (these four were collected in *Stories That Could Be True*)
James Wright: *The Branch Will Not Break*; *Shall We Gather at the River*; *To a Blossoming Pear Tree*

Robert Creeley: *For Love*
David Ignatow: *Say Pardon*; *Figures of the Human*; *Rescue the Dead*
Denise Levertov: *With Eyes at the Back of Our Heads*; *The Jacob's Ladder*
George Oppen: *The Materials*; *This in Which*

John Ashbery: *Some Trees*; *The Double Dream of Spring*; *Three Poems*
Edward Field: *Stand Up, Friend, With Me*
Kenneth Koch: *Thank You and Other Poems*
Frank O'Hara: *Meditations in an Emergency*

Gregory Corso: *Gasoline*
Lawrence Ferlinghetti: *A Coney Island of the Mind*; *Starting from San Francisco*
Allen Ginsberg: *Howl*; *Kaddish*; *Wichita Vortex Sutra*

•

Robert Duncan: *The Opening of the Field*
Charles Olson: *The Distances*
Gary Snyder: *A Range of Poems*

John Berryman: *Homage to Mistress Bradstreet*; *77 Dream Songs*
Randall Jarrell: *The Lost World*
Robert Lowell: *Life Studies*
Theodore Roethke: *The Lost Son*; *Words for the Wind*

Some of the great formalists who stayed formalists:

Elizabeth Bishop: *Questions of Travel*; *Geography III*
Anthony Hecht: *The Hard Hours*
Donald Justice: *The Summer Anniversaries*; *Night Light*; *Departures*
James Merrill: *Water Street*; *The Fire Screen*
Howard Nemerov: *Selected Poems*
W. D. Snodgrass: *Heart's Needle*
George Starbuck: *Bone Thoughts*; *White Paper*
Richard Wilbur: *Love Calls Us to the Things of This World*; *Selected Poems*

Part 5: On Translations

American poetry and the ways in which we think about it were radically changed from the 1960s to the 1990s, not solely by the examples of our own best poets, but by poetry in translation. These changes were wrought not only by the finest, most considered, and most accurate translations (Mark Strand's versions of Rafael Alberti and Carlos Dummond de Andrade, Charles Simic's of Vasko Popa, Alastair Reid's of Jorge Luis Borges, translations of Zbigniew Herbert by Czeslaw Milosz and Peter Dale Scott, Edmund Keeley and George Savidis' of C. P. Cavafy, Assia Gutmann's translations of Amichai, Greg Simon's of Lorca, Rumi by Coleman Barks, the many versions of Rilke, W. S. Merwin's translations from both eastern and western languages . . .). They came about also because of translations that, like Ezra Pound's of Li Po and Robert Bly's of Neruda, Vallejo, and Tranströmer, took liberties to better render the spirit of the poem.

Then, too, there was a range of influential anthologies of poetry in translation (Mark Strand and Charles Simic's *Another Republic*; Czeslaw Milosz's *Postwar Polish Poetry*; Hardie St. Martin's *Roots and Wings: Poetry from Spain 1900–1975*; Wu-Chi Liu and Yucheng Lo's *Sunflower Splendor: Three Thousand Years of Chinese Poetry*; Kenneth Rexroth's *One Hundred Poems from the Chinese* and *One Hundred Poems from the Japanese*; and that hoary old favorite, Robert Payne's anthology of Chinese poetry, *The White Pony*, first published in 1947 and again in 1960 . . .).

Nor was it only the finest translations, nor the most accurate, nor the most conscious of spirit and imagination, that influenced us to think more broadly about poetry, but also random translations by poets who did merely a little of this or that, using a "pony" and a dictionary to translate a few Persian ghazals or one or two poems by the Basque poet Unamuno.

In every translation, there comes to us a new wave of permission, an increased sense of freedom. Is it because we are forced to abandon prejudice and preference to enjoy travel? Is it because many cultures do not share our overwhelmingly material view of things? Is it because the pressure of empire, even a struggling empire in a desperate holding action, affects our viewpoint? No doubt it is for all these reasons and others. One thing is certain: every literature has grown fresh, and every great writer been made greater, by writers looking to other cultures and languages for new words and renewed permission.

My advice: learn the home turf, then go elsewhere.

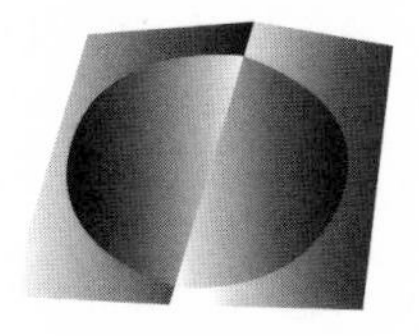

CAMPBELL McGRATH

The Cattle Raid

Poetry is not an island unto itself.

It is a free republic, a proud and independent realm, but it does not stand alone. We citizens must share this fertile land with our neighbors—a few, several, many; their number varies, their configurations shift with the passing years as new nations are born and principalities disintegrate into warring factions, ancient fiefdoms grow impoverished and young city-states amass great wealth—though these are merely political distinctions, as is widely understood, and the ground beneath our feet is continuous, extending in every direction to the horizons. It is a beautiful island, and we ought upon awakening sing its praises to the rising sun, as it is said the cattle did, in times gone by, the cattle of the Republic of Poetry being anciently gifted with the power of human speech.

Life on the island is straightforward: I do not say simple, but simple enough.

Of the several nations, poetry is the most time-honored, its roots descending beyond historical record. It possesses many fine monuments and ruins of past glory. It is largely peaceable. It harbors no malice toward its neighbors. It supports no standing army and does not seek to copyright its wisdom. Golden birds sing in its branches, golden minarets glint on distant hills, yet from the legendary power of antiquity it is much reduced.

The problem is not one of essential properties, but of politics; not of grazing lands, but of cows.

Our herds are much diminished, for we are surrounded by neighbors who profess their esteem and friendship even as they steal our cattle!

The Republic of Poetry has been generous to a fault; too reliant on courteous diplomacy, too focused on internal squabbles to recognize the dangers of the world around us, we have grown lax in our vigilance. It is in light of this sad reduction that I make the following proposal:

that we, in our turn, sally forth to steal the cattle of our neighbors.

◆

That we shift our attention outward, find what is valuable around us, and carry it back across the border—not merely for personal gain but to enrich the coffers of the realm.

A lucky day raiding the borderlands of the Kingdom of Fiction could reclaim a stray from Faulkner or Virginia Woolf—the next day Calvino or García Márquez, Cormac McCarthy, Roddy Doyle. Crossing by moonlight into the Realm of Biography we might return with Woody Guthrie or Zora Neale Hurston, or Richard Holmes' two-volume *Coleridge*, while from the vast Empire of History we could hope to rustle *The Landmark Thucydides*, or Shelby Foote's *Civil War*, or Fernand Braudel's *Civilization and Capitalism*—from which might be fashioned an epic poem of material culture! A well-aimed lasso in Nature might yield Thoreau or Darwin, *A Field Guide to the Everglades*, *A Natural History of Vacant Lots*, while a foray into the People's Republic of the Social Sciences could supply the stock for an anthropological poetry of civilization, a psychological poetry of self-realization, a sociological poetry of the self in context. Returning by way of the Highlands of the Primary Texts, we can range the wide moors in search of the wild aurochs of Etymology, seek out the beasts of pure form in the dales and hollows of Myth.

How many fine milk cows graze within the fenced fields of Folk Tales, Essays, Memoir!

Crowded grow the stockyards and feeding pens of Popular Fiction, Self-Help, and Screenplays—we will leave a thousand for every one we take and still our herds will swell!

◆

Be fearless, fellow riders!

Cross all borders! If those from whom you steal choose to quarrel, remember that they were all our cattle once, as far as the eye could see, and none should begrudge a past benefactor his simple sustenance. Even some among our own people will resist what you bring, having grown inward-looking, forgetful of the extension of our former estate, while others will never return from the raid at all, choosing to settle on the wide plains of the Novel, in the lyrical vineyard of the Short Story—

but you shall have nothing to fear.

Even if the posse captured you, how could they stop a message of such purity?

Because it does not need to be spoken, it cannot be silenced; because it does not need to be written, it cannot be censored. There is no poetry jail—and if there were, you could compose your poems there, secure in the solitude of the self—and they cannot exile you from the Island of Language because, by definition, its limits comprise the limits of our world.

Here we must confront the issue of boundaries and surveys, of Terra Incognita.

No authoritative exploration of this place has ever been undertaken; we imagine it as an island, but there is no map or chart to delimit it, though it certainly is not limitless. If you travel far enough in any direction you will come to a shoreline, in sight of which lie tumbled rocks and foundering shoals, raw islets that serve as breeding grounds for seabirds, and against the gray horizon an unknown number of other lands, places terrible or marvelous toward which, with good weather and stout craft, a voyage of discovery might be launched.

It was on just such a journey, not long ago, that I came across *The Invisible Universe*, a collection of David Malin's photographs of stars, gas clouds, nebulae, nova remnants, and other astronomical structures, an oversize atlas of celestial images so breathtaking that I could only stare at them in wonder.

Which I continue to do.

They come from across the water, and I have as yet found no means of translating their silence into poetry.

But a herdsman's life demands patience.

Vision and patience.

For now I have set them grazing on the fine grass of our renowned pasturelands, letting them wander the hills and valleys and river bottoms, mingling with the local herd, learning their ways.

One morning soon enough they will come to me, at daybreak, singing.

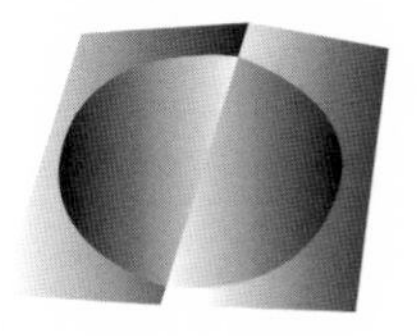

BECKIAN FRITZ GOLDBERG

Poetry and Murder

What I want from a good book is a dead body in the first chapter or I'll move on to something else that's not going to waste my time. While it's true that in the summer, when I have time to read fiction, I tend toward the macabre, the forensic, the detective-chasing-serial-killer genre, when I begin to contemplate my "serious" reading as a poet I realize this is no anomaly, but the essence of reading toward what matters. And what matters to me, as a poet, is the burden of the mystery—who's killing us—in so many uniquely intimate ways—and why? And if we want it to stop, we must understand, first, both victim and extinguisher. We must understand that everything is important—the room the way we find it, the weather that day, the casual stranger, the smallest habit. I think, too, it's that I find much contemporary poetry written without urgency, as if the conversation could be clever, amusing, anecdotal, philosophical on its way to whatever tired epiphany the author had in mind all along and that serves as enough for poetry. In my book, it doesn't.

When I was seven I fell in love with a book called *Alvin's Secret Code*. It was a ripping good story in which the young protagonist and his younger pain-in-the-ass sister Daphne get involved in some local sinister doings and meanwhile develop a sophisticated knowledge of cryptography, a subject I found so fascinating that I soon organized several neighbor children into a code-cracking spy network. Language and mystery, language and danger and rescue, language and the ways of human nature—I moved on through a series of books when I was nine and ten involving a tomboy Nancy Drew character named Trixie Belden. I reread the books in this series over and over. So I suppose it was no accident that when I came to poetry, around twelve or thirteen, I came via Edgar Allan Poe.

What the poetry had over his stories was the music, incredible indulgent music, and the romance of this sound along with Poe's perpetual preoccupation with loss intoxicated me. Even though my early poems then were highly derivative, written in purple ink, laden with autumn images and gypsies, there had awakened in me a need to pursue, in language, that sense of longing, loss, love-in-the-face-of-death. I don't think I was a particularly morbid adolescent, as adolescents go, but what caught my attention as a fledgling poet was the fact of mortality poised against the delicious beauty of the world.

I probably read every biography of Poe I could get my hands on, an obsession lasting until my early teens. And each one had a different theory about his death. With him found wandering the streets of Baltimore, delirious, and dressed in someone else's clothes, some accounts attribute his last illness to alcohol, or alcohol withdrawal, lesions of the brain; others to "cooping," a vicious mugging, and even rabies. Ultimately it came back to those secrets of the body, the level of medical knowledge of those who witnessed his death, the "evidence" lost in time. While I don't believe this had any direct "influence" on me, when I look back on it now I see that my fascination with "reading the body" has never waned.

A scalpel is a beautiful thing. Thus reads the opening sentence of this summer's indulgence, a medical thriller, *Life Support*, written by Tess Gerritsen who is also an M.D. The plot proceeds through several mysterious deaths of previously healthy residents of a nursing home as well as the death of a teenaged prostitute, and involves the protagonist's discovery of a virus that can only be spread by direct tissue exchange. Additionally, there are two highly-mutated "births," one being a living "thing" with twenty or more pineal glands. Well-written, well-paced, and provocative—that's how my review would go; but beyond simply being a top-notch example of the genre, it treats the body as a document, a whole memory that stands apart from the "mind" or "soul" and focuses on the "speech" of science, the body speaking after death.

And what speaks after death? That preoccupies me. Our teeth outlast our anger, our fear, our love. Our metacarpals outlast our sex. Our diet lives on in our hair. All sorts of history can be told from our bones. I think my hope is that language, particularly poetry, is the "body" that preserves all that disappears from our bodies: thought, impulse, feeling, memory of events, our relationship to things-in-time.

While I don't read poetry for "plot" necessarily the way I would read a murder mystery, some of the same elements seem to me necessary to each. Suspense, for example. Take the way a Stephen Dobyns poem opens: "Some people put their trust in art, others / believe in murder. Each can be in error"; or, "A man eats a chicken everyday for lunch, / and each day the ghost of another chicken / joins the crowd in the dining room. If he could / only see them. . . ."; or, "He'd not known he loved her so he let her go." The opening statements of these poems compel the reader forward—what's going on? what's going to happen? or what has happened?—as do most of the poems in his collection *Cemetery Nights*. When I look back on my reading as a student, this is one of the few volumes of poetry I read in one sitting—I couldn't put it down. What I still appreciate about Dobyns' work years later is that ability to immediately engage a reader, to do what a good thriller does, give us suspense, promise to surprise us, keep us going on. Yes, Dobyns' poetry uses the tools of narrative, and yes, he writes a pretty good mystery also; his Charlie Bradshaw mysteries kept me happy one summer on the beach. But there are a great many poets who use narrative yet do not make us feel a sense of urgency.

There is a poem by Charles Harper Webb which opens: "Djedmaatesankh—temple musician, wife of Paankhntof, / daughter of Shedtaope—died childless, aged 35, / in the 10th century B.C., of blood poisoning from an abscessed incisor." The poem gives me what I profess I want, a dead body in the first "chapter," and yet fails to really engage me. The poem moves between this "archaeological" subject and a nineteenth-century French explorer in Antarctica killed by "hot-headed naked ice-borers," which, admittedly, is a lot of fun to say. As both stories intertwine, Webb writes: "Their normal temperature / is 110 degrees. Djedmaatesankh's fever / may have reached 104." As a reader, I find "nothing at stake" here, no real reason for the connection except that the writer enjoys the idea of paralleling these two stories and then speculating on the drama that is implied by the "facts." I don't wish to engage in any sort of criticism of particular poets, or to say one *kind* of poem is innately better than another; I am primarily interested in the relationship between poetry and audience, and how one's conception of that is fed by/reflected in what one finds delicious to read or not-delicious. I'm especially concerned as a writer because I want to engage readers and I assume that most of them are as busy and impatient as I am. Do I read a long Jorie Graham poem or do I watch the late-night rerun of *The X-Files*? Or the latest *Forensic Files* on The Discovery Channel? This depends a great deal on what the poem offers, since I know that watching David Duchovny as Agent Mulder is always good for me.

It was, however, a mummy, if not Djedmaatesankh's, that led me to *The Egyptian Book of the Dead* and related texts such as Egyptian medical papyri. *The Egyptian Book of the Dead* got me thinking about what I call "ritualizing anatomy": the ceremony of opening the mouth, the drying and eviscerating of the corpse, the removal of the heart, its replacement with a "heart scarab," even the victual mummies—cow legs, for instance—all seemed a part of that human need to find our way through the body to something beyond. Perhaps no culture expressed it in such detail as the Egyptians and so I became interested in the Ebers papyrus on disease and medicine, interested in the way ancients tried to solve the mystery of the body. A section of papyrus comprises "the book of the stomach," and a wound, for instance, is said to have a "mouth" and "lips." I also discovered how people conceptualized body parts and functions before they obtained actual scientific knowledge. The brain, they thought, existed primarily to provide mucus to the nose. Science eventually proved otherwise. The Egyptians also did not differentiate between veins and arteries, but viewed the body as a system of channels which carried things from the heart—very much as a people who lived primarily off of the Nile and its tributaries would conceive of it.

The mummy of Lady Tai was discovered in China, her innermost casket filled with a yellow liquid which contained mercury. As a consequence, her body was still supple and soft, in remarkable condition for a two-thousand-year-old woman. Her body is still kept in a liquid suspension, changed regularly. During the autopsy they discovered the remains of her last meal—138 muskmelon seeds. Reading these facts feeds some sort of morbid fascination, but in reading a poem about Lady Tai, these alone would not constitute what I call "the significant gesture." And I think that's another element in the murder mystery that translates well into poetry. From Poe to the latest Patricia Cornwell bestseller, the mystery ultimately hinges on human behavior, and the "capture" of the murderer on some ritual or behavior that gives him away, betrays his identity or illuminates his vulnerability. The fact of the crime is not enough just as, sadly, in contemporary literature the fact of poverty or cruelty or incest or betrayal is not enough by itself to sustain tension. Robert Browning knew this in "My Last Duchess." It is the speaker's character that interests the reader, the implications of, "She had a heart—how shall I say—too soon made glad." In Ai's poem "The Good Shepherd," it is the moment the protagonist sits down and makes himself a cup of cocoa. In Thomas Hardy's "Neutral Tones" it is the line, "Your smile that day was the only thing / Alive enough to have the strength to die."

As a reader, my most dramatic experience of this, the "gesture," was in Henry James' *Portrait of a Lady,* when the naïve protagonist Isabel Archer walks into a room and sees her husband Ormond and family acquaintance Madame Merle standing, not intimately close, but just standing together in such a way as to alert her to the unseen, the hitherto unsuspected relationship of Madame Merle to Ormond and to her stepdaughter Pansy. Isabel, it seems, walks in on a silence—a stance, not a conversation, not an observable action. It is literally "in the air." As James says in his essay, it all can turn on the way the light hits a woman's hand on the stair banister.

Of course, James is not "genre fiction" and not murder mystery, which has its familiar conventions. But the idea of reading the body, whether it is as a forensic exercise or a psychological one, crosses genres. I found in ancient medical texts such as those by Galen, Hippocrates, Aretaeus and, particularly, gynecological texts, ways of interpreting the body's mysteries expressed in theories about the body's makeup and the function of parts. Aretaeus, for example, wrote:

> In women, in the hollow of her body below the rib cage, lies the womb. It is very much like an independent animal within the body for it moves around of its own accord and is quite erratic. Furthermore, it likes fragrant smells and moves toward them, but dislikes foul odors and moves away from them. . . .

The "wandering womb" is a "scientific theory" that reveals much about the male conception of the female body and the female "character," for it allows physicians of the time to treat most medical disorders in women as symptomatic of the "wandering womb." If it pressed upward, the woman choked. Fast-forward to the early twentieth century, and the poet Rilke writes that in woman "any lapse into a more primitive and narrow kind of suffering, engorging, and bringing forth is an overfilling of her organs with blood that has been augmented for another, greater circulation," and that she is "pulled beneath the surface of life by the weight of bodily fruit." In another ancient text, Galen concludes that the parts "that are inside in a woman are outside in a man," which means that the female body is some sort of negative of the male image, a shadow body. It is only one case of the part defining the whole as a kind of metonymy born of the mysteries of the physical.

The tendency to see the physical interior of the body as a signifier of spirit or temperament is probably nowhere more evident than in texts influenced by the study of anatomy and practice of dissection during the Renaissance. And, despite the view of Christian orthodoxy, that the spirit is pure and incorporeal, the preservation of saints' relics—St. Catherine of Siena's holy digit, for example—showed that the spiritual was still inevitably and metaphorically linked to the body. Barbara Maria Stafford, in *Body Criticism*, a book that traces the link between anatomy and art history, discusses the connection between this scientific study of the interior and Piranesi's architectural drawings. Piranesi "transplanted 'surgical' strategies into archaeological publications." He made use of "accidental holes or 'wounds' gaping in the sides of buildings, allowing glimpses into their internal structures." Piranesi also used a "dissective strategy... to exhibit multiple images on the same plate" showing different stages of building, elevations, construction types. When part of a structure was concealed, buried under debris, the artist "responsibly sutured the conjectural to the certain."

When I turn to poetry, looking perhaps for this same sort of metaphorical connection, I turn to John Donne, who wrote in the close of his poem "The Extasie," "Loves mysteries in soules doe grow / But yet the body is his booke...." Donne's poems often "dissect" the relation between the material body and the spirit in terms of Renaissance science, and are very much aware of physical disease and anatomy. One of his characteristic strategies is to place a representative object, such as a picture of the beloved, in the interior of the body, or to place his name in a glass window that eventually becomes the physical interior of his and his wife's bodies. There is, as Elaine Scarry points out in another book on my reading list, *Literature and the Body*, an additional element in Donne's work that is key, and that is language itself as both material (body) and immaterial (thought or spirit). Scarry states,

> By carrying language into the body, Donne participates in a collective project whose work is shared by religion and science.... A name or a noun is never a solitary word, but enfolds within it an entire narrative.... The same is true of medicine: when a small slippery piece of arterial matter is named "the duct of Botallo," the history of that sixteenth-century Italian physician is carried there as well.

What she calls the "substantiveness" of language is part of my own obsession with reading the body. And perhaps this is where poetry and the genre of the murder mystery are crucially different: for the feeling of the word itself in the mouth, such as in Keats's line "seasons of mists and mellow fruitfulness," or of a word like *coccyx* derived from the word *cuckoo*, the bird named for its sound, and, in the human body, the name of the tailbone for its resemblance to the cuckoo's beak. The bones "articulate." A story in Ralph Major's *Classic Descriptions of Disease* tells us that the disease syphilis actually gets its name from the name of a shepherd struck with the "French Disease" in a poem by Hieronymus Fracastorius in 1530. Language and body are inextricably linked, and this is the essence of metaphor. Take this passage from Donne:

> ...her pure and eloquent blood
> Spoke in her cheekes, and so distinkly wrought
> That one might almost say, her bodie thought.
>
> —"Second Anniversary"

and the following from Galway Kinnell:

> And the brain kept blossoming
> all through the body, until the bones themselves could think,
> and the genitals sent out wave after wave of holy desire
> until even the dead brain cells
> surged and fell in god-like, androgynous fantasies—
> and I understood
> the unicorn's phallus could have risen, after all,
> directly out of thought itself.
>
> —"The Call Across the Valley of Not-Knowing"

The latter from a poet who also writes that "yes" is "the only word the tongue shapes without intercession." Both poets, centuries apart, know that experience, beauty, time, all those mysterious things in our lives apprehend us through the body, as does language itself. Its appearance and disappearance, then, is what makes poetry an urgent art, not so much through the suspense of "who done it?" but of "how do we bear it?"

When Will Graham, the protagonist of the first Hannibal Lecter novel, *Red Dragon*, encounters a murder victim modeled to resemble a medieval anatomical image known as a "wound man," a portrayal of most of the possible battle wounds or injuries on one figure, it leads him to conclude Lecter is indeed the murderer. Graham notes that Lecter had been the victim's doctor and, during a previous interview, he had noted the old medical textbooks in Lecter's office. The end of the tale occurs when he knows "who" has done this to the body, and Lecter recognizes he has given himself away.

But the speaker protagonist in David St. John's "Study for the World's Body," leaning over

> The text of Seven's body: her skin
> Still the color of fallen apricots,
> Nipples no darker than topaz,
> The soft tattoo of
> Orphan space radiating
> From her face. That faintly metallic
> Taste of her skin; simple resonance.
> Such odd physical scriptures
> To the oblique. The braille
> Of her pain scrawled in half-moons—
> Her spine beneath my hand, cool zipper
> Of bone . . .

is led to ask, "Where is the rapture; who is the raptor?" with each word in the poem aware that the wounded and decomposed body is also the point of all possibilities, a language which desire speaks even after death.

For me, then, reading is a dialogue that involves both the mind and the body in a pleasurable seeking, and it is not separate from breathing, sleeping, eating, or taking out fresh sheets from the dryer. It is not separate from the man in the news here recently who finally confessed to the police he had lived with the body of his dead wife in his trailer for eleven years. We may be shocked or repulsed, but if we don't recognize the hand of longing here and the mystery of what the body means, we are not reading the right book.

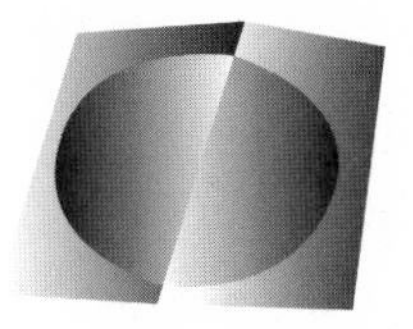

GARRETT HONGO

Reading List for American Poets of the New Millennium

Plato, *Ion*. Plato's dialogues are central in any canonical approach to poetic study, but this one is especially interesting for its critique of the poet's enterprise as a basis for knowledge. In *Ion*, the poet-rhapsode is interrogated by the philosopher, who challenges the poet's claim that all truth can be found in his recitations from Homer. The philosopher defeats these claims, showing the poet to be more an artist of memory and imitation than a genuine thinker, the purveyor of truth.

Aristotle, *Poetics*. There are terrific ideas here regarding the *dynamics* of linguistic art—ideas of plausibility, sequence, conflict/reversal, and resolution. Aristotle's terminology alone is exciting and stimulating—*mimesis*, *technē*, *perepeteia*, *katharsis*, *ekphrasis*, etc. The work is a wellspring of aesthetic concepts and an involved mapping of the turns and oxbows of classic literary creation. Aristotle makes literature seem almost a plastic art, his arguments and illustrations are so clear. And he recuperates the civic value of poetic art by arguing that—rather than corrupting truth and society as Plato argues—literature in fact enacts a purifying drama in imitation of life that "cleanses" civil society of dangerous emotions which might otherwise corrupt the political body.

Longinus, "On the Sublime." Here is the seminal essay regarding the special properties of poetry as a vehicle of transport, ecstasy, and transcendental uplift close to the supernatural. It also describes the act of the mind and the performance of language that brings about this effect. Rapture, rhapsody, and high poetic solemnity are declared to be the central principles of poetry.

Horace, "Ars Poetica." This is the sober approach as opposed to the rhapsodic. Horace ridicules the country rhapsodist, the ignorant grillot of the supernatural, and instead upholds learning, study, and more sophisticated metropolitan approaches to the poetic enterprise. He challenges the notion of direct knowledge of poetic essence, even "feeling," and defends derived knowledge, an education in poetry, law, and literature as more important for one who would practice the art of poetry. Horace is at the beginning of the Neoclassic tradition.

Petrarch, "The Ascent of Mount Ventoux." This is a fabulous essay about landscape and poetic imagination. It is a precursor to Dante's lessons on poetic allegory and ideas of ritual enactment.

Dante, "Letter to Can Grande." Here, the greatest poet of all discourses on method, and explains his compositional strategies, setting forth distinctions among the metaphoric, allegoric, and anagogic methods. It is extremely important in comprehending levels and layers of symbolic action and relations within a text, particularly one as symbolically rich and dense as Dante's.

Kant, "Analytic of the Sublime," from *The Critique of Pure Judgment*. A dense and difficult discussion of the sublime as a mode of thought and principle of art. Of seminal importance, particularly to students of Romanticism, it includes within its analyses the notions of dread, proximity to dread, contemplation in the face of dread, and, by strong implication, the supernatural as a requirement for aesthetic feeling. It also makes claims about the relationship of nature to the human mind, positing the idea of something "in-dwelling" that matches mind to something in nature that is then released or inspired into aesthetic feeling by art and/or contemplation.

Hegel, "Introduction to *Aesthetics*." This is a counter to Kant's notions of the sublime in art. Hegel sees art as a humanly constructed thing rather than something discovered in nature by the human mind. He's our "arts and crafts" aesthetician, arguing from the perspective that nature is dumb and without grace until human wiliness imposes its clever constructions upon it.

William Wordsworth, "Preface" to the second edition of *Lyrical Ballads*. One of the most beautifully written, reasoned, and illustrated essays in the English language. The great poet makes a case for a poetry of plainer, more direct speech—"of men speaking to men"—as he writes at the end of the eighteenth century, rather than the more rhetorically and allusively ornate diction of the practice then current. He also defends a poetry of humbler subjects, the intensely personal, and the treatment of the poor and the dispossessed with dignity and compassion. Finally, he introduces the grand Romantic idea, borrowed and adapted from German Romantic philosophy, of "Imagination" as the governing energy and principal aesthetic agent that inspires poetic pursuits. Though written from a perspective of great class privilege, the "Preface" stands, historically, as one of the first statements authorizing a more democratic vision, a poetry of grievance and suffering, and an accessible poetic style.

Ralph Waldo Emerson, "The American Scholar." Emerson wrote this seminal piece of American literature as a commencement address for a graduating class at Harvard. Though his rhetoric is full of grandiosity and oratory, his arguments are cogent, introducing his own version of rugged American Romanticism into our intellectual and poetic tradition. He calls for a new kind of scholar-citizen, a kind of poet of mind and action, who would take a new learning and regard for the validities of imaginative and moral insight as central to life. There is a political liberalism here, a sense of social and intellectual responsibility, and a great American sophistry of optimism that inspired Walt Whitman himself.

Robert Frost, "The Figure a Poem Makes." This is as important and succinct an explanation of and argument for the symbolic function of poetry as there is. Frost takes us through a mini-"defense" of poetry as an activity of mind that privileges the figurative properties of language over logical, sequentialized, and analytic functions (philosophy, science, history, etc.). As with Coleridge's and Wordsworth's "Preface," Frost's little essay is the source of ideas regarding poetry which have since become commonplace.

♦

T. S. Eliot, "Tradition and the Individual Talent." A large, learned statement regarding the wisdom of inscribing one's work, as a poet, within a living, learned tradition, as opposed to being "original," and without literary precursors or ancestors. Eliot nearly makes poetry, and, by extension, all of literature, one vast system of interrelated symbols, narratives, and patterns, and inspires what came to be known as the "New Criticism" of the 1950s.

Erich Auerbach, "Figura." An extraordinarily learned and insightful discussion of the practice of poetic figuration in medieval and classical literatures. While this essay is especially pertinent to those interested in Dante and Virgil, it nonetheless lays out the procedure for symbolic and allegorical layering of poetic diction such that a given poem radiates with figurative resonances throughout, that connect and build upon each other to create not only density and complexity, but, in the ways of these two great poets, an overall patterning of language as a lexical and spiritual code. It also explains notions of spiritual, religious, and moral knowledge in relationship to key moments of symbolic understanding which are revealed as one moves through life. One of the greatest pieces of literary learning and wisdom written in the past century.

Susanne Langer, *Feeling and Form.* An "Aesthetics" that is an extremely readable discussion of art, music, literature, and their principles of organization by this most lucid of Aristotelian philosophers. Langer moves the arts away from materialities into the area of "mind," and argues that its sequence of effects upon human consciousness produces that most ineffable of all things—a feeling that works upon human values, personality, and eventually, civilization itself. Art is a psychological process for Langer, a thing beyond the mere cognitive, drawn by a pull toward form—itself a process of classical "making" along the lines of Aristotelian *technē*. This gives her aesthetics a kind of central principle—that there is this universal "pull" toward form and pattern. One can see potential crossings with Kant and Wordsworth here—Langer's "feeling" is not unlike Kant's "innate" capacity of the mind for the beautiful and the sublime, or Wordsworth's notion of the "in-dwelling" match between mind and nature. Yet, for Langer, it is not the pure aesthetic moment that is central, but the full process of the accomplishment and cognitive recognition of artistic "form."

Larry Levis, "Some Notes on the Gazer Within." Here is a generous, visionary statement regarding imagination and narration in poetry, written from a distillation of thinking accomplished over several years of reading, writing, and reflection. Levis, at this time, was moving from a good deal of reading in twentieth-century phenomenology, particularly Edmund Husserl, and a selection of twentieth-century structuralist literary critics (Gaston Bachelard, Rene Girard, J. Hillis Miller), and back to the consideration of American poetic method. He looks at the work of Merwin, Kinnell, and Levine, and argues for a kind of new American romanticism that extrapolates complicated narratives out of memory and the meditative consideration of the poetic image. He argues that there are stories embedded in images and their memory, and that the poetic function is to discover and report on them. Levis' points seem very close to some of the discussions in Kant's "Analytic of the Sublime" and Wordsworth's "Preface" to *Lyrical Ballads*, except that he specifies that it is *a story* that is the rhapsodic transport and the product of the consideration of the poetic image.

◆

Frederic Jameson, *The Prison-House of Language*. This is an excellent guide to and summary of the lectures of Fernand de Saussure and the origin of twentieth-century semiotics—the science of words as signs, a kind of system denuded of "meaning." Jameson's writing here is as lucid as one could want about a topic that defies lucidity.

Frantz Fanon, *The Wretched of the Earth*. The grand statement of early postcolonialism and an eloquent cry for decolonization, full of anger and powerful insight. Fanon establishes a perspective of serious historical importance here, and gives generations of the oppressed an intellectual foundation for the continuing analysis of the dehumanization of exploited races under circumstances of colonization. The original preface was written by Jean-Paul Sartre.

Albert Memmi, *The Colonizer and the Colonized*. Another early statement of postcolonialism, this one from North Africa. Almost as much personal essay as intellectual analysis, this work is much less philosophically opaque and psychological than Fanon's.

Antonio Gramsci, *The Prison Notebooks*. A statement of class loyalty in intellectual practice. Gramsci here proposes a new kind of intellectual, "the organic intellectual," loyal to the laboring classes, wary of the influences of "tradition" as weighted toward the upper classes, ferocious in its critique of the influence of the state and capitalism.

Louis Althusser, "The Ideological State Apparatus," from *Lenin and Philosophy*. A description of the relations between literary and philosophic practices and the functions of power as played out in the practices of discourse. Here, state power is a kind of generalized magnet, while literature and philosophy and their usages of language are like the republic of iron filings Larry Levis describes in his "Notes on the Gazer Within."

Edward Said, *Orientalism*. An historical study of the Western cultural practice of deploying descriptions and accounts of "the Orient" as a cultural and political "other" such as to create a demonizable obverse of Western culture, nations, and peoples. Said demonstrates that the practice of what had been the construction of attractive "romance" easily adapts itself to the creation of damaging, obstructing, and capitalistically convenient myths regarding cultures east of the Bosporus.

Salman Rushdie, "Imaginary Homelands," from his book of the same title. An important essay on literary imagination and practice from a diasporic, postcolonial, exilic perspective. Tremendous eloquence and insight from one of the most important contemporary writer-intellectuals.

Derek Walcott, "The Muse of History." A much more cogent and precisely argued statement of Caribbean postcolonialism than the more famous Nobel speech entitled "The Antilles." Here, Walcott argues with his more nationalistic fellow writers, and champions a literature of broad, international influence rather than one of mere regional authenticity and specificity. On the one hand, he doesn't want to ignore the multiracial history of the Caribbean and its exploitations of race, and on the other, he wishes to preserve his love of and derivations from European literatures.

◆

Homi K. Bhabha, "Introduction" to *The Location of Culture*. Brilliant, Coltrane-like overture to the grandest contemporary statement of diasporic literary intellectuality. Rather than reproduce the conventional historical practice of situating cultural identities within specific regions or cultures, Bhabha proposes the *dis*location of cultures, a derivation of personal and cultural being from the "interstices"—the in-betweens of identity and cultures. He makes an argument for the situation of cultural and geographic transit as a kind of nation from which a literature can be described and written. In fact, he critiques our habits of formulating literatures out of political and national categories and boundaries. This is a new, globalized vision of literary practice in English.

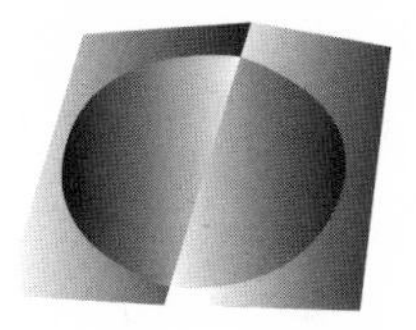

LINDA GREGERSON

Read Me a Riddle: The Light and Darkness of Poetic Form

I do not for the most part write in received, or traditional, forms. But I read them devoutly, and I take the formal contract to be at the heart of poetic discovery. Form is the poet's negotiated submission to arbitrary stricture; form is the poet's alibi, a way of looking busy while the understanding vamps and prowls; form is the poet's freedom and her pleasure and her discipline. Traditional or invented, received or "found," the formal contract is foundation to the investigative project of lyric and thus to another sort of contract, the rhetorical contract between poet and reader, bound in a complex evolution of knowing and unknowing, light and dark. Form is a social as well as a cognitive strategy. As the riddle makes explicit.

Riddle, says my dictionary: a dark saying. A question or enigma propounded in order that it may be guessed or answered. A piece of gamesmanship, in other words; a linguistic transaction based on provocation; a kind of intellectual dare. A riddle is thus a pastime or amusement, but even its playfulness retains a thread of darkness. Consider the riddle of the Theban sphinx: four legs, two legs, three; the riddle is crossbred with omen. The Indo-European root of the word *(rē)* is simultaneously the root of *read* (or *rede*, to take counsel) and *dread*. Consider the riddle Sir Walter Ralegh writes "On the Cards and Dice":

> Before the sixth day of the next new year,
> Strange wonders in this kingdom shall appear.
> Four Kings shall be assembled in this Ile,
> Where they shall keep great tumult for a while.
> Many men then shall have an end of Crosses,
> And many likewise shall sustain great losses.
> Many that now full joyful are and glad,
> Shall at that time be sorrowful and sad.
> Full many a Christian's heart shall quake for fear,
> The dreadful sound of trump when he shall hear.
> Dead bones shall then be tumbled up and down,
> In every city, and in every town.
> By day or night this tumult shall not cease,
> Until an Herald shall proclaim a peace,
> An Herald strange, the like was never born
> Whose very beard is flesh, and mouth is horn.

The language here is openly apocalyptic. The speaker affects the impersonal voice of oracle or prophet, the numerical and figurative formulas of Revelation. The riddle is technical, unnerving, predicated upon obscure point-for-point correspondences, demanding point-for-point decipherment. The hermeneutic project, like the future tense that dominates the poem, is saturated with dread.

Why is the dread so durable? The obscurity can be penetrated; the point-for-point correspondences can be solved, especially when the poem's title is supplemented by a footnote or two. The riddle refers to the Christmastide season of gaming and festivity ("cards and dice") that by tradition ends at cockcrow on Twelfth Night, or the sixth of January. The four kings are those in the deck of cards. The crosses are burdens (as in "a cross to bear"; so men shall put aside their cares for the holiday) and also coins stamped on one side with the sign of a cross (as in the comparably synecdochic "double eagles" and "American buffaloes"; so men shall lose their money at the gaming tables). The trump is a musical instrument (associated with martial activity, heraldic proclamation, and doomsday as well as with festivity) and also a trump card (the one that beats all others). The bones are dice (traditionally made of bone); the herald is the aforementioned cock, the beard of flesh his wattle, the mouth of horn his beak. This herald is not "born" but hatched from an egg (as, by means of a comparable quibble, Macduff is not "born" but untimely ripped from the womb).

What interests me most about these dutiful equations is their insufficiency. The enigmatic force of Ralegh's riddle far exceeds its point-for-point components. The riddle generates theological perturbations (the disorderly collapse of First and Second Comings, the disorderly opposition between holiday observance and holy day significance, the disorderly deferral and progressive deformation of "peace") and disquieting physical conjunctions ("beard of flesh," "mouth of horn") that cannot be wholly contained by interpretive "solution." The riddle unleashes a portent it cannot wholly dissipate or subdue when the gaming is over.

More interesting yet may be a homelier example in a lower key:

> Three things there be that prosper up apace
> And flourish, whilst they grow asunder far,
> But on a day, they meet all in one place,
> And when they meet, they one another mar;
> And they be these: the wood, the weed, the wag.
> The wood is that which makes the gallow tree,
> The weed is that which strings the hangman's bag,
> The wag, my pretty knave, betokeneth thee.
> Mark well, dear boy, whilst these assemble not,
> Green springs the tree, hemp grows, the wag is wilde,
> But when they meet, it makes the timber rot,
> It frets the halter, and it chokes the child.
> Then bless thee, and beware, and let us pray,
> We part not with thee at this meeting day.
> ("Sir Walter Ralegh to His Son")

During his lifetime, Sir Walter Ralegh was reckoned one of the notable poets of his age. No mean age. Spenser, Campion, Whitney, Shakespeare, Sidney, Sidney (sister to the brother), Marlowe, Lanyer, Donne, and Jonson: all were his contemporaries; all, or all the men, have prompted all-but-suffocating reverence ever since. Very little remains to help us judge the grounds of Ralegh's contemporary reputation. Like many a gentleman poet, he largely eschewed the vulgarity of print. A scattering of his poems appeared in anthologies, as fragmentary illustrations in a handbook of English poesy, and as part of the commendatory apparatus to other people's work. Chiefly they circulated in manuscript, and the great preponderance of them appear to have been lost. What survives is lushly sensuous ("Nature, That Washed Her Hands in Milk") and smoothly disillusioned ("The Lie," "The Nymph's Reply to the Shepherd"), immaculate in its technical ease and its ability to mimic ease of soul ("The Passionate Man's Pilgrimage"), redolent of folkway, balladry, and the ceremony of two-part invention ("As You Came from the Holy Land"), drawn to the darkness and economy of riddle ("On the Cards and Dice," "Sir Walter Ralegh to His Son").

Based on the verses that have survived, Ralegh's distinguishing aptitude seems to have been for extraordinary complexity of tone produced by extraordinary, or by apparent, simplicity of means. The prosodic features of the poem "To His Son" are all-but-transparent, fit for a nursery tale or precept-by-the-numbers. The lines are fully rhymed and end-stopped or, in Ellen Bryant Voigt's more elegant and accurate formulation, "end-paused." Monosyllabic words predominate. The tidy packaging of homiletic form (the riddle) and poetic form (the sonnet) tidily overlap: the first quatrain proposes the riddle, the second quatrain answers it, the third quatrain explains it (the couplet is a different story, but that we shall defer). The meter is highly regular, as is the manner of nursery rhyme; the dominant iambs recruit for metrical emphasis a part of speech (the prepositional *on*, *in*, *with*, *at*) that would not in ordinary conversation lay claim to musical stress. "But *on* a *day* they *meet* all *in* one *place*." Short *long* short *long* short *long* short *long* short *long*: perfect iambic pentameter, the commonest meter in English. This phenomenon is called "forcing the meter," but the concept of "forcing" is a partial distortion; it captures the push but not the pull of powerful rhythm. Let us call it leavened, or adapted, meter rather than forced. But how is it that the artificial simplification of metrical surface can heighten rather than deaden the language? Line three, for example ("But *on* a *day*") is odd to modern ears, or would be were it not for its haunting proximity to the formulas of fairy tale: "on a day," as one might say, "once upon a time."

A note on meter, while we're here. In the ordinary analysis of English meter, we count both syllables and accents; hence, accentual/syllabic verse. We pretend, for the sake of analysis, that syllables are of only two kinds: accented or not. This is of course a patent falsehood: there are infinite shades of emphasis, manifold degrees of sonic weight. But we say—we agree to pretend—that accent is a binary code, like the zeros and ones of digital programming. What we gain from this vast oversimplification are highly sophisticated musical effects, since even in the simplest verse, and even discounting the variations of pitch and pacing that do not translate into "accent," the ear discerns two overlapping patterns: the actual, complex variation of emphasis, and the underlying (or superimposed) disposition of syllables across a binary pattern that constitutes "meter." All verse is in this sense syncopated.

Does this mean there is no such thing as tedious regularity in metered language? Of course not. But it does mean that the most masterful poets often achieve their most subtle effects by a near approximation of the obvious. "And *let* us *pray*, / We *part* not *with* thee // *at* this *meet*ing *day*." *At* is eminently debatable: it is either so lightly accented as barely to secure the iamb at the center of Ralegh's final line or, unaccented, it contributes to a slightly quickened run of short beats ("at this *meet*ing *day*") that in turn depends upon a slight anticipatory caesura at the middle of the line ("*part* not *with* thee // at this *meet*ing *day*"). In either case, the surer consequence of the adapted accentual pattern, at least to my ear, is a subtle setting-apart of the first two metrical feet in the line ("*part* not *with* thee"), a heightened conjunction of "part" and "with." These two words are profoundly at odds, of course; the first bespeaks a destined separation ("*part*"), the second a wished-for continuance ("*with*"). The union ("with") so poignantly enacted here, and so patently threatened throughout the poem, constitutes the poem's rhetorical ground.

Poetic practice and rhetorical practice were understood to be aspects of a single encompassing discipline in Ralegh's day, which is why his poems and those of his contemporaries tend to be so vividly *voiced*. The poem is spoken *by* someone and *to* someone; it does not drift in a vague interior space. The audience of readers is typically third party to a dramatized negotiation between poet and mistress, poet and patron, poet and "soul" or deity, poet and particularized internal auditor. This doubling of audience is supple, porous, and not to be confused with later, hardened conventions of dramatic monologue (see Browning). The riddling poem we're focused on at present gains edge and resonance from the unfolding relatedness of speaker and auditor; indeed, that unfolding relatedness may be said to be the poem's real subject. But we do not know at once, perhaps not even in the end, exactly what that relationship is. The title does not appear in all transcriptions; it may be the surmise of later copyists. Even if we take it to be authorial, we must move through several lines of progressive inference before we can confidently propose a "fit" between the title and the body of the poem.

What we hear at the outset is distance, a puzzle proposed by one who knows the answer to one who does not know, a rhetorical structure of asymmetrical authority. This authority, accruing chiefly to the riddler, is augmented by the potent formulas of number and alliteration: two-beat metrical units, two- and four-line units of rhyme, "*th*ree *th*ings" so conspicuously aligned (*w*ood, *w*eed, *w*ag) as to bear the force of omen. Progressively unspooling its dark prefiguration, the poem simultaneously reveals an intimate connection between speaker and internal auditor. The riddle is all third person to begin with, its nouns near-ciphers: "they," "three things." Line by line, these "things" assume the materiality of vegetable and animal life (wood, weed, wag) and then the wrought momentum of dramatic scene (a gallows, a noose, a he-who-is-hung). (A fourth thing, "bag," or hangman's hood, assumes its eerie prominence by force of rhyme and intimation: covering the head of the condemned man on the scaffold, the "bag" consigns him to darkness and anonymity, thus mimicking the blinkered ignorance induced by riddle.) Third person gives way to first ("my") and second ("thee"). *Thee*, the second-person familiar, is "dear" and young (a "boy"), familiar enough to be teased ("my pretty wag"). So the two, the speaker and the listener, are at once distinguished, by age and understanding, and yoked, by affection and mutual entanglement in fate.

The affection, in context, is disturbing. What is the answer to the riddle? Death. And whose death? Yours. It tolls for thee. Who tells me so? One who is close and ought to protect you. Why frighten a child with news like this? The darker predictions of homily and nursery tale are sometimes thought to have disciplinary or didactic force; they may tether the child to virtue. But what can virtue do when punishment is certain? The "meeting" destined to "choke the child" (a sinister piece of onomatopoetic alliteration if ever there was one) seems not to be conditional ("if") but inevitable ("when"). Perhaps the fear has something to do with pleasure? The manipulated tension between fear-of-knowing and eagerness-to-know propels a great variety of story-bearing genres. But whose is the pleasure here? Child's? Adult's? And at what point does the pleasure fail to sustain the conceit? For the poem breaks faith with its own incantatory premise. It turns on itself; it does not like what it has seen; it tries to wrest an exemption from the future it has summoned. It abandons the language of riddle and spell for the language of prayer, the language of wishing-against-all-odds. It converts, in the couplet, to the optative mood. Or was the optative always implicit? Does the grammar of the poem derive from another, more mysterious, instance of the subjunctive ("there be" and not "there are")? Has the spectral "meeting" been conjured by way of inoculation?

Ralegh's own endgame worked something like a riddle itself, or like the labors put to heroes in quest romance. Outmaneuvered by rivals and condemned for treason in 1603, he spent the next thirteen years of his life in the the Tower of London under sentence of death. In 1616, he persuaded King James to grant him a final high-stakes bid for pardon and for New World wealth: he would sail to Guiana, secure a gold mine he had never seen but swore to believe in, load his ships with ore, and deliver this treasure in triumph to the English king, all without offense to the Spanish, who claimed Guiana for their own. The voyage was a spectacular failure: ten of fourteen ships were lost, a key Spanish settlement sacked and burnt, large numbers of English killed, including Ralegh's elder son, no treasure whatsoever secured. James had promised the Spanish that Ralegh should "be hanged" if he willfully broke the peace between England and Spain but, with Ralegh again in custody, was informed by his counselors that a man under sentence of death could not legally be tried for new offenses. So Elizabeth's sometime favorite, warden of her stanneries (or mines), recipient of forty thousand acres of Irish land, lord lieutenant of Cornwall, governor of Jersey, vice-admiral of Cornwall and Devon, captain of the queen's guard, and, not so incidentally, her frequent military champion and backstairs plotter against the enemy Spanish, was, in order to placate the Spanish, executed by order of the queen's sovereign heir on a fifteen-year-old treason charge, a charge that included conspiring with the Spanish against the English crown. The traitor was not hanged but beheaded, a prerogative of rank.

Ralegh writes a riddle on the brink of an abyss. Since the man also lived his life on the brink of abyss, or multiple abysses (the years of imprisonment under James were if anything more placid than earlier phases of his career), one is tempted to read the gallows at the heart of his riddle as a figure for dangers the man knew something about. We cannot assign a date to the poem, though most assume it was written well before the final venture to Guiana; we cannot be sure which son it has in mind, if indeed it is addressed to a son; the poem in any case disdains mere topicality. But thus far the life is pertinent to the poem: their shared foundation is political. Ralegh's talent, his instinct and intelligence, took light from the perilous intersection of private and public affairs in early modern England. That intersection is quite simply all we know of him, all that is visible in the fractured but extensive remains of his actions and his pen. It is not death alone that is cast as inevitable in the riddle spoken "to his son," nor even death-by-violence: it is death-by-state-violence. Where does one turn when the consolidated powers the self has played to, pitched its measure to, exploited and served, turn cold? In another surviving version of the poem, the sudden appeal to an alternate power shatters poetic form: three quatrains that culminate in "chokes the child" are followed by a single half-line: "God bless the child."

Four manuscript versions of the riddle "To His Son" survive, all posthumous. One is a twelve-line poem. Two are twelve-and-a-half lines, as above. The fourth, a sonnet, and favored if only for that reason by most modern editors, is the version under discussion here. In this version, the final couplet retains the petitionary force of that shorter half-line utterance ("God bless the child") but maintains the ceremony, the social contract, of meter and line length and sonnet form. The speaker calls down blessing, counsels wariness, and leads collective ("let us") prayer. "Beware" is all but nonsense in the light of inexorable prophecy (beware of what? to what end?), but it mimics the consolatory formulas of precept and cautionary tale, which posit an elder whose wisdom can help. The final line of the couplet coincides with the words of the spoken prayer: optative mood, as we noted before, is natural for prayer, and possibly tinged with that other subjunctive, contrary-to-fact. But note the new layer of underwriting: "meeting day," the dreaded conjunction with death, has picked up another resonance. In the formulas of faith, the meeting of consequence is no mere matter of hangman's tools, whatever these bode for bodily h[illegible] It is rather the meeting of Soul and Maker, a source of hope [illegible]ead. In life, Ralegh sometimes played more hands than h[illegible]le of sustaining; his faith was thought to be doubtful; h[illegible]oets had a way of going smash. In the sonnet whose cr[illegible] by-hanging, the precarious balance of worldliness and oth[illegible]ailout will seem to some readers to be too clever by half. [illegible] shadow that gives the poem its particular chill, gives the [illegible]vado of a privately vested *we* its danger and its tender, t[illegible]strength.

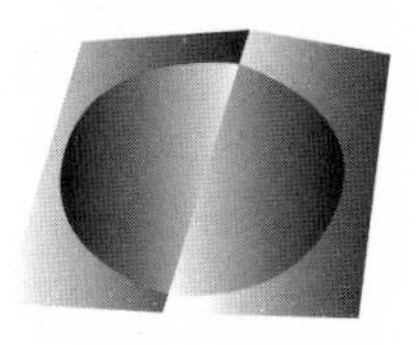

MARK HALLIDAY

Perverse Reading

My approach to reading in my twenties was absurdly inefficient and embarrassingly incoherent. A reasonable and simple version of an essay on my reading during those formative years would analyze my follies as a reader then and sagely warn today's twenty-somethings—graduate students in creative writing, especially—against making my mistakes.

That would be a clear procedure, and would have a sober, mended-my-evil-ways all-grown-up tone. But it would not be in good faith—because vestiges of my early bad habits linger in my reading now in my fifties; and (more importantly) because I secretly *love* those bad habits, or aspects of them, and can't help feeling they're deeply connected to what has made me a poet.

I can't honestly tell a young reader, "Do the opposite of what I did at your age." But I can say, "Think hard about your choices of what to read, and about what reading is." Well, a person can think *too* much about the many choices involved in the activity we call "reading" and this consciousness can become paralyzing. But still I hope it may be useful to someone if I describe in detail how my reading in my twenties was un-serious and even perverse.

What a splendid and absurd thing it is to be a writer in one's early twenties! Infinity of possibility spreads before you. In your desk drawer, or (nowadays) on your old floppy disks, there are not yet hundreds of pages of failed prose or failed poetry. No one yet knows how great you might be! No one yet has clear evidence that you won't be great.

But greatness itself and also half-greatness and very-goodness in creative writing cannot emerge except in relation to literature of the past. What past? *All* the past? All the English-language past? Including Chaucer? All of Chaucer? Around the time you graduate from college you're waking up enough to realize that the reading you need to do in order to have *any* smart, deep idea of what you can write—not to mention any smart, deep idea of what life is really all about—heaps into mountain beyond mountain. You sense that most writers, including some of your brighter friends, will get lost in the foothills of reading, will meander in confusion or delusion—or else abandon the quest and become practical moneymakers who read (or write) only romances or crime novels. Wanting not to become one of those fadeaways, wanting to be a serious mountaineer, you cast about for a method.

Of course if you were an English major as an undergrad, you've already participated in a procedure which offered itself as systematic—but even if (or perhaps especially if) your English professors were good, you still graduated with an echoing, daunting awareness of holes in your learning, chasms, craters, many of the craters larger than the total of your reading so far.

So the early-twenties reader is liable to get depressed. Reader-depression will threaten your thirties and forties and fifties, too, I can say from experience; but I remember a kind of wild-eyed, sweaty depression as a constant threat defining the condition of being a fledgling writer. I'll distinguish four dimensions of this psychological threat: chronology; contextual dearth; oeuvres; conversational anxiety.

1) *Chronology*: There is the endlessly telescoping chronology question—how to understand and appreciate any writer without having already taken in the writer's forerunners—or at least the greatest forerunners....

Can you read Austen without having read Richardson? George Eliot without Charlotte Brontë? Joyce without Homer? Can you read any twentieth-century American poet without "knowing" Whitman and Dickinson? Dickinson without "knowing" the Bible? Keats without Shakespeare *and* Milton? *Anyone* without most of Shakespeare? (And we're not even letting ourselves glance at the crushing monuments of European literature—but as soon as you study any great English or American writer you find that he or she delved deeply into French or Italian or Spanish or Russian or German literature....)

2) *Contextual Dearth*: There is the huge problem of contextualizing—when you read a book "by itself," that is, outside of an organized set of books, without a scheme such as a course syllabus, without a file already established in your head, most of your impressions of the book turn out to be

written-on-water, they dissolve within a few years, or a few months!, into some soft, useless, overall impression.

3) *Oeuvres*: there is the more specific, seemingly finite but still maddening problem of multiple works by one great writer. No sooner do you take satisfaction in having read *Great Expectations* than you start feeling shoddy for not having also read *Bleak House* and *Our Mutual Friend*. (Eliot used a line from *Our Mutual Friend* as a working title for what became *The Waste Land*—then surely you, a young poet, must soon read *Our Mutual Friend*?) Briefly proud to have read *Hamlet*, *King Lear*, and *Macbeth*, you soon feel ashamed of your ignorance of *Othello* and *Antony and Cleopatra* and five other plays you hear knowingly mentioned. (I in my fifties remain embarrassingly ignorant of *Coriolanus* and recently read *Richard III* for the first time.) You've read *Paradise Lost*—bravo, but what of *Paradise Regained* and *Samson Agonistes*? You've read *The House of Mirth* and it mattered to you, but what of *The Custom of the Country* and *The Age of Innocence*, let alone Wharton's less famous novels? You meet annoying people who claim to have read "everything" by X. You wonder if they're fibbing—but still, how can you say you "know" or "love" a certain writer until you've read all of her or him? (I still haven't read all of Dickinson's 1,775 poems though I say I love her and I've taught her several times.)

4) *Conversational Anxiety*: You want to talk with people about books; since you want to widen and deepen your perspectives, naturally you often want to talk with persons who have read (*really* read) much more than you. Some of them are

> professors, and a few are (more disturbingly) writers only five or ten years older than you. Of course you want to be able to contribute to the conversation, and so you may urgently want to read particular books which interest your friend or teacher. This makes sense; indeed, a wretched aspect of contemporary postmodern pluralist culture is that in a roomful of interesting people it's rare to find that two of them have read the same contemporary books, and so conversations keep stopping too soon with "Yeah, I want to read that." But somehow when you read the books your friend or teacher cares about, they may not *mean* for you because you lack a context, a history of associations, in which to place a given book. Meanwhile, you're not reading all those great tomes on your list.

The above account of reader-anxieties is all obvious, but I burned up so many hours of my twenties (and still burn hours in my fifties) obsessing about all this, hours of bookstore bafflement, library paralysis, hours of list-making and new-list-making, that it feels therapeutic to summarize the whole smog-bog.

At least grad school gave the anxieties more of a structure, and gave me obligations instead of too much maddening freedom, and I had a few fibers of emerging maturity to help me along. But in the preceding years I was constantly tortured (melodramatic word, but it seems right for my sweaty memories) by all four of the above issues of what-to-read-when.

And behind them all loomed a great question that a reader usually, from minute to minute, needs to forget: What *is* reading? When have you read a page? Is it enough for your eyes to register every word on the page with some notion of its "main" or denotative meaning? No? If not, if some thinking is required, some reflection, some comparison with other pages, other texts, then *how much?* When are you reading too carefully, too slowly? Some lucky people seem able (as early as their early twenties) to answer these questions intuitively, without getting hung up. One minute per page for journalism or history, two minutes for most fiction, three minutes for criticism, four minutes for great poetry.... Such guidelines, whether intuitive or conscious, have always felt impossible to me. Instead, I've almost always read all texts as if they were equally significant, and read them all with compulsive, fanatical thoroughness. You'd think the result might be marvelous retention of everything read. Alas, it's very possible for me to read one novel lingeringly for two months and forget its plot and characters entirely within two years, just as if I'd dashed through the book. (Ah, but the texture? Maybe the compulsively slow reading allows some good, long-lasting appreciation of a narrative style, even if this appreciation is hard to demonstrate? Let's hope so!)

Anyway, the question *What is reading?* turns out to be a labyrinth once you stop to worry about it. On the moment-to-moment level, a huge proportion of reading is actually rereading, as your eye and mind flick back to reconsider each word or phrase in the context you are perpetually building and reshaping. An anxious young reader, a reader who feels that marvelous keys and clues and secrets and meanings float somewhere in the print ocean, perhaps under the surface, may wonder: When is it okay to turn the page? A serious reader often glances back, flips back—but beyond *some* point this rereading of what you just read becomes neurotic, perverse. Thus it was often for me in my twenties (and since, too, oh Lord).

I want to sort out four regrettable aspects of my reading in those years, presenting the charge (saying why the behavior was perverse, unwise, counterproductive) but also the defense (why the behavior seemed necessary for me, so that I can't wholly regret it).

◆

1) Fanatically Slow Savoring
2) Tokenism/Fetishism
3) Frantic Au Courant-ism
4) Instant Judgment

1) *Fanatically Slow Savoring*

I've already said that in my twenties I refused to read anything fast or even with reasonable momentum. I acted as if every sentence, every line might hold a clue to some essential pattern of human life, *and* a clue to how I should write. Virginia Woolf, E.M. Forster, Kurt Vonnegut, Ronald Sukenick, Rex Stout, Ursula K. Le Guin—they were all Writers and I wanted to be a Writer, so I felt they all deserved equal attention. Reading a novel I felt to be mediocre or worse, I required myself to skip nothing. I was paying my dues. In those years I hadn't chosen between being a poet and being a fiction writer—maybe I could be a star at both! A double genius! The kind of fanatically slow reading I did has sometimes been described as "reading like a poet"—but some fiction writers confess to similar tendencies. When I picked up a book of poems, I lingered and stared, reading ten poems instead of thirty or fifty. I realize this seems inconsistent with the compulsive thoroughness of my fiction-reading; but for me it was as if every poem was a tiny book. The psychology involves my deep desire for any single poem to be a Very Big Deal. By this I don't mean a nobly austere demand that each poem should attain the profundity of "Ode on a Grecian Urn," but only an instinctive recoiling from the suggestion that *any* poem can be glanced at and lightly tossed aside.

In my middle age, though, I've developed a healthy skill: the ability to quit reading a bad novel after the first thirty or fifty pages. Okay, but what about abandoning someone's poem? Well, yes, I now do so shockingly often, to tell the truth, because I now imagine that I know so quickly what a given poem is likely to do, and I do think this early dismissal of some poems is better than the compulsive magnetized obligedness of my poetry reading (in little journals as well as thick books) in my twenties; but still I never quite shake off guilt about this. Even the most shallow or derivative poem still gets a hook into me just by being a poem, just by whispering *poem* into the ear of my conscience.

2) *Tokenism/Fetishism*

I worked in a bookstore in Providence for several years during and after college. I liked the job but it was a kind of delicious torture—every day exposed to the radiation from hundreds and hundreds of crisp new books I SHOULD READ if I were really to become a writer. This was the early seventies and the market for "quality paperbacks" was booming fabulously and all kinds of serious literature sprang from the boxes in handsome yet affordable paperback editions. I really felt as close to crazy as I've ever felt in that realm of dazzlement and blazingly renewed frustration. I, who could manage to read one book in one week only with the most Spartan commitment, made lists calling for me to read a book per day. Several of my fellow clerks were young writers, too, and we all needed coping strategies. A normal coping strategy is simply to decide that many categories of literature are not interesting to you; you're only interested in, say, the Romantic poets, or contemporary American fiction by hard-drinking hard-living men. But I kept wanting to imagine myself as an omnivorous appreciator of *all* literature. Books taunted me from every shelf of College Hill Bookstore (except maybe Health and Self-Help).

Omnivorous appreciation of all literature is impossible for anyone (isn't it? even Harold Bloom, even Denis Donoghue, even William

Pritchard?) and wildly impossible for a fanatically slow reader. So I coped by way of Tokenism/Fetishism.

Confronted with a category, or an oeuvre, maddeningly unknown to me, I seized upon some tiny bit of it—preferably *not* the most famous bit, preferably something unpredictable—and read it repeatedly with a nutty, burning concentration. I chose one obscure novel by any celebrated novelist and fixated on it. *Despair* rather than *Lolita* or *Ada*. *Between the Acts* rather than *Mrs. Dalloway*. *The Man Who Died* rather than *Women in Love*. *When She Was Good* rather than *Portnoy's Complaint*. I wanted to be the aficionado who had read everything, not the average reader who had read just what everyone else read. This approach leads, of course, to some weirdly skewed notions about the writers. By skipping the best-known books and focusing on minor books I could resemble (I imagined) the reader who had already gone through the major books. I applied this clever strategy to whole genres such as Science Fiction and Fantasy (burgeoning in the early seventies) and Contemporary Drama and History and Criticism—and indeed poetry.

I wanted to have favorite poets. I wanted this because I understood that serious writers always *love* certain forerunners and older contemporaries. I experimented with the notion of "loving" so-and-so—"I love Roethke," "I love Richard Wilbur," "I love Adrienne Rich," "I love Ted Hughes," "I love Gregory Orr"—but I didn't seriously love any of them. I hadn't thought enough about what serious love might be. My identity was so plastic—I won't say I was incapable of *loving* someone's work but I wasn't alert to the traces of potential real love in me. This point crystallizes around Kenneth Koch's wonderful poem "Fresh Air." I read this poem—Koch's tour de force of nerve and wildness and insouciance and satire reacting to conventional poetry of the fifties—in an anthology in 1969. It made a strong impression—I never forgot it—but in some way failed to realize that I *loved* it. I was too distracted by a succession of other hypothetical affiliations. Not till the eighties did I understand that for *me* Koch's poetry was really important.

Hypothetical affiliation . . . Merwin! The books of W. S. Merwin were sacred in College Hill Bookstore in the early seventies. My fellow clerks revered him. He was handsome, angelic, his books had an aura. He was the prince of Deep Image. Hundreds of times I picked up *The Moving Target* or *The Lice* or *The Carrier of Ladders*—and tensely read one or two poems. I couldn't bring myself to read one of the books entirely. I now think that a big reason for this was that the poetry didn't really mean much to me, *for* me. But at the time the reason for such skittish reading seemed to be the unbearable spooky magnificence of Merwin. I said I "loved" Merwin, but what did this mean? Mainly it meant I loved the idea of him filtered through book jackets and conversations with other bookstore clerks; I loved the creaminess of his Atheneum paperbacks.

I was too bedazzled to be more serious. I had favorite lines of Merwin, and of many other poets, and favorite sentences in many novels and stories—including many I hadn't read—and a month later, a new set of favorite bits. Often I picked up a book and turned to an arbitrary page with an occult determination to cherish some nugget on it. Once I wrote an essay for a little journal celebrating (with tongue partly in cheek) the gems to be found on page 77 of dozens of books.

What defense for all this? Not much, I guess, except to say I was so young and bedazzled that I needed ways of coping with the onslaught of literature and I needed to feel my ways were *my* ways, idiosyncratic, eccentrically reflecting my wonderful (albeit confused) sensibility.

◆

3) *Frantic Au Courant-ism*

Writing about Tokenism/Fetishism I suspected I was describing an immaturity that would seem merely peculiar (and maybe sick) to the reader of this essay; but surely very few of us have escaped Frantic Au Courant-ism.

A brand-new book comes to your attention—suddenly you crave to read it *immediately*, before anyone you know has read it. Next week will be too late! If you read it *now* you'll be—well, you'll be the person who knows the latest. After all, you want to write the poems (or stories, novels) that will succeed this year and next year, not three years ago, so you need to know what's cooking. This idea is not purely silly but it can lure you into piles of regrettable reading. You could be reading the *Iliad* and the *Odyssey* and the *Metamorphoses* and *The Divine Comedy* and *Measure for Measure* and *Essay on Man* and *The Prelude* and *Leaves of Grass*, but instead you're reading slim volumes of newness with whooshy blurbs, blurbs you imagine being written about you just three years hence....

Frantic Au Courant-ism and Fanatically Slow Savoring are painfully inconvenient to each other. And I'm still prey to this illusion. In a bookstore I see the newest book of poetry or fiction and my credit card starts pulsing in my wallet before I've read a single page.

I could advise grad students to invest only in classics—nothing since Stevens and Faulkner? Nothing since Elizabeth Bishop and *Gravity's Rainbow*? No, that would be *too* "serious" or too timelessly mature. If Abraham Lincoln or George Eliot were an MFA student today, he or she might read only classics—but you and I are more nervously caught up in the glitzy flux. We're bound to crave some au courant-ness. It does at least help us avoid writing poems and stories that are blithely, unwittingly just like others published last year—doesn't it? Besides, sometimes your reading can be more energized and imaginative when you're not intimidated by the book's classic stature.

But perhaps our Au Courant-ism need not be Frantic. Perhaps I can learn to take steady deep breaths in Borders—and to read carefully several pages of a new book before whipping out the Visa.

But looking back at myself in the seventies, I can't honestly picture a big change in this department—*unless* I had met a great teacher sooner. On my own, I wasn't able to say, "All these glossy new books will soon be forgotten, but the great books won't." In 1978 I met Frank Bidart. He turned out to be the great teacher who enabled me to think hard about what mattered—about what "serious" would mean for me. I really don't know how a twenty-something writer escapes Frantic Au Courant-ism without the influence of a great teacher.

4) *Instant Judgment*

Despite my fetishizing, intense attention to many bits of text, *and* despite my compulsively slow reading, it is somehow also true that I became, by age twenty-two, a monstrously quick evaluator of new books and of anyone's new poem or story. I announced the shortcomings of almost everything. When you feel overwhelmed, there's a strong temptation to declare that most of what overwhelms you is worthless or insignificant. I alienated quite a few acquaintances with my hyper-decisive judgments of their manuscripts and chapbooks and books. (I haven't altogether outgrown this tendency, as my friends and ex-friends will attest.)

Now, I am in favor of evaluation. I'm repelled by an indiscriminate embrace of all new writing, the attitude that finds everything admirable "in its own way." I think a writer, young or old, should feel that some new writing is *much* better than most new writing and that this superiority needs to be pointed out and pondered in detail. My habitual mistake was (and is?) not evaluation but such quick and rigid evaluation.

According to what criteria? Well, my favorite criteria were clarity and moral purport. Frequently I judged a poem or prose work to be too obscure. Or, too unconcerned about social injustice—particularly sexism (the feminist wave of the early seventies was a big force in my life; I lived with a radical feminist for three years).

Strangely, I often made these stern complaints against poems and novels on the same day, even at the same moment as I cherished a fetishistic "love" or delectation of a certain portion of some similar poem or novel or even of the *same* poem or novel. Consistency was not my hobgoblin.

What drove me toward rigorous quick judgments? I was scared, like any young writer: I felt in danger of smothering under the piles of other people's books; also, scared of not being smart enough or deep enough to understand mysterious literary profundities; also, scared of the cloudy moral relativism of maturity; I wanted to cut with a bright clean sword! I wanted to clear a space for young Mark.

It has often been observed that the not-so-hidden agenda of many book reviews is to make a space or protect a space in the world for the kind of writing the reviewer himself does. Negative evaluation tends to say implicitly: "This text is not conducive enough to a social and literary world in which *my* particular personality and imagination seem likely to thrive." That subtext perhaps can never be eradicated from literary evaluation, but it can be less dominant and less bellicose than it was in the countless evaluations I dished out in my twenties. I *think* I've learned, in middle age, to be more aware of a fabulous variety of ways in which literary works can illuminate and investigate human life, including versions of human life interestingly different from my own.

Yeah, but this still doesn't become a pluralist everyone-is-groovy open-arms boosterism. There's a criterion I was groping toward in my twenties which became more clear to me in the years after I met Bidart: *truthfulness*. To say it flatly is to sound dumb, but I want to mean it unflatly. I believe there is no escape from the idea of *truth* in the evaluation of literary art (any more than in other human affairs); no matter how contingent and subjective any statement is, still we can't live—can't live intelligently, interestingly, morally, seriously—without feeling that certain statements at certain times ("I love you," "Milosevic is guilty of genocide," "The worlds revolve like ancient women / Gathering fuel in vacant lots") are true, while others (in advertising, for instance) are not. There is a truthfulness of truth-telling and a truthfulness of truth-seeking. There is loyalty to the effort to speak truly to other human beings about human experience. ("Speak" can include many kinds of speech, including theatrical speech.) This loyalty is a definition of seriousness.

In the early seventies I knew the word "serious" counted for me, I knew it had some meaning beyond any number of jokes made by my friends and me, but I hadn't yet learned to distinguish seriousness from various shams—mandarin pomposity, self-admiring moralism, voguish mystification, repressive solemnity. Learning and relearning to be serious is an ongoing struggle, and the ongoingness of this struggle is one reason why someone without humor is unlikely to succeed in it.

What is the upshot of all my 'fessing? I strongly suspect that a young reader whose habits are all plainly unembarrassing and commendable will be more likely to end up a critic or journalist than a good creative writer. If you're a poet or fiction writer, you will need to be perverse—or at least peculiar—in your reading, in some way.

You may need to read fifty murder mysteries, or twenty books on animal reproduction, or the libretti of fifty operas, or every translation of Euripides . . . or page 99 of every book you see. Just try to make sure the perversity or peculiarity is *yours*, not a fad or pose laid on you by teachers, friends, or Zeitgeist; and try to keep an eye on it so that it is, on the whole, however unreasonable, more enabling than disabling.

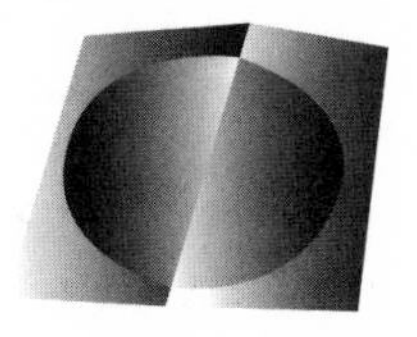

RICHARD LYONS

A Loose Net: Some Meditative American Poets

When discussions of canonicity arise, I can't help but see stubby cannons perched on the hillsides above some Florentine city. I imagine plenty of fine writers slaughtered when the explosives detonate. Poetry should do more than measure who's in power. I want poems to arise from blank space, not a tabula rasa, but some smaller, more nebulous staging area as if there were no aesthetic, historical, political, racial, gender, or linguistic precedents. Of course, there are always precedents. Of course, the space for a poem is never really blank, but, from training perhaps, from habit, for sure, I want a poem to delude itself that it has no palpable design upon the reader. Even a writer as thoroughly engaged in his writing and activism as Albert Camus writes that a person is defined as much by his "make-believe" as his "sincere impulses." I want a poem to exist in the fiction of amoral experience at least as it begins to assume its shape. For me, it is in its fictiveness that a poem's wisdoms—even its ethical wisdoms—take on experience. That fictiveness is best served by the credible treble of a human voice. I admit that there is an arrogance and self-indulgence in the confessionalism of some contemporary verse. But there is also an arrogance and self-indulgence in verse that presumes to speak for all of history and culture. The best polyphonic verse, if it is true to itself, does not petrify into the monolithic. Whether a poem has one voice or many voices, a poem's persona is both a magical *and* fabricated way for the individual artist, in the act of composition, to strive to strike a balance, in Camus' words, between the "values of creation" and "the values of humanity."

Meditative verse is an ambitiously discursive medium always conscious of itself as a "made thing." Conversational and allusive at the same time, the meditative poem includes parts of narratives, fictive or historical, or parts of myths, but it does not develop complete stories or complete characterizations for their own sakes. My project here must allow itself a loose net. My guess is that most writers do not want to be categorized at all. I have grouped them here as performers, talkers, or visual artists because those different strategies seem to shape the poems and illuminate consideration of them.

PERFORMERS

Emily Dickinson

The performers are unusually conscious that their made thing "exists" on some sort of dramatic stage, whether the subject matter is intimate or political. Emily Dickinson's poems are trajectories passing into viewlessness. They are performances of consciousness, "Like looking every time you please / in an abyss's face!" (#1400). Dickinson's poems are radio waves broadcast from a person who has shed any sense of personality and ego in the self-aggrandizing sense of these terms. She writes, "Faith is a fine invention," and her more than seventeen hundred poems, at their best, seem like agnostic explorations of a universe that is held still for a second in each poem's intimate enlargement of consciousness.

Robert Lowell

Robert Lowell's poems bridge the gulf between so-called confessional poets like Anne Sexton and so-called language poets like Susan Howe. Some of his poems are oratory; they are concerned with public declarations of history. Other poems are prayers whispered by a person inside an oratory—a room for private devotions. The poem "For the Union Dead" is both a public and private prayer that coheres around the image of a hole: the old aquarium tank, the excavation for an underground garage, the classical underworld, the grave hole for Colonel Shaw and his men, the "city's throat," and the photograph of the Hiroshima blossom of smoke above its almost unimaginable chasm. This poem, in the manner of a number of Shakespeare's sonnets, wrestles with the difficulties of humanizing a monument. Lowell's poems continually try to bridge the chasm between the individual self and history. How does one make one's suffering useful? How does the self withstand becoming a part of the deathly flow of time and history? The stone faces of Shaw's Negroes seem to come alive as the poem contemplates their visages.

Adrienne Rich

Rich's *An Atlas of the Difficult World* is, I think, a deliberately motley performance, a verbal melting pot. Section I, if it stood alone, would surely best be described as a song of myself as the other. But Rich increases the degree of difficulty by challenging the unity of the title poem with an additional twenty-eight pages of assorted portraits.

Ghandi has written that we must *be* the change we seek. In this statement is a radical activism and idealism not lost on Adrienne Rich who, in this atlas, tries to visualize away the differences between nations, races, genders, ages, even historical periods. Rich assumes, as Whitman does in *Song of Myself*, that these differences are socially manufactured constructions. But Rich goes beyond Whitman's sympathy—even Keats's sympathy, I think—by becoming her subjects as wholly as humanly possible without writing dramatic monologues.

The second section of the book is also meant to challenge the utopian venture of sympathy itself. There is a grand modesty at work in Rich's and Whitman's atlases. In both, the persona insists on juggling the individual parts, stories, and invented beings so that those parts have an integral existence apart from the performer's skill. In the "intricate losing game of innocence," if I may conflate some crucial lines, Rich claims, "A patriot is a citizen who wrestles for the soul of her country / as she wrestles for her own being." Rich knows that a poet should not separate the personal from the historical because to do so would be fatal for the body politic as well as for the body itself.

Richard Howard

Richard Howard's books are poetic dramas, operas, performances with the mask nearly pried off, the very dance of the mask as it coasts the ridges of the face and holds on, persona intact but troubled. As much as any other poet working today, Howard is sensitive to the expectations we place on one another, and his poems meticulously measure the cost and worth of human relationships in determining a character's self-esteem, even existence. Having adopted the masks of players from history and literature, Howard continues his affection for the dramatic monologue in *Trappings*. In one poem, he speaks in the voice of Browning's interlocutor Nikolaus Mardruz from "My Last Duchess." In Howard's rendition, Mardruz debriefs his employer, the Count of Tyrol, applauding his own deployment of *semblances* while deriding—at a safe distance—the old Duke of Ferrara for the transparency of his. Mardruz's scrutiny penetrates the ugliness behind the Duke's masks, mirrors, and effigies while the envoy exacts a dowry transaction that will preserve the life of his employer's daughter and ultimately effect a transfer of all the Duke's esteemed "objects" to Tyrol's heirs.

Howard is even tough enough to scrutinize his own status as sophisticated poet and consummate performer. In "For Mona Van Duyn, Going On," he tells the story of his fainting at a poetry festival. At first, the social flutter of embarrassment and speculation on motivations seem like devices to propel the poem to its frightful possibilities. But when the poet denies the glamour of blacking-out and tells us he has no contact with the "Other Side," he gives us a double payoff. We shudder at the ultimate depths that he is not eager to plumb—literally or aesthetically—while he uses Van Duyn as a way to talk about and accept the flawed "community of pain to which we all / belong." The poem concludes with the poetry festival going on, but Howard has shot a chill down the spine of the platitude "the show must go on." The players are still a bit weak in the knees, but they go on stage.

John Berryman

John Berryman's poems are part stand-up comedy, part high-wire act, and part vaudeville. They juggle the tragic and comic masks. There's the speaker himself, Berryman's persona, Henry, and his compatriot who calls the speaker Mr. Bones. He uses these and a host of other manifestations of the self as dramatic personae. Like the British painter Francis Bacon, Berryman does violence to our sense of self-portraiture by continually highlighting the poem's staginess. Berryman is also continually toying with his persona as artist *and* worthless object. Berryman even calls Henry "itself" in a number of his songs. Sometimes Berryman's persona is the narcissistic artist among other members of the pantheon. At other times, the persona is the frivolous poet, professor, and drunken womanizer whom the average American loves to berate. More than any American poet of his generation, Berryman seems to have internalized and amplified his nation's disdain for the world of letters.

Berryman's pyrotechnical manipulation of the sense of self also makes use of the tradition of the somber European clown to sharpen, even radicalize, moments, of vulnerability and moments of defiance—sometimes in the same breath. The tough, rude side of Berryman is like a lowlands mother bird that performs suicidal displays in front of predators to distract them from her nest—Berryman's vulnerable side.

TALKERS

William Matthews

Like Wordsworth, Coleridge, and Keats, talkers use the illusion of natural speech to reduce the distance between speaker and listener, whether the listener is an interlocutor, an absent auditor, or a reader. William Matthews' poems are gregarious and cordial. As with Charlie Parker's sixteenth notes, Matthews' lines think swiftly down a page, seeming to improvise their various colloquial wisdoms. Matthews' poems, like Berryman's, know that they are "chummy with dread." Matthews' poems lust for life as much as they fear silence and death. The human body—like language, like memory—is a rickety old machine we love to push beyond its limits. Matthews spent a career challenging the layers of self-deceit in our embodiments of truths. In "Euphemisms," the speaker warns us against clinging to an antiseptic, monolithic, self-protective use of language. He writes, "one touch of smugness makes the whole world kin." He urges himself to be as careful with words as he can in his enthusiastic lunge to express what he thinks he means. Playing with many of the euphemisms surrounding the subject of cancer, one speaker says, "if I could make it like something else, / I wouldn't have to think of it as what / in fact, it was: part of my lovely wife."

Jon Anderson

Jon Anderson's poems speak outside of time, yet somehow speak intimately. With a rigorous plainness of speech, the speaker of his "Tucson: A Poem about Wood" affirms a friendship by watching men work on the house next door. Speaking of his verse with a series of end-stopped lines that could stand up to the most sensitive carpenter's level, he claims "I hate it, I do it for pleasure, I'm not even a part of it." This sort of poetic self-abnegation pleases because it happens outside the stingy parameters of the usual group flagellation. His absence in the frame of the poem's everyday activity is an act of love. He is not ashamed, not embarrassed, and not self-congratulatory. A similarly sweet pulling-back in the poem "Cypresses" lets us see beyond the trees some clouds assuming familiar shapes, "In time, upon all the possible / Faces of all possible things." With an almost Buddhist not-acting, Anderson concludes "Lives of the Saints" with his speaker saying "Give me a little time— / Eternity— / & I will mend." Though the point of view may seem to be retreating, this gesture neither protects the self nor trumps itself with irony. Anderson's restraint perfects the very act of sympathy.

Stanley Plumly

In Plumly's field guides, everything is adrift on the breath that names things as they go: leaves, smoke, soot on currents of air across sinuous and sinewy bodies of water. The rhythms are insistent and patient, always listening to themselves hum, always listening to nature's rhythm section—piano, bass, and drum—waiting for the signal that loneliness and loveliness are the same thing, the wholeness of experience turned back upon its sources. Air, earth, and water recover a spark of life often inside the very flame of loss itself. These poems insist that wisdom become experience, and a particular experience so that wisdom can flow through the veins and nerves into the wonderful and inconsistent agility of the human body, "so much of a piece / with the whole it is wood for a fire."

James Wright

Poetry may not be plain speech, but James Wright's rendering of a colloquial working-class cadence is nonetheless unsurpassed in the history of English verse. The reader is swept up in the naturalness of speech patterns, but the poetry isn't swept away by the fluidity and wastefulness of ordinary speech. Wright is able to give colloquial phrasing just enough starch that it seldom sounds flaccid or stiff. In Wright's verse, the colloquial American tongue can drawl and clip the rigor and vigor of a metrical line.

Besides plainness of speech, what has drawn imitators to James Wright is his insistence on sympathy, especially for those on the downside of the America Dream. In Wright, we get ordinary people speaking almost ordinary language. But for me what separates Wright from his imitators is his rigorous examination of guilt and violence—cultural, natural, and individual. I am thinking in particular of the credibility Wright manages when his personae participate in unsavory activities: "On a Phrase from Southern Ohio" in which Wright and friends row out to an island and beat up some black kids they find there; or the emblematic "Autumn Comes to Martins Ferry, Ohio," which shows the human cost of industry's rape of the heartland.

Mona Van Duyn

The poems in Mona Van Duyn's *Letters from a Father and Other Poems* are plainspoken and metrically rigorous. Most are harshly-whispered missives dealing with the familiar—with the family, with ordinary, even basic events and details, an elderly father's growing devotion to birdwatching, cats wandering Proust's grave, an eye test for a driver's license, the awkward anatomy of a female moose, even Ozark gossip. In fact, Van Duyn's aesthetic project, at least in this collection, seems to set itself up as a wholesale antidote to imaginative flights of fancy. She is willing to expose our most awkward vulnerabilities.

The two long poems that seem to serve as pillars for this collection focus on the speaker's aging parents. The title poem, spoken in letters by the father-character, and the poem "Streams," addressed to the mother, both seem to eschew the customary grief of the elegy so as to celebrate human endurance and grit as fact more than consolation. I imagine Van Duyn reading Dylan Thomas's poem "Do Not Go Gentle into that Good Night" and saying to herself it's easier said than done. In fact, Van Duyn's two poems enact, manifest, and embellish the challenge that Thomas issues to his dying father. Van Duyn's poems teach the reader to be ready for what will inevitably fall upon him or her: "responsibility for his own life / and a share of responsibility for the world."

VISUAL ARTISTS

Wallace Stevens

The visual artists de-emphasize voice and voicing to enhance the sense of the poem as object. Instead of an emphasis on the "made thing" as a system of sounds, this kind of poem declares itself as a system of scapes or sculptured views. Not surprisingly, then, this kind of poem often describes an actual landscape or idealized realm. Wallace Stevens' poems make me trust his confidence in the human imagination because in them there is just as much distrust of the imaginative function. Early and late, in "The Snow Man" and in "The Plain Sense of Things"—to name two examples—the same mind that can conjure the palace of Hoon can project an oblivion, where "the absence of the imagination had / Itself to be imagined." The integrity of Stevens' faith in the mind's imaginative power requires a qualified homage to chaos in which the person "knows desire without an object of desire, / All mind and violence and nothing felt."

Charles Wright

Dual impulses are also crucial to the work of Charles Wright, especially in the poems after *Country Music*. In Wright's discursive, episodic meditations, the symbolist and surrealist love of the image is juxtaposed with the mystic's distrust of language, thought, and image. Unsurprisingly, Wright presents the landscape as an abstraction even in poems that use homely backyard settings. There are very few extras on stage: his army buddies, off and on, and the occasional cameo appearance of family members. These characters, when they do appear, are more figures in a larger depiction of landscape as a state of mind—as in, say, the landscape paintings of Breughel—than they are characters in subplots. Wright seems to have steeped his verse in Eastern philosophy, at least as much as Ralph Waldo Emerson, Walt

Whitman, and Gary Snyder have theirs. Taoist and Buddhist aphorisms and practices manage, at their best, to reconcile the simplest, perhaps menial tasks of daily life with the mystic's non-striving for the peace of the invisible.

Elizabeth Bishop

I do not agree with readers who think that *Geography III* was a sincerist breakthrough for Bishop. *Geography III* is a continuation of her lifelong investigation of the tension between the private self and the world as landscape. Like Charles Wright, Elizabeth Bishop does not want her poetry to be overtly autobiographical, and this wish is neither a failing nor a cowardice. Like George Herbert, she is concerned with the idea of poetic utterance as an edifice threatened by the world and even by the poet's depth of feelings. In "2000 Illustrations and a Complete Concordance," Bishop uses a sentence fragment to tell us that she suspects that the world and our renderings of it are "Everything only connected by 'and' and 'and'." Bishop made a career of these misgivings, and she celebrates this negative capability in the last stanza of "Poem," too. The literal painting in "Poem" is both precious and worthless. The dramatic monologue "Crusoe in England" resonates with the same tensions: Crusoe's artifacts are both everything and nothing. Bishop's greatness lies in the delicate balance she has struck to keep her house of cards standing despite the self, the self's tumult, and the world's uncooperativeness.

Beckian Fritz Goldberg

Goldberg's painterly ventures may give us a surreal pleasure, but what is really special about her poems is the inkling of what is not present in what is. The objects in Goldberg's poems are certainly rendered for what they are, but they also point elsewhere, to haunting absences whose light is still discernible. Goldberg's poems are about the impossibility of fulfilled desires—as one of her book titles, *In the Badlands of Desire*, makes explicit. Her poems yearn for what is absent and at a distance, not for what is dead. This collection also seems deliberately framed, beginning with "Possibilities" and ending with "In the Badlands of Desire." "Possibilities" is a catalogue of negative *if* clauses, each of which removes the image it has just given to replace it with another in the *then* clause: "These are," the poet writes, "the possibilities, the immaculate / like miracles which are nothing / in themselves, but in this world a sign / of angels, ghosts, supernatural beings / who watch us." In the title poem which concludes the collection, Goldberg confirms my suspicion that any number of elsewheres motivate the evocation of sensual imagery: "if there is a tongue / moving toward its mother silence . . . I will be the look given to a door / when it closes by itself." Goldberg is not a mystic because her poems do not ache for a wordless, thoughtless, transcendent realm to replace this one. Instead, they maintain this synapse between self and other, presence and absence, world and ghost world.

Frank O'Hara

O'Hara's poems come in a multitude of shapes and sizes and radically different linguistic attitudes, from street jests to cerebral ruminations. But for me his odes, which struggle with the poet's assuming the mantle of creative genius, are the cornerstone of his aesthetic. "Ode To Michael Goldberg ('s Birth And Other Births)," and "Ode To Willem De Kooning" follow the arduous labor of a poet giving birth to himself even though the ostensible project is to celebrate the art of each painter.

O'Hara celebrates a Whitmanesque American self, but one whose ultimate project is to liberate art from death by creating a community of selves inside the self. Alongside these invented selves, O'Hara invokes a host of actual persons from his autobiographical life—jazz greats, poets, and painters from the New York art scene, and personal friends. In the epithalamium "Poem Read at Joan Mitchell's," for example, O'Hara looks forward to the birth of a child for whom he can serve as godfather; he also helps us see marriage and childbirth as artistic ventures when he writes "for this life and these times, long as art and un- / interruptable." He aspires to an art that will not petrify into a monument to individual personality. In his elegiac poem "In Memory of My Feelings," O'Hara orchestrates multiple selves he refers to as "transparencies," and seems bent on creating an aboriginal, multiple personality. This otherness within the self is O'Hara's strength. Though there are moments of self-torture in O'Hara, these moments do not seem born of a fabricated or autobiographical anguish. O'Hara's best poems are ultimately paeans to all aspects of life, including the terrifying.

Michael Burkard

Michael Burkard's poems are fiercely introspective. But if this introspection is solipsistic, no poet is more aware of his isolation than Burkard himself. Somehow Burkard makes neuroses cordial and welcoming. The objects in the poems are so conscious of their illusory status as nouns that the boats, the donkeys, the houses seem ever-ready to become verbs, to surrender to the processes of loss, disintegration, memory-shift, perspective, motion, and transformation. But Burkard's poems are never hermetic or surrealistic. He is aware how quickly the act of utterance congratulates itself for its elegance and eloquence, and this scrupulous honesty creates a unique realism. The authenticity arises in part from Burkard's treatment of abstractions as if they were as palpable as clay, oil, or splintered wood. Like the imagery, the abstract ideas are so mercurial that when he challenges, for instance, the way he articulates a phrase, the manneredness he questions remains part of the composition's whole. By exposing the seams of his artifice, Burkard insists that artmaking partake in life's volatility.

Some poets here borrow the trappings of theater and oratory. Others talk or whisper. Still other inhabit images, objects, and landscapes. Still others try to paint with words what Paul Klee called the "prehistory of the visible." Performers. Talkers. Visual Artists. Now I unloose my already loose net. . . .

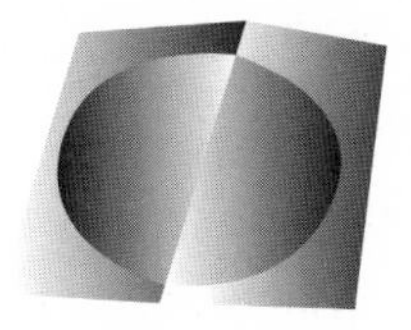

CYNTHIA MACDONALD

The Compass of Association

None of us can read all that we wish we could. Of the poets I know, Edward Hirsch and Richard Howard come closest—they seem not only to read everything, but to remember all of it as well. Of course, you must read poetry—imbibe it and, if it makes you drunk, use the observing part of your mind to understand it. Read it aloud to listen to its music, memorize as much as you can so you will have it inside you. Poets need to know poetry first, but also fiction, essays, history, news of the day, week or year, biography, autobiography, mythology, art, theater, movies, music, architecture, and so on. The possibilities might range from Ovid's *Metamorphoses*, Cervantes' *Don Quixote*, Sei Shōnagon's *The Pillow-Book*, and Walter Benjamin's *Reflections* to *Guinness World Records* and *The New York Times* obituary pages.

What I want to talk about here, though, isn't only how to choose what to read, but how that choice will lead you to decisions about what to read next. It could be described as an associative process, letting your subconscious or unconscious lead you from one thing to the next, instead of following an orderly list. I think that's particularly appropriate for poets because that's the way a mind moves when it's reading poetry, and also when it's writing it. The mind meanders, instead of moving in a straight line. Straight lines . . . like soldiers marching in a parade . . . and when they need to turn a corner, the right angle turn is precise. I can see them turning from 86th Street onto Fifth Avenue.

Suddenly a scene of a child sitting in bed, playing with toy soldiers comes to mind: an unconscious connection. The association is probably right angle corners: soldiers marching. Though I guess it might also relate to "square corners," the military way to make a neat bed. But the boy in bed exerts a stronger pull. It comes from a poem by Robert Louis Stevenson, one I first heard when my mother read it to me from *A Child's Garden of Verses*. The poem, "The Land of Counterpane," is about a little boy, sick in bed, who uses the hills and valleys of his body under the covers as a landscape in which to arrange his lead soldiers and villages:

> And sometimes for an hour or so
> I watched my leaden soldiers go,
> With different uniforms and drills,
> Among the bed-clothes, through the hills. . . .

There is a picture, on the page opposite the verse, of the boy leaning against his pillows watching the soldiers he's arranged going this way and that, some falling over, some in ranks, some not keeping to the marching order.

One association from "The Land of Counterpane" is a pun: against pain. Then Israeli poet Yehuda Amichai's poem, "Evening Promenade on Valley of the Ghost Street," comes to mind. Why did I think of that poem? I think it begins with something about marching. "Evening Promenade on the Valley of the Ghost Street, German Colony." "Weariness gives way to the pomp of parading up and down the street—a ritual almost." Yes, I see the connection; it's obvious. But there is also something less obvious. Israel . . . the German Colony. What seems to introduce the reader to the pleasant scene of people strolling down a street, leaving the weariness of the day behind, is shadowed by "the pomp of parading" and the mention of the German Colony. Even without knowing the many poems Amichai has written about Jews and Germans, I think most readers would make that association. The title page of that section in the book is:

> I Wasn't One of the Six Million:
> And What is My Life Span?
> Open Closed Open

You will see that I have gone from orderly ways of choosing what to read, to thinking about right angles to the boy with the toy soldiers, to Israelis promenading. I could let these associations lead me—reread *A Child's Garden of Verses*? Amichai? Find a biography of Robert Louis Stevenson? Probably I would choose the latter. Or I might read a book or books of Holocaust literature. What keeps this from being a random, meaningless process is that I trust that at least some of the associations are driven by a powerful emotion, that it acts as a magnet, drawing words and images to itself. In the grip of these emotions, we often seem to find what we need, and to see new associations in familiar passages.

When I was making some notes for this essay—not long after the events of September 11th—I marked some passages I found in *The Poet's Notebook*, edited by Deborah Tall, Stephen Kuusisto, and David Weiss. It was only after I went back to those notes later, though, that I could see how my unconscious had shaped my choices:

> VIOLENCE (Transformations require destruction: like that Tibetan deity in the Museum of Fine Arts trampling on a necklace of skulls in his marriage with Wisdom. He has the slavering, fanged mouth of a monstrous bull as he leans over her, waving his forty-odd arms; she, in his lap, twists upward, her legs twining around his waist, melon breasts pressed to his chest. The museum label helpfully notes that the figures are "anatomically correct" and that they can be separated and fitted back together in their copulation. A crowd of schoolchildren tromps by the statue; two ten-year-olds linger to peer at it while their myopic and harassed teacher tries to show them into a farther room. "What's that bull doing to that Lady?" asks one girl. "That's Asia," says the teacher with a vague wave of the hand. "Come on." "Look," says the other girl, "that bull is eating that lady.") *Rosanna Warren*

> At fourteen I read the bible through twice, and then abandoned it because there seemed to have been too many contradictions. Six years later I read it through again, and this time came away convinced that Jesus Christ was a socialist and that is what got him nailed to the cross. True, admittedly, I didn't become a model Christian, but I learned a great deal about imagery and metaphor. The Old Testament is pure surrealism. *Yusef Koumanyakaa*

> October 13, 1983. Once you turned off Ocean Drive you felt the difference. The sun was no less dazzling down those side streets, but it was no longer welcomed. Old people sat behind drawn Venetian blinds, diminutive fans turning. In the heat of the afternoon nothing moved. Cats slept in the shade of shrubs and occasional great tree roots. Once I stopped to watch a train of tree ants maneuvering torpidly across the pink stucco of a storefront, spelling out in insect hieroglyphics some cryptic message. Probably a warning about the future.
>
> *Donald Justice*

Now Warren's description of the marriage of Violence who tramped over a necklace of skulls to marry Wisdom reminds me of the horror that I felt as I watched a plane hit the first tower. How strange, yet perhaps not. My unconscious evidently made the connections before I recognized what I had found. Koumanyakaa's description of the Old Testament as surreal matches the incredulity I felt as I watched the plane hit the side of Tower Two, then vanish into it as if it were raping the building. That was surreal; everyday reality turned upside down. As was the towers' collapse and all that followed. And Justice's heavy, hot afternoon where nothing moved except tree ants maneuvering across a pink stucco wall, creating hieroglyphics that warned about the future, makes me think of all the warnings we had that the United States was hated in many parts of the world. The hieroglyphics were scarcely seen and when they were, they were ignored.

Trusting the unconscious, using the surprises it brings you, does not mean that the conscious abdicates. It's like dropping a fishing line in the stream and catching a trout. You had an expectation you would catch something, but you didn't know what it would be—it could have been a minnow or an old shoe. But your conscious mind would tell you not to cook the minnow or the shoe. If you choose the associative method to discover what you might explore next, you'll often need other, more organized ways of reading as well. Chronologically. By country. By genre. But if, after a while, those ways of organizing begin to make you feel as if you're marching, use association. It will invite you to dance or to make love. That doesn't mean it is what I've dubbed "sweety-floaty," a shampoo commercial of a young man and a young woman, her golden hair bouncing as they run, arms outstretched, across a lush, green field toward each other. Rather, it means that you will open yourself to surprise, and surprise often connects to fresh emotion, emotion not fading to gray because it is too familiar.

You may feel that the method I've described sounds overly orderly to be called associative. That is partly because using it to describe a way of reading has necessitated going step-by-step through processes that are more fluid when you or I are using them. It's a matter of picking a place to start, and assuming that from that place will come another. If, in reading a poem, I suddenly thought of fish, I would imagine that I was hungry; or might want to read Izaak Walton's 17th-century book *The Compleat Angler, or the Contemplative Man's Recreation*; or had forgotten to load the lunch dishes into the dishwasher. How about fish in the dishwasher? For me, unconscious material is best explored further by reading whatever it has yielded that gives a feeling of excitement and curiosity.

In fact unconscious connections are, in most successful poems, vitally important, and often create the lyrical or narrative structure of poems. As I said earlier, surprise is central to my feelings of delight in both reading and writing, no matter how dark the subject may be, no matter how deciding which of many places to go presents a dilemma. As Robert Frost writes in "The Road Not Taken": "Oh, I kept the first for another day! / Yet knowing how way leads on to way, / I doubted if I should ever come back."

So is this essay about reading, or writing poems? Both. It's about a way of expanding your choices of what to read, and a way of reading that opens up the secrets embedded in the poems. We were asked to write about reading for poets. If the task had been to discuss reading for cartographers, the task would have been different. Cartographers. Oh, that sounds interesting. I think of all the maps in Vermeer's paintings. . . . I must look at the Vermeer reproductions in the books I own, *Johannes Vermeer*, *Vermeer and Rembrandt*, and *Vermeer and the Delft School*, and read the essays in them.

Those maps . . . I want to start a poem.

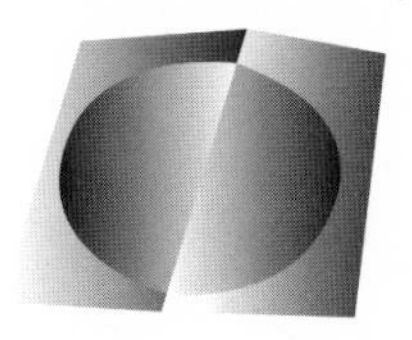

REGINALD GIBBONS

A Few Cells in the Great Hive

Someone asked me to suggest a reading list for a young American poet. Before I can suggest what anyone should read, I think I should ask what sort of reader I am, since preferences inevitably depend on temperament and formation. There are many simultaneously existing and developing kinds and genealogies of poetry in the world and within this country, and no set of readings can speak equally well to all practitioners of the art. Simonides is supposed to have said that the more bees there are bringing honey to the hive, the better. And I agree. So I think I am able to speak only to, and for, poets whose sense of things is already somewhat, or may turn out to be somewhat, like my own. Also, age has shown me that much of what I thought was still contemporary, and still very much believe to be valuable to anyone writing in our era, may already feel gone to many poets who are much younger than I. (In the short span of years from the middle 1500s to the early 1600s, and again from the late 1700s to the early 1800s, and once more from the years of World War I to the 1930s, English poetry changed very much, and didn't both poetry and the novel change greatly from about 1960 to about 2000, in many languages? Now, too, we can sense that since September 11, 2001, some of the imposed structures of our society are beginning to change in a particular way, and with them some of our ways of feeling and the acculturation of our spirits and our imagination will change. All this affects what we write and how we read.)

So what sort of reader am I? I discover the answer partly by looking at what sort of readers others are. To grasp how deeply writers younger than I might be affected by their formation in a later, media-saturated culture has taken me a while, because their experience is so different from my own. And this difference continues to be shaped as we live on—I cannot guess how differently from me they may be affected by a new stage, in America, of a more militarized, more policed society. I matured as television did—which in any case I did not see so very much of, because when I wasn't in school, I was reading or making music with friends, and it was easy to be where TV was not, but young poets have matured in an environment of electronic media. I took the low production values of live TV for granted, and as a boy I watched the end of the period when improvising whirligigs like Sid Caesar and Imogene Coca risked the whole illusion of performance in front of the camera—and when they lost it, I don't think there was much irony in the moment, either for them or for us, but instead a kind of burst of released psychic energy and connection with them as performers. I watched the filmed horrors of attacks on civil rights demonstrators and of combat scenes in Vietnam. I listened to music in "hi-fi," which went stereophonic for consumers during my teens, or on bad small radios or car radios, on little scratchy 45-rpm players, or occasionally in performance; while in college, I listened to music on speakers in my homemade cabinets—to the Stones and the Beatles and Dylan, when the energy of song seemed to me as creative and as intimate as it was rebellious—not staged in order to be filmed; and to Beethoven and Falla and Tchaikovsky, as I found my way to realizations of how complex feeling is, how vast the inner realms might be. It did seem then, as it apparently has not seemed since, to most Americans, till now, that a hard rain was going to fall. Now we can all hear music or a simulacrum of music reproduced with startling qualities of fidelity or with electronically exaggerated audio range, anywhere we want and in lots of places we don't want, as day in and day out we are forced to endure artificially saturated sound-spaces all around us, and songs that once burned with ardent dissatisfaction and idealism are melody lines for Muzak arrangements. I thought of film, too, as more capable of relatively intimate effects than it seems to be now—for me this meant old films by Cocteau and Chaplin and Keaton, it meant *Grand Illusion* and *Blue Angel* and *Nosferatu*, and it meant some of the French film noir, then early films by Fellini, Truffaut, Godard, Rohmer and others; there weren't nearly as many films, altogether, as there are now, although then as now, Hollywood formed strong fantasies in young minds. (The substance of those fantasies was not so filled with explosions as now, nor were as many movies made for twelve-year-olds of all ages.) Classic foreign films were still circulating to provincial audiences for the first time; in all of Houston, where I grew up and where I returned for the first few summers of my college years, only one theater—the seedy (but well air-conditioned) Alray—showed films by Fellini and Truffaut in the evenings, and by day it screened pornography.

All this experience of recorded music and of the images of film and television was not only an education in musical rhythms and in the pace and style of film and television, but also in language, which I'm sure had a decisive effect on me as a writer of poems. I was not lucky enough to grow up where there was strong speaking—telling of story, rich metaphor arising from everyday life, regional accents that were a form of resistance, instead of what I heard—a form of sociability and conformism. I listened to voices around me, but their way of speaking gave me little. I went to oddballs and foreigners and media from somewhere else to hear other ways of speaking. And I think that persons formed emotionally and culturally by more recent TV and film—and technically, such as by a pace of cuts that I still have trouble catching up to—have understandably become accustomed to a very different linguistic environment and different ideals both true and false, both civilized and puerile, both noble and crass. Accustomed to a different sort of standardization on the airwaves, which co-opts non-mainstream language ways. Listeners to language who are younger than I have been educated in different linguistic environments and have learned different production values in media (which, whether we're comfortable with this thought or not, are also human values), and I think they are steeped in an often ironic allusiveness in commercial mass culture ("intertextuality") that allows very few to take the risks of live, more improvised performance or more complicated language, or win for such risks the exhilarating payoffs for sheer human rather than technical virtuosity. All of this gives the poet some of the artistic assumptions that determine how she or he writes poems. When I work as a poet, I don't believe I am caught in my past—I believe I'm looking, actively scanning, both backward in experience and forward. But my particular personal history does affect how I write, what I write, and what I am recommending as reading for other poets. And my personal history is what orients me toward the unknown into which we are advancing, each day.

Perhaps the most telling of all my retrospective Personal Poetry Facts is that when I graduated from high school, and my two favorite English teachers jointly gave me a copy of T. S. Eliot's *Collected Poems* and another gave me Ezra Pound's *ABC of Reading*, Eliot and Pound were still alive. Larger than life but at the same time somewhat marginalized by their obsolescence (after *Howl*, etc.) and, in Pound's case, perhaps senility, they were nevertheless living presences who still reminded me convincingly and constantly not so much of their own work but of their sense—as I understood it—of how poetic works were made: out of reading widely among works of the past in order to renovate the dulled or hollow present-day language (in every present—that of the modernists or our own), the routine language of ordinary description, emotional expression and ideas, the language of received opinion. The poet produced from older *literary* models (not necessarily canonical ones, and not very many models in the other arts) a revived freshness of language and especially of descriptive powers and technique. One applied that freshness to, and developed it out of, one's own perceiving, feeling, thinking, and one's own historical moment. I accepted their assumptions about how all this worked, for a poet, and then gradually I learned how to train my ear for language in present-day life and in contemporary literary works, especially the quirkier writers of fiction; and then, I tried to learn how to coax language out of the future, also.

I mostly assign readings to students in order to (1) push their sense of the timeline of poetry back a hundred or four hundred or four thousand years, and (2) lead their awareness of poetry's infinitely various modes out beyond English and also toward what has not yet been articulated. And I assign or suggest readings in order to try to

(3) instill an artistic value that to me seems important—that one writes poetry not only to convey something (a feeling, an idea, a way of speaking, a choice—however vaguely the poet apprehends it or longs for it, at first) but also to join an ongoing exploration *in* poetry not only of feeling and thought but also of language itself. During my many years as the editor of a literary magazine, when I worked on each issue, whether of writers from the U.S. or elsewhere, I thought of my motto as, "It's a conversation."

"It" meant writing, reading, reading about writing, writing about writing and reading—a process not only linguistic but also allusive, echoing and responding to other writing as well as to reality and desire. (Before there was the word "intertextuality," I think, and before there was the phrase "anxiety of influence," there was Walter Jackson Bate's lovely and illuminating little book of thirty years ago, *The Burden of the Past and the English Poet*.) But to me, *this* intertextuality does not seem especially ironized, unlike so much intertextuality of film nowadays, and of poetry and fiction, too. Also, because I believe there are truths of lived experience, I don't much like the postmodern assumption that there are none. I think literary canons have value, and I favor a postmodern openness of multiple canons, without, I hope, any superciliousness on my part about any of them. I don't very often "appropriate" scraps of *mass* culture (true popular culture is filled with marvelous work yet "appropriating" becomes more like theft). I don't see great value in stances of postmodern irony, nor in welcoming the supposed emptiness of the "subject position." But I will "appropriate" anything and everything that leaves a trace of lived experience and human regard, that resists the diction and rhythms and motives of "commercial speech"—because I believe one must with all one's artistic and human might resist the imposed artificialities of mass media (all forms), the outbreaks of ignorant "othering," and all forms of chauvinism—national, religious, regional, ethnic, etc. I see the ideas of biological uniqueness and human capacity as the ground of human rights, the worth of the individual life and truth of individuality. The books I read and recommend often have to do with all that, too.

Language is the common capacity and property of us all, yet it can be bent to a surprising and memorable blue note by the uniqueness of a line or a whole poem, and our use of it in poetry—so as to mark it as different in some way from its utilitarian use—offers us at least the possibility of an oblique (Emily Dickinson famously called it "slant") communication worth having. Language is serviceably functional among us all, yet it can lead into a vertiginous exhilaration of self-reflexiveness. Language is sometimes a game we all play, yet it reaches into our being with soul-shaking utterances of grief, love, pain, promise. Writing in general, and writing poetry specifically, is a conversation, a making of language into verse with others—"verse" meaning something shaped, made out of "language in the dimension of time" (Antonio Machado's definition of poetry), and often labored over (which is itself an artistic value that has become precarious). Writing implies having in mind "others"—as sources (the voices one does hear), as models of other possibilities of being, as addressees, forebears, colleagues (dead and alive, looking over one's shoulder), distant listeners and imaginary interlocutors. Thus a Sterling Brown brings into his work models from both the blues and the English canon; thus a Derek Walcott grasps the King's English and turns it to a new use and sends it triumphantly back to the King's subjects. Thus a Paul Celan immerses himself in the language of the murderers of his family and a million families, and turns it back toward the expression of humane feeling. Thus an Aimé Césaire transforms surreal French, or César Vallejo Andeanizes Spanish. Yes, it's all so complicated, in those moments of listening, of hearing, of seeing the traces, of realizing that a feeling is opening up, of finding some first words, or final ones.

I believe that our faculty or instinct of language, as Stephen Pinker calls it, is astounding for its usefulness and complexity, inventiveness, reliability despite inevitable confusion, and for the pleasure it makes possible in the creation of language-objects like poems and novels. The power of language to shape thought is both liberating and frightening, in the range from a convincing authenticity and scrupulousness all the way to dishonesty and demagoguery. This is not new. Sophokles wrote of the human creature, "He has taught himself speech and thoughts swift as the wind.... Full of skills and devising, even beyond hope, is the intelligent art that leads him both to evil and to good." For the writer, perhaps what is most important is that the use of language is also an implicating process—for we register incomparably (even when unwillingly) a multitude of feelings and ideas that arise ceaselessly in our own unconscious processes (personal and cultural). In our writing we do record—whether or not we wish to, or pay attention to this recording, or make anything out of it—much that comes to voice *through* us impersonally *from* our culture, *as well as* from our deep personal, individual, experience of the intimate relations, successful or failed, loving or brutal, of our families-of-origin and mates and children, and of our power relations to our fellows, nearby and remote, similar and dissimilar. We bring to the page much more than we can manage to make the most of. And some of what we bring is from our playing around in, and serious wrestling with, language itself.

Then the questions for each poet are, what sort of poem do *I* want to write? And: how have I come to feel that I want to write *that* sort of poem? Or: why is it *I* who want to write it?

◆

1) Because I think the *sound* of language in the poem is one element that is essential to distinguish it from other uses of language, I would begin my suggestions with some ear training—a kind of *solfeggio* of language, although it cannot be as clearly structured as it is in music. I would listen to the short poems of the English Renaissance, with attention to the differences between the poets of the plain style (like Ben Jonson and Walter Ralegh) and those (like Philip Sidney and Edmund Spenser) who favored Italianate ornament and rhetoric. Almost any big anthology would do, but there's an especially rich selection of the period in which the iambic rhythms of English and of poetry that we still hear were first being heard and artistically deployed, in Emrys Jones, *The New Oxford Book of Sixteenth Century Verse*. And I would listen to the syntax in *Paradise Lost*.

One guiding poet is Yvor Winters, in his long essay, "Aspects of the Short Poem in the English Renaissance" (*Forms of Discovery*, 1967). Winters was notoriously cantankerous when judging modern poetry, but for poets he was a useful guide to the Renaissance, despite his narrow preference for poems that versify a moral argument. He had a great ear, so he was an excellent guide to scansion, too. And without hearing the rhythms of the Renaissance, a poet can't hear what was done to those rhythms by the artistic choices of the prodigious Shakespeare, then John Donne and John Milton, then the eighteenth-century poets, then the Romantics and Victorians. True, poetry in English gained the free-verse resources of the King James Bible and the democratic impulses (in line and diction and structure) of Walt Whitman, the abbreviated, sometimes syncopated hymn rhythms and mind-Möbius strips of Emily Dickinson, and the prose poems of Charles Baudelaire, and the very different sorts of rhythmic (and artistic) freedom discovered or created by Arthur Rimbaud and Stéphane Mallarmé, and the rhythms of modern vernaculars from Mark Twain to Gwendolyn Brooks. But through all that, American English is still an iambic language, just as British English was in 1590 or so.

In fact, modern poetry in English also took several different rhythmical paths; one goes through the metrical practices of William Butler Yeats and the free verse of Ezra Pound. This free verse is especially keen to represent vivid sense perception and to make use of the incomplete, the fragmented. At first, this path leads to a freely lineated iambic verse; later it arrives at a mostly free verse using some of the small-scale metrical devices of iambic verse. Soon H. D., Mina Loy, Williams Carlos Williams and others were writing true free verse, leaving metrical echoes behind. But others continued to write metrical poetry—again, I would look for the richness of variety rather than the confusion of sometimes heated differences in any historical moment when many kinds of poetry are being written.

Later, after the American poets who began publishing around 1950 broke yet again with the inherited traditions of metrical verse and went to their own true free verse—rather scant on speech stresses, sometimes, with scarcely anything of a metrical ghost in it (like the post-metrical writing of W. S. Merwin, Adrienne Rich, James Wright and others)—the sense of writing free verse as a way of going *against* another insistent rhythm (iambic) seems to have gradually drained out of many American poets' sense of rhythm. So although the English *language* continues to be thoroughly iambic, one historical irony in the art of American poetry is that, because the feeling of free verse as a fresh *counter*-rhythm is gone, many free-verse poets today write very flat language that has very little rhythmic energy at all; meanwhile they and many others can end up falling unwittingly *into* iambic rhythms without seeming to have even heard them, for they often leave these iambic passages trotting regularly along for several lines, amidst other lines (and rhythms) that are free, instead of choosing *either* to use those iambic rhythms deliberately *or* deliberately to avoid them. But one can still train one's ear to hear linguistic rhythm, by reading aloud the kinds of poetry I am mentioning, and moving from the rhythmic discoveries of the late 1500s by steps and stages all the way to the highly deliberate, repeated reinvention of free-verse rhythms by William Carlos Williams—in both what we might call his impersonal free verse in *Spring and All* (the complete version, including both prose and poetry, in his *Collected Poems*) and in *Paterson*, and in his personal free verse (his many short poems)—and by listening also to his best followers in several different poetic genealogies, from Black Mountain to African American.

In twentieth-century poetry in English there is every conceivable model of how to achieve expressiveness with the sounds of language, from Robert Frost's colloquial yet decorous, smooth yet by no means tame, use of meter, to the verbal collages of Ezra Pound (reinvented for new purposes by Gary Snyder and Charles Wright, for example) and the very precisely prosy rhythms of Marianne Moore; from Wallace Stevens' brilliantly disguised feeling tones to John Ashbery's chatty refusals to "make sense"; from H. D.'s sometimes icy couplets to C. K. Williams' warm, capacious contours of thought-working-itself-out; from Allen Ginsberg's pelting pantomorphic metaphors to Geoffrey Hill's grave, nearly impacted compression of polysemous meaning-making; from Kenneth Fearing's or Louis MacNeice's openhearted, fast-paced ironies (ironies of pain, vulnerability, and sheer intelligence rather than of the condescension that rots so many later ironists) to the cool tone of a performed casualness in the poems of Elizabeth Bishop or the measured elegance of perception and expression of

Seamus Heaney; from the slow deliberate movement, packed with speech stresses, of Basil Bunting to the helter-skelter diction of our contemporaries Campbell McGrath and Dean Young, and others of similar almost bebop swiftness or surreality; from the calm, meditative pace of late poems by James Wright to the agitated but melodious ballads and blues of Sterling A. Brown; from the energetic word-cracking of Heather McHugh to the very different but equally inventive meaning-doubling line-breaks and blues beat of Sterling Plumpp. This list could be expanded *enormously*. I am only trying to suggest a little of the available *range* of attempts to create particular sounds of language. The best single anthology of modern American poetry of which I know is Hayden Carruth's *The Voice That Is Great Within Us*—best because it keeps alive so many relatively recent sounds of the language not found in other anthologies any more, and because it includes excellent poets whose work seems to have been abandoned by far too many readers, including poets. This anthology is a sampling of the sounds of poetry in American English, but for a comprehensive survey one also needs supplements like Arna Bontemps' early anthology of *Negro Poetry* and also a collection like *Every Shut Eye Ain't Asleep: An Anthology of Poetry by African-Americans since 1945*, edited by Michael S. Harper and Anthony Walton, and some examples from black American poets working the edge of an aesthetics of simultaneity or "spatial form," like Ed Roberson and Nate Mackey.

2) Why spend so much time on the *sound* of it all, when it's about "images" and feelings and moves of the psyche? You might say that since we—unlike Shakespeare or Coleridge or Dickinson or Yeats—live in an overwhelmingly image-saturated culture (images false and true, unreal and real, images spun with ulterior motives or raw with

news value or both at once), shouldn't poetry get hold of some of that? But for me, poetry is words, and is not, strictly speaking, visual images, even though it creates what we call mental images. It seems to me that a poet tries to do in a poem, with language, things that visual images can't do. Some "images" are only conceivable in language—the French surrealists were the first to try deliberately to articulate "primary process thinking," as Freud called it in *The Interpretation of Dreams*, and so to give central importance to mental images contrary to reality (although such images can be found even in ancient works, even if not so frequently). So yes, there is indeed something worth hunting down that is not *sound*. But just as many photos are faked, visual ads (as well as verbal ones) are fake in intent, and what we see in nature, to say nothing of culture, often is only projected there, so "images" in words are not covered by a guarantee of validity. Even the usual images that dreams and automatic writing give us are—as Freud pointed out—already *censored* access to the unconscious. Since we swim amidst innumerable visual images of indecipherable or dubious validity, we can resist perhaps by reading poetry for metaphor and image that belong to unfamiliar life-worlds, so that we can try to stand briefly outside our own. I mean the imagery of the ancient Greek tragedies, of oral poetry (ancient or modern, e.g., Homeric or Zulu), of cultures not yet industrialized but making use of the book. Or this could mean poetry from outside the mainstreams of England, Ireland, the US and Canada. One picks the texts that might answer a whispered doubt in one's own psyche.

Why, for that matter, did surrealism take so long to catch fire in English? Why does much of its imagery feel forced or superficial rather than profound? I think something got in the way of surrealism in English (in the US and in Great Britain) because of Anglo-American pragmatism—I mean not the formal philosophy but a habit of being—and because of customary repression, culturally enforced, of some kinds of feeling (even among poets, who, like all artists, live by conventions within the art, however much some of them may flout social conventions outside it). Yet there's no forcing, and there's at least a different *set* of repressions from what we are used to, in the Spanish-language surrealists—in Federico García Lorca, César Vallejo (who did torque the language itself, mightily) and Pablo Neruda, for instance.

3) At this late date in the history of studying the psyche, it seems that the next crucial ingredient of the inevitably elusive recipe for poetry is training one's ear and eye to read one's own work for the sake of finding in it the touches, traces, moves, preoccupations, obsessions, that have entered one's draft from the unconscious rather than from the poet's inevitably rather limited conscious intentions—whether these are "images," expressive sounds and syntax, or aspects of structure. We look for what gives away, in its awkwardness, an attempt to get hold of what doesn't want to be got hold of—the very thing we want. The excitement of moves or turns of psyche or feeling in the poem will then be expressive of movement in the unconscious as well as the conscious mind (goodbye, Yvor Winters!). That is, expressive of the lived experience of fleeting, self-contradictory, elusive feeling. And of the lived experience of the familiar, incomprehensible, fascinating affection and violence, creativity and destructive rage, of which the human being is capable.

And by unconscious I don't mean only the most private feelings of intimate desire, but everything, especially all that habituated responsiveness in us to the mainstream mass culture and electronic media that constantly saturate the thought-world of sales and marketing and political masquerade. When I write a poem, to what degree does it confirm, or fail to disagree with, the publicly reinforced attitude—which since Sept. 11, 2001 we have seen revealed more clearly—that since we (well, some of us) are (were) OK, then isn't the world OK, too? It is not OK. It is beautiful and horrible. When I write a poem, to what degree does it confirm, or fail to disagree with, the established habit of feeling that my particular decisions about my own life can be made without reference to much else besides consumer product availability and whether I feel "happy" or not?

But yes, even so, I suppose, the unconscious will add into the poem, will finally make visible, for those who have eyes to see, some intimate, more private preoccupations of the poet that otherwise would have remained behind the impenetrable screen between our conscious awareness and our unconscious thought and feeling. For example: I read over another poet's typescript to give him some responses to its shape as a book, and I happened to notice that half a dozen poems ended with the *image* of the human hand. Of this, the poet seemed not to have been fully aware. I did not suggest that all the poems be revised solely to get rid of what could seem repetitious, but instead that the poet try to trace the path of that hand, so to speak, back to its origins in his memory and feelings, in order to try to see in which of those half dozen poems the hand was truly important, and in which it was simply his own personal gesture, made toward himself, as if to remind himself of something that he felt and didn't realize that he felt. As when getting a sense of how American one is by going abroad, one could look for some vantage point from which to see what in one's poem may be typical of one's particular Americanness in addition to (or instead of!) being individually expressive. What if what I have taken for my own isn't "my" own, in part? And to what extent might it represent what psychoanalysis calls a "consensual object"—the result of my trying to please others whose demands and expectations I carry around with me in my attitudes and habits of feeling? And which of those demands and expectations bring out what I hope will be brought out, in myself, and which only return me to old ideas? I am assuming a willingness in the poet, in fact an appetite, which not everyone has, to see oneself as working with all of one's psyche, not just the manageable part (but I would not want to romanticize the unmanageable part!). I think it's essential to bring more of one's own full being to consciousness; to ponder—given who one is and where and who and what one came from and where one wants to go, in every sense—what it is that one wants to write. And why. Not so much in order to "get ideas for poems," but simply in order to prepare the mind and the ear for writing.

(The unconscious content might be an idea, an image, a counter-feeling, a rhythm, or a structural device—one could find one's own techniques of revision that would make it more possible to come at any of these, and other things, as well. Catching hold of some of the unconscious content of the draft is something that the great writers seem to do without nearly as much trouble as the rest of us have. I am certain there is some gift of self-transparency of intuition in them, even if they may say or think in their conscious minds that their creative process is otherwise. This intuitive gift is apparent in poets as different as D. H. Lawrence and Rainer Maria Rilke, Paul Celan and Marina Tsvetaeva, Antonio Machado and Nazim Hikmet, but it's not limited to twentieth-century writers—it fills Shakespeare's plays and sonnets, too. Apropos the French surrealists I mentioned above: as Freud pointed out, dreams and free association are already altered (by "secondary revision"); they can't really reveal directly something within us; they are only clues. So I am not suggesting that we transcribe dreams and call the transcriptions poems, thinking they are somehow more honest, but that we ponder, in the same way as dreams, the drafts of poems. In their verbal swervings—approaches and evasions—we can hope to catch a trace of something: that vague feeling-idea that lies behind what we *thought* we were doing. Then the trace can be pursued further, and it will reveal another trace. The poet becomes an internal tracker. Christopher Bollas's psychoanalytical book *Cracking Up* seems to me a remarkable exploration of the work of the waking unconscious. And in fact I recommend all his books.)

A painter will turn a work in progress upside down and study it. And as I mentioned, there are devices of composition, or rather of revision, that many poets use, and teach in workshops, for turning the draft of the poem in such a way that one can see something in it that had not been visible before, such as experimentally or provisionally altering points of view, lines, rhythms, and structure; making lists of the sorts of things that are in the poem(s); looking for the boundaries between those sections of the poem (from a phrase to a large block) that are the steps the poem takes, through turns of feeling, subject, narration, voice, image, metaphor, etc. (so as to consider the proportions of the sections to each other, and the order of the steps). And then the truly surprising power of focus of both conscious and unconscious mind, holding ready at the same time a hundred different figures, feelings, choices of diction, etc., can do its work.

So the poet's reading list has to include the poet's own poems (both finished and in progress). But the poet has to read them for what she or he did not already know is in them. Not easy!

4) The next issue for the poet is how to situate his or her own artistic goals—which don't have to be especially clear, but do have to be recognized, felt, as truly pressing. There are some books that *model* this. In Hayden Carruth's *Selected Essays and Reviews* we can see a bracingly

learned but antiacademic and independent response to contemporary writing. Unorthodox and brilliant, Carruth retraces his own path through the great contemporary changes in American poetry. By contrast, the French writer and theorist Hélène Cixous, in *Rootprints* and also in *Three Steps on the Ladder of Writing*, shows us a very different but also exemplary mode of self-scrutiny, as well as philosophical speculation on the ultimate location of the impulse to write, and a caution not to take for granted our straight-ahead narrating of this and that while not allowing ourselves to think through and to feel what the language itself is doing, while we are writing. She is a good corrective to the American foibles of either wanting to read nice books or wanting to slum in easy lowlife downhill escapades (which is the same impulse, in opposite manifestations, I think). Among her favored writers are Franz Kafka, Clarice Lispector, Jean Genet, and Thomas Bernhard—all of whom I too think are able to break the frozen sea within us, as Kafka said a great book should do. To her favorites of the sea-breaking kind, here I would add a few of my own favorite utterly independent works: stories and diaries of Isaac Babel; Edwin Muir's *The Story and the Fable*; William Goyen's *The House of Breath*; and Thomas McGrath's *Letter to an Imaginary Friend*.

Related to our trying to set ourselves an artistic project is the idea of vocation. I have been told that the German writer Gerhard Falkner has written a book about the saving resistance of poetry to commodification, the title of which in English would be *The Worthlessness of Poetry*. True, poets can trade on renown, get teaching jobs on the basis of their publications, and even sell, in a few cases, many books, but the rule for most poets is mostly that the making of poems has to be its own reward. And the making of poems requires stamina over years. I was especially interested in the question or problem of vocation when I collected the poets' essays in *The Poet's Work* (1979). Some poets continue to write about it, from Adrienne Rich in *What Is Found There*, a published journal of responses to artistic and political issues, to Geoffrey Hill in *The Enemy's Country*, a very densely argued series of lectures on poetry's use of language and its nearly (nearly) inextricable ties to commercial or instrumental speech and writing.

I said I wanted to send students back as far as four thousand years and out beyond poetic practice in English. How do we go there? The vehicle for such time-travel is the poem itself—our encounter, necessarily through translations, with the metaphor and other tropes, allegory, narration, poetic forms, etc., in epics, in Greek plays, Native American myths, hymns and prayers, and those of the Rig Veda, lyrics of the T'ang dynasty, Bessie Smith's blues lyrics, and so on. I especially recommend one astonishing work of scholarship: Calvert Watkins, *How to Kill a Dragon: Aspects of Indo-European Poetics*. This is a massive, analytical compendium which we poet-readers can study as a trove of hundreds of examples of the earliest known poetic texts in the family of languages in use from Celtic Ireland to ancient South Asia known as "Indo-European"; Watkins describes many poetic devices apparently invented hundred and even thousands of years before there was writing, some of which we are still using. No less interesting is his distillation of the core poetic themes of the most ancient poetry still available to us by example and conjecture. Wouldn't it be interesting for us, in trying to understand what it is that comes through us, as distinct from what it is we create, to consider "the totality of themes" in our work, and then in the work of all our contemporaries taken together? Watkins says, "the totality of themes may be thought of as the culture of the given society." What are the major themes of American society? Where do I position myself amidst or against those themes, as I write?

Also for dipping into rather than necessarily reading straight through, is the hoard of statements in T. V. F. Brogan, *English Versification, 1570–1980: A Reference Guide with Appendix*, an annotated bibliography of every known text by poets in English on the rhythms of poetry.

In addition to all the writers and specific books I have mentioned so far, I will recommend a few other favorite books by writers of the past and by our contemporaries, for stretching or refining one's sense of language, of poetry as an art requiring craft, of artistic possibility: James Baldwin, *Go Tell It on the Mountain*; Roland Barthes, *Mythologies*; Thomas Bernhard, *Gathering Evidence*; Gwendolyn Brooks, *A Street in Bronzeville*; Sterling A. Brown, *Southern Road*; Stanley Burnshaw, *The Poem Itself*; Albert Camus, *The First Man* (it is fascinating to watch as one reads this unfinished book how his artistic project changes as he goes further into the draft); Donald Davie, *Articulate Energy*; W. S. Di Piero, *Shooting the Works*; Robert Duncan, *Selected Poems*; Erik Erikson, *Identity and the Life Cycle*; Euripides, *Bakkhai* (may I be forgiven for recommending my own translation); Allen Ginsberg, *Howl* (the facsimile edition); William Goyen, in addition to his *The House of Breath*, his collection of stories, *Had I A Hundred Mouths*; Michael Hamburger, *The Truth of Poetry*; Danilo Kiš, *A Tomb for Boris Davidovich* and *Hourglass*; Lawrence Lipking, *The Life of the Poet*; Thomas McGrath, in addition to his *Letter to an Imaginary Friend*, also his *Collected Poems* and *Thomas McGrath: Life and the Poem*, edited by Reginald Gibbons and Terrence Des Pres; Czeslaw Milosz, *The Witness of Poetry* and his poems; Michel de Montaigne, *The Complete Essays of Montaigne*, translated by Donald Frame; Vladimir Nabokov, *Speak, Memory* and *The Gift*; Walter J. Ong, *Orality and Literacy*; Octavio Paz, especially his essays, such as *Convergences*;

Katherine Anne Porter, "Pale Horse, Pale Rider"; Marcel Proust, *Swann's Way* (especially the first forty or so pages, read very slowly; poems of Rumi; poems of Nazim Hikmet; Adrienne Rich, in addition to her *What Is Found There*, also *An Atlas of the Difficult World*; Joseph Roth, *The Radetzsky March* (in the translation by Joachim Neugroschel); Jean-Jacques Rousseau, *Confessions*; Muriel Rukeyser, *Out of Silence*; Bruno Schulz, *The Street of Crocodiles*; W. G. Sebald, *The Emigrants* and *The Rings of Saturn*; Charles Segal, *Oedipus Tyrannus*; Wole Soyinka, *The Man Died*; Wisława Szymborska, *View with a Grain of Sand*; Patrick White, *The Tree of Man*, *A Fringe of Leaves*, and *The Solid Mandala* (well—all of them, if you have a taste for them); Raymond Williams, *The Country and the City* and *Keywords*; George Oppen, *New Collected Poems*; Richard Wright, *Black Boy* and *American Hunger*. Two recent large anthologies achieve some redress of the omissions of more mainstream editors: Cary Nelson, *Anthology of Modern American Poetry* (Oxford, 2000) and Keith Tuma, *Anthology of Twentieth-Century British and Irish Poetry* (Oxford, 2001). The sixth edition (1993) of M. H. Abrams' invaluable *A Glossary of Literary Terms* also has a useful section summarizing some critical theories and methodologies used in academic literary studies.

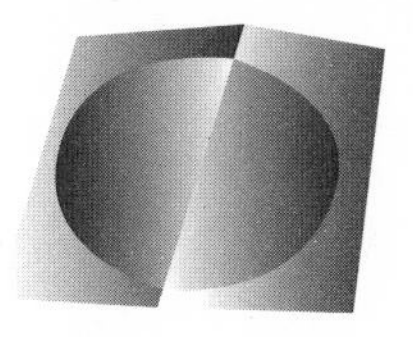

STEPHEN DUNN

Reading: Preparing the Mind for Possibilities & the Soul for Tenderness

The poet . . . gives to life the supreme fictions without which we are unable to conceive of it.
—Wallace Stevens

If one's very early reading is largely a pursuit of what's going to happen next, mixed with a desire to be enthralled, then those motives must have been easily satisfied by my exposure to fairy tales, the Arthurian legends, the Hardy Boys, and the series of *Chip Hilton: Sports Hero* books as I came of age in the late 1940s, early 1950s. The Sherlock Holmes mysteries would follow, and the Christ story would be ever-present, making me worry and dream.

I suspect those original motives are never wholly superseded, though as we get more sophisticated what it means to be enthralled and intrigued takes on different properties. The next stage of my early reading was a desire to experience otherness, which included my own. At most I was only half-conscious of this as a motive for pushing forward in a book, and even less conscious that I was also involved in a kind of apprenticeship in the art of reading, each book preparation for another. At the time, if asked, I probably would have said that I read simply for the pleasure of it, but most of what we say out loud isn't true, or not true enough. It's one of the things reading makes us aware of.

It was the Somerset Maugham books, when I was in my midteens, that began to introduce me to other worlds and to myself. *The Razor's Edge*, *Of Human Bondage*, *The Moon and Sixpence*. Then it was Salinger's *Nine Stories* and *The Catcher in the Rye*. And Kerouac's *On the Road.* All those sufferers and outsiders were nourishment for empty spaces within and without. Soon, for their heat and forbiddenness, I would read *The Amboy Dukes*, *God's Little Acre*, *Peyton Place*. And perhaps for the same reasons, *Wuthering Heights*. Jane Austen was in the mix, too. Issues of class and the manners of such—very much on my high-schooler's mind—raised to the level of pathos and wit. Then Hesse, those extended hushes of seeming profundity. Jack London's moody *Martin Eden*, Steinbeck's *East of Eden*, Mailer's *The Naked and the Dead*, Dreiser's *An American Tragedy*, and importantly, Melville, especially his *Billy Budd,* who couldn't speak when he needed to, a problem of mine. All of these were my first "poets" and "poems," the fictions—not necessarily supreme—that helped me conceive of the life I lived and observed.

It seemed like normal reading, or less than normal. I was aware of the vastness of my ignorance, but I can't remember what or who made me aware. I was an athlete and spent an inordinate amount of time at the schoolyard and at basketball practice. I don't even remember how I learned about the aforementioned books (except, say, *The Amboy Dukes* ["Hey, there's this dirty book"]), or when I found the time to read them. Certainly no one in my family would have recommended them to me, and I wasn't the kind of student who often inspired a teacher to take me aside, except to admonish me for being so quiet. No doubt television's slim pickings helped, as did going to a rather high-powered, albeit public, high school. And a few girls I dated who actually had libraries in their homes. Perhaps a certain osmosis of the literate? After all, it was the 1950s. People read serious books back then, and talked about them. Literature still mattered.

Not speaking of which, I read all of Ayn Rand's books during my seventeenth and eighteenth years, around the time I gave up being a Catholic, thus substituting one system of belief for another. I became an Ayn Rand proselytizer. I bought her whole. Perhaps one's intellectual life begins when his first freely-chosen god fails, and he finds himself navigating among the terrors of a pluralism. Rand created memorable single-minded characters, like Howard Roark in *The Fountainhead*, whose integrity was never compromised by compassion or historical circumstance. He was who I wanted to be, fearless and stoical, his disregard for other people, if Rand would have her way, a measure of his respect for them. It wasn't long before social experience itself and competing philosophical ideas would confound my certainties (my simplicities?). Still, she had taken me into her world, made her imagination mine. And gave me, eventually, the great pleasure of feeling superior to both my earlier self and to her books. I couldn't be more grateful.

But a reader can't feel superior for long. Dostoyevski and Melville, together with a few philosophy courses, took me into the extremes of moral complexity (where Ayn Rand did not tread). *The Brothers Karamazov* and *Moby-Dick* overwhelmed me when I encountered them in Professor Chalfonte's Great Books course my sophomore year at Hofstra. I wasn't ready for them; they took their place among the necessary unfairnesses that our educations provide for us, an exposure to a largeness that, with luck, we might catch up to in time. Chalfonte was their agent, who showed how a first-rate professor can unlock doors, then open them just enough. In the same course, he introduced us to *Don Quixote* and *The Education of Henry Adams*, two entirely different examples of greatness. Hemingway's stories, which I was reading on my own, became emblems of style and stance that same year. I didn't yet know how to read Chekhov. One of my favorites now, who seemed dry then, he marvelously thought that the function of reading was to prepare the soul for tenderness. Time and a more disciplined contemplative life would be needed for him. Kafka, Beckett, Borges, and Pinter were several years ahead for me. When I read them, experience suddenly seemed stranger and more familiar. I felt I'd been introduced to my life. There's a book side to everything, Frost said. I was unprogrammatically in the business of finding out what that was.

I minored in English, majored in History. In my senior year, a historiography course significantly changed the way I read. History got deconstructed. There were versions! For starters, there was a Marxist bent, a Toynbee slant, there were people like Carlyle who believed history was the study of great men. Why hadn't I known this before? Depending on your world view, you would see and isolate different things. Truth was from where you stood and from what distance and from what you believed before you observed and collected. In those senses, it wasn't much different from fiction. One needed many stories to understand experience. One might even need *many* stories to understand *one* experience. Not only did I need to look for authority of voice and command of detail in order to determine the feel of the true, I had to know the background and philosophical biases of the teller. And, if I could, I needed to be hip to the various strategies of persuasion that were being employed, and be able to divine the niceties of how I was being manipulated. To become such a reader takes years, of course, but this was a start.

I brought some of that cognizance to literature, but not with the same sense of discovery. Nevertheless, I did read literature with an ever-increasing awareness of narrative stance and point of view. Then (and it's even more essential now) the trick was how, if possible, to not let your sophistication prevent you from being transported, from being wowed. How to still have a primary reading experience, an Oh-my-God-isn't-this-wonderful! response. Such is the deconstructionist's problem, or the Marxist's or the feminist's—anyone who reads with a singular agenda. But it increasingly became my problem, too, and why I long for the stories and poems, those sustained illusions, that enthrall and yet invite many critical responses, the latter not delimiting the former.

I think of *One Hundred Years of Solitude* in that regard. And recently Jose Saramago's *Blindness*. And a few poems almost every year, which go in my special folder. This year, Louise Glück's "The Ruse," Sharon Doubiago's "How to Make Love to a Man," Billy Collins' "The Night House," Lawrence Raab's "Damage," and many of the poems in Jane Hirshfield's book, *Given Sugar, Given Salt*.

I didn't begin to read seriously the poetry we call poetry until I was in my midtwenties. In school I had read it as literary artifact, or as code-breaking, a code that the teacher knew and I had to figure out. As a result I didn't know that poetry impinged on my life, or that there might even be other reasons to love it. I remember being excited early on (after college) by E. A. Robinson, Kenneth Patchen, Cummings, the brilliant nonsense of Lewis Carroll, Dickinson's distilled mysteries, William Carlos Williams' experiments in a language I could recognize. I liked Frost, but wasn't yet ready to appreciate his depths and his slyness. I liked *Prufrock*, but was lost in *The Waste Land*. In 1967 I took Wallace Stevens' *Collected Poems* with me to Spain where I went to write a novel, and was happy to read them precognitively for their music and idiosyncratic verve. It was around that time that I started to write poetry with an amateur's seriousness.

But it wasn't until I read James Dickey's poem "The Sheep Child" in a late-sixties issue of *The Atlantic Monthly* that I felt I'd been given permission to be a poet. It seemed that if you could write about farm boys fucking sheep, and imagine the product of such a union, even give it voice, well, you could write about anything. Sure, I had read "Howl," but that was a different kind of permission, and the incantatory quality of its language was some distance from my ear and my temperament. I recognized its considerable power without thinking I could come close to emulating it. Dickey's poem was also bold, and written with a measured lyricism and inventiveness I felt more kinship with. I thought it was gorgeous, and still do.

If I found myself as a reader coming to poetry for the elusive news of the world, for the unspoken finally spoken, then as a would-be poet I simultaneously became a different kind of reader, someone who found himself trying to be alert to a poem's moves and formalities. I increasingly read with an eye toward learning to perceive the various ways meaning could be orchestrated. Or if not meaning per se, how a poem might be a series of "sudden rightnesses" that might disabuse us of ideas and feelings calcified by complacency and convention. A poem, I discovered, might move us into a new mode of regard for what we thought we knew. It might even be a verbal romp, what Paul Valéry called "a holiday of the mind." Sometimes it was just strangely beautiful.

Yet when trying to discern what a poem was up to, I still found it useful to bring the strictures of fiction to the occasion, especially to those poems that purported to tell stories. What authorial signals were there? What was the author's tone? What patterns of imagery or concern were underway? What were the tensions, complications? Where did the poem turn?

Did I want to know what was going to happen next in a poem, as I did in a story? Yes, but *next* was tied up as much with linguistic surprise and the pleasure of cooperative sounds as it was with "plot" and content satisfactions. And the totality of the poem had something to do with voice and style and the spirit behind them, with how a poet earns your trust. Did I wish to be enthralled by a poem? I did, but that meant being enlarged, startled, delighted, persuaded, in ways that were measured against both the masters of the past and the masters of the present.

Early on, I probably half-knew that a successful poem was some amalgam of content and handling of content, that to be a good reader you had to train yourself to be alert to how one serves the other. I may have vaguely known that the power of "The Sheep Child" resided in Dickey's management of effects as much as it did the exotica of his subject. But I wouldn't have been able to articulate that then. When reading Stevens, Berryman, Creeley, I found myself thinking of syntax and diction, of framing and phrasing. I read Frank O'Hara as a model for playfulness and for his handling of tonalities. But I think it was Roethke (whose work I had known casually for many years) in whom I started to see an ideal. His blend of music and sensuality, his mixture of play, existential edginess and gravitas, his formal dexterity, all were thrilling to me. Over and over I would read "I Knew a Woman," "The Waking," and "Elegy for Jane." I lived with the mysteries in "Meditation at Oyster River" and "In a Dark Time." Mysteries that had clear surfaces. Here was a poet who had everything that I wanted for myself.

Roethke led me to Yeats and Hopkins, Eliot to LaForgue and Apollinaire, Williams to Whitman. I read backward into the tradition.

First, someone or something modern, then their luminous predecessors. I wonder if that's a typical arc in others' reading lives. In graduate school at Syracuse, eight years after I graduated from Hofstra College, I received a heavy dose of New Criticism, which in retrospect I value as one way among many to read. But more important was the catholic teaching of Philip Booth, Donald Justice, and W. D. Snodgrass, practical in nature and buttressed by the examples of their poems. And George P. Elliott, too. Though he was more novelist and story writer than poet, he might have been the most valuable of them all. To have a curmudgeon approve of you is an exciting thing indeed, and approve he did. But he would also regularly share his reading enthusiasms. Read Anthony Hecht's *The Hard Hours*, he'd say. Read Nadezhda Mandelstam's *Hope Against Hope*. Read Mandelstam himself. Read *King Lear* again. And of course I would read everything he recommended.

Meanwhile, my fellow graduate students had put me on to the poems of James Wright, which seemed like soul-notes in a new American idiom. Robert Bly was translating Neruda and Vallejo. Merwin and Kinnell were in their compelling ascendancy. The journal *kayak* was delighting us with a strangeness that seemed utterly kindred. It was 1969. An exciting time to be an apprentice. I read everything whispered, alluded to, championed, everything that came my way.

Thinking of myself as a poet while reading poetry certainly made reading an even more self-conscious act, a process that had commenced some years earlier in my historiography course. It was distracting and delimiting until it became assimilated. Before long, though, I could enjoy the steak without thinking too much about the chef or the cow, or how many times I chewed. A good reader, I must believe, can be simultaneously aware of a multitude of factors inherent in a work, and still be swept away. Perhaps even swept away the more. Obviously the more one reads away from his area of expertise the greater the possibilities of reading with uncritical joy. Within one's area of expertise the large pleasures will necessarily be fewer, but more intense when they occur.

In the broadest sense, Kenneth Burke was right: literature is equipment for living. The welter of experience—the good, the bad, and the enormous middle in between—arranged for us in a series of enactments. My life as a reader has been gradually to understand that authors enact situations and moments that are as compelling for their angles of regard as for what is being regarded. But I desire and need the filter of their sensibilities as well, the infusion of their spirits—finally, the world according to them.

Recently I finished a novel called *The Reader* by Bernard Schlink, which satisfied in many such ways. His positioning of his narrator (as someone looking back, meditative, self-indicting, yet poised amid the sensational details of his story) was crucial, maybe especially so because I suspect that the author and narrator are one in the same (more on that shortly), and that the telling of the story was not only an evocation of a sensibility, but perhaps a history of the education of that sensibility, Schlink's own. It is a disturbingly beautiful story, in it a delicacy complicated by factors which militate against any simple response to them. And I think it helped me to understand what Chekhov must have had in mind when he suggested that reading could prepare the soul for tenderness: a tenderness that arises from deep understanding, yes, but implicit is an aesthetic element as well, the soul increasingly refined by its encounters with artfulness.

If I ever encounter facsimiles of Schlink's protagonists in "real life," would I now be less inclined to judge them? Be better able to judge them? Did I in the act of reading discover or recognize in myself capacities, if not actual tendencies, not very different from theirs?

Could I now better imagine circumstances in which I wouldn't be sure how I'd behave? The answer to each is yes. As a reader, I found myself companion to the narrator's quest to understand. Once again I was made aware that at the end of understanding is complicity. Certainly part of what equipment for living means is the discovery that others have thought and felt what we've thought and felt. We may be no less troubled after such awareness, but it's likely we've been brought more into the human fold, feel less freaky and alone.

The Reader is narrated by a man who as a boy of fifteen was happily seduced by a woman twenty-two years his senior. Both are postwar Germans. She is "the reader" the title refers to, and the story recounts their love affair and how he lives with both the memory of it and her eventual imprisonment. By novel's end, we learn not only that for most of her life she couldn't read or write, but that she'd been a Nazi, a guard at Auschwitz. Her inability to read is intertwined with her becoming a guard and, finally, with being convicted. (She turns down a promotion to foreman in a factory, which would have exposed her illiteracy, and joins the SS instead. And at her trial she verifies as hers a damning signature because she finds doing so more bearable than admitting she doesn't know to write.) The novel would have us believe that—in spite of seducing fifteen-year-olds and having been accused and convicted of war crimes—she is a decent, caring woman, maybe even one with integrity. I was persuaded to believe just that.

In the telling Schlink enacts the narrator's education in moral complexity as he deals with the above circumstances. We sense that it is Schlink's story, one that's based largely on fact, if for no other reason than that he has Hannah, the woman, commit suicide in prison just before she's to be released. It's the novel's only flaw, insufficiently prepared for or worked in; we suspect it occurs only because it did in real life. But it's interesting to note that the suicide occurs *after* she has taught herself to read. (Schlink doesn't sentimentalize the greater consciousness that can arise from reading; he shows there can be a corollary between it and misery.) With his narrative equilibrium, his sensibility no doubt honed by the very circumstances his story delineates, he accomplishes what the best novelists accomplish. In his book, fixed designations like *criminal*, *seductress*, *Nazi*, dissolve. He deprives us of our certainties, disturbs us into a Chekhovian tenderness.

The novel reminded me that my introduction to otherness is ongoing. And that I, like the narrator, am in constant search of how to live with what I know. "After such knowledge, what forgiveness?" Eliot asked. Like all great questions and like *The Reader* in toto, it has many resonances, and is best entertained *as* a question, a constant provocation to thought. The latter is one of the things that reading should provide for us, and most certainly has provided for me.

Novels or poems are not the real world, they are evocations of the real world. In them we can bear the unbearable and entertain the sublime in ways we rarely can in our daily lives. They are places to live for a while. Without them we would not be able to conceive who we are or have been or long to be. And when we learn that a sadness, for example, well-rendered, can be as satisfying as any triumph equally well-rendered, it's likely that we're hooked. A serious reader is someone, it might be said, who over the course of time develops an ever-increasing inclusive sense of what pleasure means.

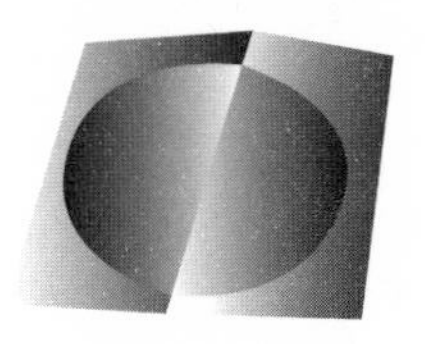

MADELINE DeFREES

Pleasure Dome

In Xanadu did Kubla Khan
A stately pleasure dome decree
Where Alph, the sacred river, ran
Through caverns measureless to man
Down to a sunless sea.

For the first thirty years of my life, there was almost always some authority figure, some poverty of circumstance, some roadblock between me and the books I wanted to read.

We play the hand we're dealt, and mine, as I've written elsewhere, was a home with a mother who had dropped out of high school and married at sixteen, and a father whose crowning achievement was a blanket-size diploma from the Behnke-Walker Business College. Aside from the usual nursery rhymes and fairy tales, books were scarce in our home, but my mother did the best she could. She bought from a door-to-door salesman the six-volume *My Bookhouse* set and three oversize collections with more color plates than text: *Tales from Far Japan*, *Nursery Rhymes from France*, and something I've forgotten *from Holland*.

Except for these and an inadequate, dogeared dictionary, we had only three books: *The Circle of Knowledge*, a novel by Zane Grey, and Gene Stratton Porter's *A Girl of the Limberlost*.

When I started school, I only pretended to read. As Coleridge might say, "It was a miracle of rare device." I knew my *Peter Rabbit* book by heart, right down to the exact point in the narrative where the pages turned. It was this kind of "reading" that gained me entrance to the first grade two months before I was five.

St. Matthew's Catholic School was unaccredited, taught by the Sisters of St. Mary of Oregon. Awake or in dreams, I still navigate that old building in search of something to read. On the main floor are a classroom for grades one through four and another for grades five through eight. Outside each is a steel-mesh-enclosed cloakroom where we left our coats, hats, galoshes, and lunch boxes. Upstairs in what is known as the parish hall, stacks of folding chairs and card tables, a small stage for school productions, and the old Beacon charts used for singing instruction and choir rehearsals. The basement contains a large open space for lunch, restrooms, the furnace room, and a kitchen the school used for the annual taffy pull in the spring. Nowhere do I find a library—only a few stray volumes in the classrooms, most likely publishers' freebies.

I loved my first-grade teacher, Sister Mary Cyrilla, but as I advanced to higher grades, both the teachers and the classes, like the poet's river, ran "down to a sunless sea." I must have discovered the Hillsboro Public Library fairly early. I remember making my way through the *Bobbsey Twins* series, paced by my Portland cousins. I read the fourteen *Oz* books by L. Frank Baum, and Jules Verne's *Twenty-Thousand Leagues under the Sea*. The Peter Rabbit factor was still paying dividends as I memorized reams of Longfellow, Oliver Wendell Holmes, and Edgar Allan Poe. The language was even more dated than my mother's and, like hers, often had some message attached.

Coleridge's dream vision is more persuasive, by contrast, because it links poetry and pleasure. Rote memory had turned into a famished vacuum cleaner that gobbled up indiscriminately everything placed in its path, whether by accident or design, especially anything in verse: "The Village Blacksmith," limericks, "The Chambered Nautilus," Burma Shave roadside ads, the Gettysburg Address, "Peter Piper" and "Theophilus Thistle," the Curfew that Must Not Ring Tonight.

All these memorabilia, in turn, stocked the mind with images: the village smithy stood under the horse-chestnut tree that overspread the train loading platform where boys in my hometown rolled newspapers before packing up their bikes to deliver the *Oregon Journal*. The chambered nautilus was like the abalone hidden among starfish at Rockaway, but it had almost as many rooms as an apartment building with mother-of-pearl wallpaper. Basil Underwood, sentenced to die when the curfew rang, was a roughed-up version of Gary Cooper. His lady love, she of the golden hair, white lips, and torn-and-bleeding hands, was first cousin to Mary Pickford.

Then as now I might find myself mentally reciting a passage from Longfellow:

> The day is done and the darkness
> Falls from the wings of night
> As a feather is wafted downward
> From an Eagle in his flight.

As I walked home from the late matinée at the Venetian Theater on a winter Sunday, I could see it *wafting*. Because I didn't always understand what I memorized, I made mistakes in the text, like that of dropping three commas in the first line of this stanza:

> This is the ship of pearl, which, poets feign,
> Sails the unshadowed main.
> The venturous bark that flings
> On the sweet summer wind, its purpled wings
> In gulfs enchanted, where the Siren sings,
> And coral reefs lie bare,
> Where the cold sea-maids rise to sun their streaming hair.

I didn't know that *feign* meant faking it, so I couldn't understand why poets *feigned* a sailing ship. The final stanza of "The Chambered Nautilus," however, survived intact:

> Build thee more stately mansions, O my soul,
> As the swift seasons roll!
> Leave they low-vaulted past!
> Let each new temple, nobler than the last,
> Shut thee from heaven with a dome more vast
> Till thou at length art free,
> Leaving thine outgrown shell by life's unending sea.

My outgrown shell was already bursting at the seams, to mix a metaphor. All those *thee*'s and *thou*'s. I must have resented these lessons in verse for Little Americans—the imposition of a false self, the myth of the Perfect Child. Else, why would my eyes fasten on my mother's lips, moving in synch with my own, as I delivered the poet's lines from the stage with a wooden indifference like a puppet in thrall to her ventriloquist?

High school was, compared to what came before and after it, a Golden Age of reading. For the first time, I had access to a good library, that of St. Mary's Academy, Portland, and to teachers who had read the books. When I worried about not remembering what I found in my history textbooks, my teacher suggested novels and short stories that would help me to immerse myself in the relevant period. I read Thomas Nelson Page's stories of the aristocratic Old South and the Civil War. I read Walter Scott's *Kenilworth*, *Waverley*, *The Heart of Midlothian*, and *The Bride of Lammermoor*. Best of all, I discovered George Eliot (Mary Ann Evans), whose erudition and unconventionality won me over completely. I still think that *Middlemarch* belongs on any list of ten greatest novels in English. I even loved the length of the books because they allowed me to disappear into "caverns measureless to man" and emerge only when I had reached the final page.

When I entered the novitiate, it was the novice-mistress and the rigid regulations of Canonical Year—when we were allowed only theology and philosophy and works considered religious—that limited what I could read. I would have been happy to avoid anything on the official *Index of Forbidden Books*, later abandoned after Vatican II, if only I could have read ordinary novels and nonfiction that interested me. I remember after I had left the novitiate, asking my local superior's permission to read A. J. Cronin's *The Keys of the Kingdom* and being told to go, instead, to the library and check out a life of the foundress, Mother Mary Rose.

Until 1950, the year I began teaching at Holy Names College, I had to ask permission to read any book that was not required for a course I was taking or teaching. This, in spite of the fact that I was thirty-one. Even our spiritual reading had to be cleared with the novice-mistress or local superior, lest we go off the deep end, lured by the siren song of the mystics—Meister Eckhart, Teresa of Avila, John of the Cross.

Reading the Bible required no permission. Each of us had brought to the convent a copy of the New Testament, and the novitiate and college libraries had enough complete Bibles to meet the demand. Years later, I was shocked to discover that a graduate student—Jewish no less—in John Berryman's class, had no Biblical knowledge. "Well, after all," Berryman said, "there is such a book as the Bible." And from then on, each time a Scriptural reference surfaced, Berryman would say, "Let's ask our Biblical expert. Stuart?"

Nor did I have any strictures about reading Gerard Manley Hopkins, the nineteenth-century convert, poet, and Jesuit priest. My friend and mentor, Sister Christine Mary (Kathy King) was a Hopkins fan; she introduced me to his work, which soon filled the whole screen. Soon I was using lines from the "terrible sonnets," first presented to me as the "sonnets written in blood" to fuel my morning meditation. To spend half an hour every morning internalizing two or three lines of a poem is a life-giving transfusion that alters the chemistry of the beginning poet. I began doing my best to imitate the Hopkins style, and though I would not recommend the practice, I finally emerged more or less unscathed after an apprenticeship of a year or so. As mysteriously as I had come under the Hopkins spell, I began to pull away in the search for my own voice.

After the novitiate, I took classes only in summer, occasionally on Saturdays, and once or twice by correspondence. That meant twelve years to get the B.A., the courses often nonsequential, classes in French sometimes including students at several different stages of instruction. In this helter-skelter education, there were a few lucky breaks: courses in Chaucer and Dante from a poet friend in the convent, who was also my religious superior; a class at the School of Letters (much later) in Poetry and Narrative from Robert Fitzgerald, shortly after he completed his translation of the *Odyssey*. A class in Minor and Major Forms in Poetry from John Berryman. Being assigned to teach World Literature at Holy Names College, and, later, at the University of Montana.

Somewhere along the line, I took a Survey of Twentieth-Century French Literature. The course allowed me to read novels like *Joy* by Georges Bernanos and *Thérèse Desqueyroux* by Francois Mauriac. The effect was like that of being given meat after a diet of fictional pablum.

In the "twice five miles of fertile ground" I equate with my eighty-two years on the planet, the physical feature that looms largest is the dictionary. This is due to more than the poet's characteristic love of words. Early on, I was embarrassed by my mother's mistakes in grammar, her dated vocabulary, and occasional mispronunciation. I had been humiliated by a teacher who challenged my pronunciation of the simple word *been*. "Ben!" she said. "It's not a boy's name. *Bin*, B-I-N, Bin!" From then on, I made sure to check everything in the dictionary.

Several years ago, one of my former journalism professors, conducting a *Time-Life* survey on Americans' best-loved books, asked me to name a single favorite. With little hesitation, I selected the dictionary. He must have thought I was putting him on because my choice didn't make it into the survey. So it was with a feeling of vindication that, on returning to *The Dyer's Hand*, a book I prize, I encountered a passage in which Auden discusses the different ways one might read a work of literature. He considers some "truer" than others, some "doubtful" and "some, like reading a novel backward, absurd." He adds:

> That is why, for a desert island, one would choose a good dictionary rather than the greatest literary masterpiece imaginable, for, in relation to its readers, a dictionary is absolutely passive and may legitimately be used in an infinite number of ways. (p. 4)

Aside from considerations of purchase price and shelving, poets can never have too many dictionaries. Mine are in the bedroom, the dining room, and my basement study. In my dream home, there would be sturdy floors and yards of bookshelves on the main level, with the multivolume *Oxford English Dictionary* conveniently enthroned for frequent recourse. Instead, I've had to settle for a Merriam-Webster unabridged on an oak stand upstairs and that maddening two-volume condensation-cum-magnifying-glass in slipcases in weak basement light. My dictionary collection includes five college English versions, five of foreign languages, one each of art, biography, foreign phrases and abbreviations; music, mythology, slang, and zoology as well as the essential Brewer's *Dictionary of Phrase and Fable*.

But dictionaries are merely tools—keys to a kingdom no longer forbidden. The avid reader makes her way through that wide-ranging prospect, attentive to Coleridge's ancestral voices, to the "deep delight that weaves a circle round [her] thrice." Meanwhile, the "stately pleasure dome" looks less and less like a palace and more like a library to which the reader returns for re-creation and refreshment.

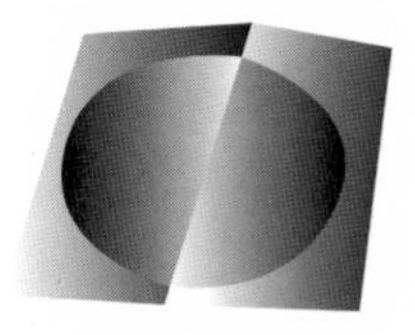

RICHARD JACKSON

Dancing As If Free: Reading, Imitation, and Influence

In a letter from 1928, the great Italian poet, Cesare Pavese, writes: "You have to create a world of books for yourself, a world of poetry written by people who have lived their lives in much the same way as we do our own, people we remember because they possessed the power to leave behind them books of immeasurable value. We need to love their spirit, talk about their ideas, dream their dreams, and so create our own spirit on the poetic foundations they have already laid for us, making our own ideas by discussing theirs, hoping our own dreams, our desires, will be finally worthy of theirs" (my translation). Indeed, his letters are filled with discussions of books, sometimes lists of what he's been reading. In October of 1926, for example, he mentions the Italian medieval writers Berni and Boiardo, also Hugo, Goethe, Carlisle, Leviticus, Herder, a vocabulary book, *Othello*,

Whitman's *Leaves of Grass*, Horace, the medieval Ossian, and the *Decameron*. In these letters he is always asking friends for new books to consume, particularly a few years later when the Fascists put him under house arrest.

I think I first understood the power of reading when I sat, in the fall of 1966, in the Andover Public Library, discovering the poems of Randall Jarrell, especially "The Girl in the Library," only to look up and see the kind of vision he saw sitting a few tables over. What power, I thought, words have, and I was hooked. Despite later failings. For after that episode followed my imitations of Dylan Thomas, worse than one could ever imagine, horrific word and syllable splitting that would have shamed even the E. E. Cummings I stole that method from, rantings to make Corso blush, folksy pastorals that would have sent Frost into a rage, and later, by the time I was a senior in college, images so deep no mind could ever retrieve them, not even the Merwin I stole that idea from. Seeing no luck in that, after a while I turned to reading only short stories and trying to duplicate the sentence flow of writers like Faulkner and Welty. But each failing was also a good lesson, because I did after all learn the passion in Thomas, the attention to detail in Cummings, the rhetorical skills in Corso, the structures of Frost and Jarrell, the evocative power of Merwin's *The Lice*. And that allowed me, later, to appreciate a poet like James Wright, whom I still believe to be the major influence of my reading and writing life.

When I escaped college, the first poet who looked at my work was Miller Williams, who suggested that perhaps Merwin had been too strong an influence and that I might try reading a poet who put some other words between the images—Wilfred Owen being a prime example, and William Meredith, who became an early and important mentor and who introduced me to the work of Berryman and Bishop and a host of other writers. In a way, all my early mentors were walking libraries who helped me create the kind of world Pavese describes. My only poetry workshop was with Robert Pack, in a class where we spent most of the time talking about "real" poems we should try to measure up to rather than our own quite limited visions. It's a method and an attitude that has influenced me ever since. Pack kept pushing Stevens, Williams, and Shakespeare, and my love at that time, Keats.

Keats was certainly a poet who found friends in books, especially as he suggests in his "On First Looking into Chapman's Homer"—

> Much have I traveled in the realms of gold,
> And many goodly states and kingdoms seen;
> Round many western islands have I been
> Which bards in fealty to Apollo hold.
> Oft of one wide expanse had I been told
> That deep-browed Homer ruled in his demesne;
> Yet did I never breathe its pure serene
> Till I heard Chapman speak out loud and bold:
> Then felt I like some watcher of the skies
> When a new planet swims into his ken;
> Or like stout Cortez when with eagle eyes
> He stared at the Pacific—and all his men
> Looked at each other with a wild surmise—
> Silent, upon a peak in Darien.

What an amazing poem! Look at how it moves from a sort of vague myth set in "realms of gold" the poets have created in their pastoral poems, through the poetry of Homer he read translated by Chapman and into history, reality. It is a poem about how reading leads us back to the real world, to ourselves, and allows in that historical world a new discovery, a new vision, a kind of oxymoronic wild surmise that is the poem itself. The sonnet, in moving from pastoral to literary to historical worlds, transforms the epic vision into a lyrical one.

Reading the classics—unfortunately, most of the reading that students do today is of poems from the past ten or twenty years. I can't count how many times I have visited a writing program where the students don't know who Wyatt is, or Sidney, even Pope. How few realize that the Miltonic line is the basis for their own poetry whether they write formal or free verse, for today's poetry works within or against that masterful presence. Or take the influence of Horace: one can trace the odes through Pope's "Moral Essays" (Horatian poems that make use of a sense of order in nature) through Hardy's poems (which see nature as a disorder) down through James Wright's last three books. On the other hand, if we start with the satires we can see them reemerge in Pope's satiric poems, Byron's "Beppo" and "Don Juan," and in a contemporary like William Matthews. Not to understand this lineage is to fail to understand the poetry of Wright and Matthews and to see what possibilities we ourselves might create from a lineage of our own making. So I think I want to emphasize these older poets here, and, true to my belief, quote a lot of opinions of others that I have taken to heart.

I suppose that's why in every undergraduate workshop I teach there is a reading list that varies from semester to semester. One time we focused on forms; another on the way the careers of Montale, Pavese, and Wright developed; another time on classic poems. In that last class, for example, we looked at the poems of Pindar, Sappho, and Kallimachus to see how the ode, the lyric, and the satiric epigram developed, and then followed that up with poems by Horace to see how all three modes merged, and then the self-conscious irony in Ovid, the savage satire in Juvenal and Martial, the complex and contradictory visions of Propertius and Catullus, and finally glanced at how Dante and Petrarch revisited some of these issues in their shorter poems. In another workshop we looked at poems by the epic writers Homer, Virgil, Lucian, Dante, Ovid, then Milton and Chaucer to see different ways narrative might be constructed. We always spent more time talking about these poems we were reading than the poems we were writing. Of course there were imitations galore, some better and some worse than the ones I had done in college, but then the students' own poems also grew in resonance and maturity, borrowing a technique here, an idea there, then transforming it into their own.

And of course I was doing the same thing, being particularly enthralled by the discontinuous and surreal elements in Ovid's *Metamorphoses* and the sudden leaps in Petrarch's *Rime*, a study that led to a book of poems based on Petrarch, *Half Lives*. John Ashbery describes a similar situation in *Other Traditions*: "In addition to the poets one has at times been influenced by, there is also a much smaller group whom one reads habitually in order to get started; a poetic jump start for times when the batteries run down." Or as Charles Simic says in "A Fly in the Soup": "I liked so many different kinds of poetry. One month I was a disciple of Hart Crane; the next month only Walt Whitman existed for me." Simic goes on to say: "I am only mildly exaggerating when I say that I couldn't take a piss without a book in my hand. I read to fall asleep and to wake up. I read everything from Plato to Mickey Spillane. Even in my open coffin, some day, I should be holding a book. *The Tibetan Book of the Dead* would be most appropriate, but I'd prefer a sex manual or the poems of Emily Dickinson."

I remember William Matthews looking at a review of his work that described him as urbane and witty and ironic, and how "purely" original all this seemed to the reviewer. The reviewer simply had not read Horace. And of course Horace has been a major influence on a lot of poets. Indeed Matthews has an entire essay, "Horatian Hecht," devoted to showing how the spirit of Horace is recreated in a new fashion in Anthony Hecht's poems. James Wright, probably the major American poet in the last half of the twentieth century, in his "Prayer to the Good Poet" calls Horace his "good secret," contrasting and comparing him to his own father, to his neighborhood friends—in other words, absorbing Horace and his vision into his own life. At the end of the poem he can exclaim:

> Quintus Horatius Flaccus, my good father,
> You were just beginning, you quick and lonely
> Metrical crystals of February.

A more conscious form of influence is "imitation." Catullus's adaptations of Kallimachus, Virgil's imitation of Homer's *Iliad* and *Odyssey* in the two halves of his *Aeneid*, Horace's borrowings from Lucilius, Petrarch's use of Dante and Cino di Pistoia, Wyatt's and Surrey's use of Petrarch, and so on. Pope said he turned to imitation to tighten his own verse and to find a voice to say things he was not ready to speak in his own voice. Petrarch, an early champion of learning from the past, writes in a letter to his friend Boccaccio: "An imitator must see to it that what he writes is similar, but not the very same; and the similarity, moreover, should not be like that of a painting or statue to the person represented, but rather like that of a son to a father, where there is often great difference in the features and members, yet after all there is a shadowy something—akin to what the painters call one's air—hovering about the face, and especially the eyes, out of which there grows a likeness. It may all be summed up by saying with Seneca, and with Flaccus [Horace] before him, that we must write "just as the bees make honey, not keeping the flowers but turning them into a sweetness of our own, blending many different flavors into one, which shall be unlike them all, and better." Imitation, in other words, is creation: just take a glance at what Samuel Johnson does to Juvenal in his "Vanity of Human Wishes" or what Frost does with Virgil's Georgics in his *North of Boston*.

Even more loosely, we can see a number of influences: Kunitz, Horace, and Robinson on James Wright; Greek and Roman epigrams on Linda Gregg and Jack Gilbert; Vallejo, Rimbaud, and the Beats on Tomaž Šalamun. Longinus, the Roman critic, wrote: "Emulation will bring those great characters before our eyes, and like guiding stars they will lead our thoughts to the ideal standard of perfection." One great example is the way Petrarch borrows the idea of creating an evolving self in a sequence of poems from Horace's *Odes* and his sense of how to address the reader from Cicero's letters. Not to read, not to "emulate," is to isolate one's art, to leave it static.

So how exactly do we allow influences, even consciously imitate, without becoming slavish? As Theodore Roethke notes in "How to Write Like Someone Else," imitation is not of the surface: for some young poets, he says, "any alliteration, any compounding, any enthusiasm before nature equals Hopkins; any concern with man in society or the use of two 'definite' articles in a row is 'Audenesque'; any associational shifting or developing a theme alternately, as in music, is Eliot; sexual imagery or dense language structure, Thomas; and so on." What Roethke would have us do is "take what you will with authority and see that you give it another, or even better life, in the new context." What Octavio Paz says about translation holds just as true for imitation and influence: "After all, poetry is not merely the text. The text produces the poem: a sense of sensations and meanings.... With different means, but playing a similar role, you can produce similar results. I say similar, but not identical: translation is an art of analogy, the art of finding correspondences. An art of shadows and echoes . . . of producing, with a different text, a poem similar to the original." As he says, "poetry is what gets transformed." What Paz is talking about is transforming the unsayable, as Rilke calls it in his ninth elegy, or what Pound called "logopoeia," into one's own vision.

Earlier, Ben Jonson had defined imitation in his *Timber* as merely a poem loosely based on another poem. In his "Preface" to his translation of Ovid, Dryden later defined three kinds of relationship a poet could have to a prior text. "Metaphrase" for Dryden was a slavish, "word by word" account. "Paraphrase" was a "translation with latitude" that kept the original meaning but often with "amplification." "Imitation," on the other hand, meant, for Dryden, a process where the "translator (if now he has not lost that name) assumes the liberty, not only to vary words and sense, but to forsake them both as he sees occasion; and taking only some general hints from the original, to run division on the groundwork, as he pleases." This is precisely the sort of thing Robert Lowell does in his *Imitations* from various poets, and what Pound does in his "Homage to Sextus Propertius," a sequence of loosely translated lines rearranged into a sequence of totally new poems. And it is related to what Stephen Berg does in gathering images, tones, and lines from Anna Akhmatova in his *With Akhmatova at the Gate*. Dana Gioia has an essay describing how Donald Justice makes use of various lines, poems, and forms of previous poets in over a fourth of his own poems.

In some ways the poem enacts what T. S. Eliot meant by balancing tradition and the individual talent. And Eliot's essay "What Dante Means to Me" provides an excellent description of the depth of vision transmitted from one author to another: "the greatest debts are not always the most evident; at least, there are different kinds of debt. The kind of debt I owe to Dante is the kind which goes on accumulating. . . ." He cites, for example, "width of emotional range," and "that the poet should be the servant of his language, not the master of it." He finds in Dante "a constant reminder to the poet, of the obligation to explore, to find words for the inarticulate, to capture those feelings which people can hardly even feel, because they have no words for them; and at the same time, a reminder that the explorer beyond the frontiers of ordinary consciousness will only be able to return and report to his fellow citizens, if he has all the time a firm grasp upon the realities with which they are acquainted." One could add Robert Lowell's essay on Dante's influence, in increasing degrees, on Pound, Eliot, and Browning and the Romantics. Robert Pack in the introduction to *Touchstones*, notes "how poets necessarily feed on earlier poets, and how they inevitably attempt to redefine the tradition to make room for the poems of the kind they would like to write." Harold Bloom has fully schematized such a process where the stronger poet "swerves" away from his or her master until it seems the master is but the imitator of the later poet! But isn't this the point? Here's Roethke on how he imitated Leonie Adams: "I was too clumsy and stupid to articulate my own emotions: she helped me to say something about the external world, helped me convince myself that maybe, if I kept at it, eventually I might write a poem of my own, with the accent of my own speech." And who now reads more Adams than Roethke: indeed, it almost seems as if Roethke was her influence!

I am of course self-consciously putting this piece together as a patchwork of quotes that I myself have found influential about influence. For example, Joseph Brodsky writes in his essay "In the Shadow of Dante" that "ghosts of the great are especially visible in poetry, since their words are less mutable than the concepts they represent. A significant part, therefore, of every poet's endeavor involves polemics with these shadows whose hot or cold breath he senses on his neck." The essay is actually on Eugenio Montale and how that great and original poet "created his own poetic idiom" out of the *dolce stile nuovo* of Dante, Petrarch, and the Italian Renaissance as it in turn was transmitted through poets like Leopardi. John Berryman describes how he came upon the form for "Homage to Mistress Bradstreet": "The eight-line stanza I invented here after a lifetime's study, especially of Yeats's, and in particular the one he adopted from Abraham Cowley for his elegy 'In Memory of Major Robert Gregory.' Mine breaks not at midpoint but after the short third line; a strange four-beat line leads to the balancing heroic couplet of lines five and six, after which seven is again short (three feet, like line three) and then the stanza widens into an alexandrine rhyming all the way back to one. I wanted something at once more flexible and grave, intense and quiet, able to deal with matter both high and low" (*Freedom of the Poet*). In the end we want what one anonymous critic wrote of Pope's versions of Horace and Homer, that they were "bound hand and foot and yet dancing as if free."

In the end, it's the dancing free that is so important. I remember after my first book I was chagrined to hear a new friend at that time, David Wojahn, tell me he could see I had been reading a lot of Stafford. Of course, I was, but I had hoped it didn't show. So nearly ten years later I was delighted when my friend Bill Matthews said in the early nineties that I was doing something no one else was doing. Marvin Bell once said that you should try to write a poem that doesn't sound like a poem, which means we have to cast off our influences, to read not to imitate or to copy, but to transform, to make new. Reading is a sort of intellectual osmosis where the mind absorbs the past only enough to forget it as it was and so to create something new. We don't grow by watching the marks and numbers our parents draw on the door frame; we grow by growing where we have to grow.

And not only by reading poetry. Petrarch was enthralled by

Cicero's letters, Simic has an excellent essay on reading philosophy, Mark Jarman has transformed *Ecclesiastes* into a major contemporary book of poetry, Albert Goldbarth seems to have read everything, especially science and history, Miller Williams makes use of his science background—as Dante did. Matthews would always describe how he thought young writers should read eclectically—about "jazz, science, cooking, detective stories, history, geography, odd facts, devour it all." And of course one might think too about the poor "imitatee" as Petrarch ironically did in a letter—he borrowed the form from Cicero—to Homer, telling Homer he should not be distressed at all of Homer's imitators (he mentions just about every major poet until his time)—"You grieve because you have been so greatly mangled by your imitators. But do you not see that it could not possibly have been different? How could anyone deal fully and fairly with so great a genius?"

I myself like to look at topographic maps to imagine what it must be like to live in various places. And I regularly look at *Natural Science*, *National Geographic*, *Sporting News*, *Civil War*, *Archeology*, *Astronomy Magazine*, the Bible, art books. As a kid I loved to read cereal boxes—again and again. Charles Simic got me hooked on Schopenhauer, I've read most of Derrida and Heidegger, some Lacan and Kristeva, and the philosophers who influenced them from Plato to Freud. Right now as I read this I am reading Unamuno's *Tragic Sense of Life*. But I would also suggest the following philosophical and critical pieces:

Bachelard's *The Poetics of Space*. Heidegger's *Poetry, Language, Thought*. Hirshfield's *The Nine Gates*. Most books in the Michigan Poets on Poetry series, but especially the ones by Simic, Matthews, Meredith, Tate, Bell. Auden's *Lectures on Shakespeare*. Rukeyser's essays. Letters of Rilke, Keats. Wordsworth, "Preface" to the *Lyrical Ballads*.

In a class once someone proposed naming our favorite English poems, limiting one per author in each of the several categories, and so here are the ones I chose. The only rule was that the poets had to be mostly from before our own age, that they could be considered classics, or that we felt had a 150% chance of becoming classics.

Twenty-Five Short Poems (good to memorize)

Wyatt, "They Flee from Me." An incredible number of tonal twists and turns, zooming in and out. Jonson, "On His First Son." An epigram in the tradition of Catullus that derives its power by speaking so tersely. Shakespeare, Sonnet 94 "Those that have the power to hurt. . . ." A poem that thinks aloud, changing its whole image structure after the eighth line; perfects the sonnet as a poem of process rather than reportage. Wordsworth, "She Dwelt. . . ." Look at the way the meter forces you to say the word "difference" in the last line, which is the point of the poem in the first place—redefines the ballad as a lyric. Dickinson, "After great pain." For its mastery of syntax balanced against meter, phrase, and line, and its last line that so accurately imitates its idea, and its playing off of psalter meter. Whitman, "When I Heard the Learned Astronomer." A characteristic poem that keeps expanding frames of reference ideologically and rhetorically. Blake, "London." For its incredibly powerful meter, its controlled outrage. Keats, "To Autumn." For the way the images redefine time as circular and renewable as opposed to linear; it links the ode from then on with the elegy as a poem that defeats time and death. Millay, "If I Should Learn. . . ." Such a cold, calculated poem, yet such hurt must have been hidden behind it—what a twist on the Petrarchan love poem! Frost, "Stopping by Woods." It redefines pastoral. Thomas, "Refusal to Mourn the Death by Fire. . . ." For its incredible rush and build up of passion and rhetoric, and its sudden heartbreaking turn at the end. Stevens, "The Snow Man." With such simple phrasing Stevens manages to produce a paradox at the end where all and none become one, in a poem as philosophical as those of the Romantics. Bell, "To Dorothy." This is how you write a love poem today. Yeats, "Lake Isle of Innisfree." Its perfect use of sound to move the poem forward is perhaps unmatched in English. Hardy, "Neutral Tones." One of the prime process poems where the images in the first stanza are redefined in the last—Wordsworth with an edge. O'Hara, "The Day Lady Died." A poem whose rush of movement reminds one of Swift's city poems, so immediate and diverse. Sidney, "Loving in Truth." The first in his "Astrophel and Stella" series, it is a sonnet against imitating others, yet of course it does—Petrarch, Wyatt, and others. Tennyson, "Crossing the Bar." Like Yeats's "Lake Isle," it is a musical, simple poem about finding a resting place, here beyond death, but with a yearning that seems to realize it won't happen. Bogan, "Medusa." A lyrical monologue where the speaker, turned to stone, straddles immortality and mortality. Meredith (William), "The Illiterate." Perhaps the most powerful Petrarchan sonnet in our age. Matthews, "Landscape with Onlooker." A poem that derives from both Yeats's and Tennyson's poems mentioned above, but seeing that pastoral world as doubled, ironic, both earthly and heavenly. Simic, "Jackstraws." A complex poem that flirts with the surrealism of Breton and Prévert but ends up being a sort of anti-parable. Bishop, "One Art." One of the most masterful villanelles around; see also those by Roethke and Thomas. Merwin, "When You Go Away." The first poem I memorized outside of school, and one of the best examples of a deep-image poem around. Gilbert, "Adulterated." A wild card entry, epigrammatic but in a way Catullus never imagined, for its use of images of enclosure and sound that metamorphose into its stunning last lines.

Twenty-five Medium Length Poems

Donne, "The Canonization." For its irony, its sly turning of Christian terms into sexual ones. Marvell, "To His Coy Mistress." For its ironic use of syllogism. Wordsworth, "Tintern Abbey." For its redefining a healing time and space as continuing toward the future; one of the very great poems in English, it moves from plaintive to prayerful by constantly meditating on itself, turning in on itself. Coleridge, "Frost at Midnight." A companion to "Tintern Abbey" where Coleridge tries to link heaven and earth through the frost image, the poem is almost a prayer in soft, pleading tones. Keats, "Ode to a Nightingale." THE great meditation on reality and dream in English, Keats's music acts on us as much as it did his speaker. Bishop, "In the Waiting Room." THE poem about finding an identity. Tennyson, "Ulysses." One of the great monologues, it builds rhetorically in a masterful way. Browning, "My Last Duchess." THE monologue of monologues, but look especially at how the listener in the poem is defined by what the speaker says and does with his verbal gesturing. Eliot, "Journey of the Magi." One of the great poems of doubt, also a monologue, yet with a tight-lipped, epigrammatic resolve. Stevens, "Connoisseur of Chaos." A poem that covers an enormous distance, from a sense of chaos and disorder to a transcendental vision in the end. Frost, "Directive." Like so many of the Romantic poems, this poems moves us back in time to move us forward, into myth to see reality, in speech that is as everyday-ish as it is formal. W. C. Williams, "The Yellow Flower." A paradigmatic meditation poem; look at its parentage in Wordsworth and Coleridge's conversation poems and its heritage in a poem like Robert Hass's great "Meditation at Lagunitas." Auden, "In Memory of W. B. Yeats." If you want to know how changes in rhythm can change tone, this and

Blake's "Mad Song" are your choices. Hardy, "Darkling Thrush." This poem takes Keats's ambiguity in "Ode to a Nightingale" and makes of it a profound despair. Arnold, "Dover Beach." Okay, Hecht has rightly written a masterful parody, but the poem is still unmatched for its quiet beauty, its way of seeing the particular in a larger context, love in the face of doom. Wright, "The Journey." One of his last poems, a sort of self-elegy in which the idea of dust goes through several permutations until it becomes almost salvific, in a language that moves from occasional to necessary—one of our great poems. Dickinson, "The Soul Has Bandaged Moments." Almost surreal, yet formally structured by its rhetoric, incredibly haunting, with several turns and twists that move the reader toward an overwhelming fear. Jarrell, "Woman at the Washington Zoo." A monologue whose tension builds gradually until the release of the last line. Yeats, "Wild Swans at Coole." A poem of incredible yearning: an earlier draft had stanza three as the final stanza, with a more optimistic turn. Gray, "Elegy in a Country Churchyard." Perhaps the paradigmatic elegy after "Lycidas." Levine, "The Mercy." The name of the ship in this poem becomes the central conceit that governs the poem in Levine's typically emotional and yet tough-minded style. Hecht, "The Hill." The two hills in this poem finally merge as the poem itself, a simile vision become a metaphoric vision. Levis, "The Smell of the Sea." This haunting poem redefines the possibilities for narrative in our time. Matthews, "A Happy Childhood." Matthews' gift was to use everyday images to reveal the most important aspects of our inner lives. Ashbery, "Self-Portrait in a Convex Mirror." For me this overshadows Auden's great poem on a painting, for taking the inner impulses of the artist's vision and transforming them into a rich tapestry. Stern, "Soap." This poem, with all its anaphora and changes in tone, its synecdoche and its other figures, make it the most powerful holocaust poem ever written. Plumly, "The Boy on the Step." Plumly rewrites Keats for our age in every poem, and yet he is a real original; this meditation goes through time in order to save the narrator, and us. Tate, "Constant Defender." Lest anyone think Tate is simply a poet of verbal high jinks, look at the loneliness and pathos of the last lines of this poem and how they force us to reread the poem as an elaborate attempt to hold off despair.

Twelve Longish Poems

Milton, "Lycidas." Our most famous elegy, defines the elegy not as a lament but as a poem that creates optimism from despair. Pope, "Epistle to Dr. Arbuthnot." In over 450 lines he moves from shutting off the world to embracing it, from cold distance to earned sentimentality. Stevens, "The Man with the Blue Guitar." A sort of surreal meditation based on Picasso's work, it tries to look at all the facets of the reality we half see and half create (Wordsworth's terms), and how they depend on each other. W. C. Williams, "Asphodel." Auden called this the most beautiful love poem in English, and he may be right—Williams' use of his variable foot is at its height here. Frost, "Home Burial." A dark psychological study with masterful use of blank verse. Eliot, "Love Song of J. Alfred Prufrock." A great dramatic monologue, a great narrative, a great surreal description of the mind's fears, masterful free verse. Wordsworth, "1797 Prelude." The best, most powerful autobiographical poem, it examines the growth of the poet's mind more succinctly than later, longer versions. Whitman, "Crossing Brooklyn Ferry." A great meditation that defines time as something the American spirit can create as much as he himself creates American poetry. Blake, "Auguries of Innocence." The greatest aphoristic poem we have. Chaucer, "General Prologue." For its characterizations. Bogan, "Summer Wish." A dialectic between the mind and the heart, abstract rhetoric, and the language of nature in the tradition of Yeats. Simic, "White." A surreal narrative with no characters or plot, except that the words and images act like characters in a drama that includes us.

Ten Long/Epic Poems/Sequences

Shakespeare, *Sonnets*. Because he's THE master of the form. Pope, *Essay on Criticism*. Filled with good advice for poets. Milton, *Paradise Lost*. Besides the line, look especially at the way his epic similes undercut the plot, how he sets up the reader to sympathize with the wrong characters and so fall with them—the ultimate poem that involves the readers in its action, only to show them what they read wrong; a poem that teaches us how to read it as we go along. Berryman, *The Dream Songs*. Look at the variety of voices, rhythms, and strategies—and compare to his "Homage to Mistress Bradstreet," a more overtly structured narrative. Millay, "Sonnets from the Ungrafted Tree." Anti-love poems that constantly play in tension with the form. Roethke, "North American Sequence." An incredibly powerful free-verse sequence that rewrites Whitman and moves from the physical to the metaphysical in breathtaking leaps. Whitman, *Song of Myself*. Redefines the self in American poetry as something beyond a simple autobiographical and confessional "I," redefines the line, the language, the possibilities of poetry itself. Sidney, *Astrophel and Stella*. The earliest story-novel-in-verse, based upon Dante's *La Vita Nuova*. Bell, *The Book of the Dead Man*. Redefines the line as a sentence, and the rhetorical and imagistic weavings are unique and powerful. Levis, *Elegy*. These poems redefine elegy, and create a sense of narrative at once both fragmentary and coherent.

I suppose that's as good a set of lists as any. But it leaves out a lot. What else do I have my own students read—that is, what other poems have formed the world that Pavese described for me and which I hope to pass on not as a world but as stepping stones?

Homer, especially the *Odyssey*, for the use of narrative. Sappho, for her uses of image, the leaps in thought. Horace, for his balance, and his later influence on contemporary poets like William Matthews and James Wright. Catullus, a couple of epigrams. Martial, epigrams, translated by William Matthews. Lucan, *Civil War*. Bleak exposé of a country tearing itself apart; plain style epic. Propertius, *Love Poems*. Great sudden shifts in tone; see also Pound's sequence "Homage to Sextus Propertius." Perseus, satires. See the superb translation by W. S. Merwin. Lucretius, *On the Nature of Things*. An epic with many scientific and historical similes, whose hero is ultimately a philosophy of life. Juvenal, satires. Pretty harsh about Roman life. Ovid, *Amores*, *The Art of Love*, or a couple of stories from *Metamorphoses*. *Heroides* (dramatic monologues where shafted women from various epics get to speak). Petrarch, for the beginnings of the sonnet (Petrarchan conceit). See Musa's translations. Dante, *La Vita Nuova*. (Poetry sequence with prose self-interrogations and explanations on what he is doing—a must!!)

The list goes on. Other Americans like Steven Crane and Hart Crane. South Americans. Eastern Europeans. Earlier poets like Vaughn and Hopkins. I write this surrounded by piles of books, not sure what to pick up next. Here is Milosz's new book, *A Treatise on Poetry*, maybe that will help? And here are some contemporaries—a new book by Dara Wier, another by Dean Young, one by Mary Ruefle, another by Mark Halliday, here's David Rivard. It never ends. Nor should it. That's the point, isn't it? Simic said he'd like to be in his casket with one of two books. I haven't decided on mine yet, but whatever they are, the pages will be dogeared, and I'll have a pencil in the other hand.

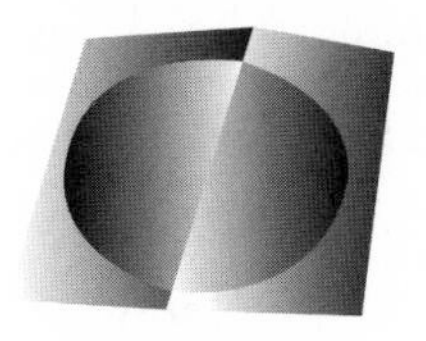

MAXINE KUMIN

Peripheral Vision

My advice to young poets, both those in graduate programs and those writing outside the academy, is to read widely in other fields. Of course I would say this to any well-educated person, but I urge this catholic approach on poets in particular because it is so important that they not lose their peripheral vision of the universe.

Read botany, astronomy, popular physics. Idle through a good dictionary. Read sociobiological studies, such as Sarah Hardy's *Mother Nature*; read fiction that dissects social mores—here, all Jane Austen's and Alice Munro's fiction qualify. Investigate comparative religion, modern medicine, ornithology, American history. Reading omnivirously will sharpen your senses; if you come across accounts of the extinction of the passenger pigeon and the Carolina parakeet, for instance, you will have gone beyond mere birding into issues of industrialization, shrinking habitat, and so on.

To come to terms with the twentieth century, read Susan Sontag, James Baldwin, Joseph Ellis, Mary McCarthy, David McCullough, and Carolyn Heilbrun, among others. Passionate social history not only has a civilizing effect on readers, but may also prompt them to develop their own passionate convictions. For a refresher course in your roots as poets, go back to John Donne and George Herbert. A powerful poet writes out of staunchly held convictions, and none are more strongly held than those of the deeply religious poets of their age.

As an unrepentant old formalist, I recommend paying attention to a good poetry handbook. There are literally dozens available; the most recent and accessible one I've come across is *The Making of a Poem*, edited by Eavan Boland and Mark Strand. Lewis Turco's *The New Book of Forms*, Miller Williams' *Patterns of Poetry*, and *Strong Measures*, edited by Philip Dacey and David Jauss, are also excellent.

The best abstract painters came of age studying anatomy and painting still lifes; this provided them with rich material to draw on when they began to develop their own styles. Even for poets who intend to write only free verse, it is important to first take instruction in form. Prosody is a dear school; it pains me to see that, like the study of grammar, it seems to be going out of fashion, since it is crucial to reading poetry. Understanding metrical structure will inform their writing in free verse as well.

Nothing infuses the poem as deeply with feeling as time out in the world. I always advise students who plan to go on for an MFA in creative writing to take a year off from the university cloister and garner experience on the job. Working a nine-to-five job can also invite the poet into ever more luxuriant reading, a practice to look forward to and long for late at the end of the day. The young poet now craves books as a reward after toil. They provide an avenue into experiences far removed from the poet's own, emotions he or she may recognize but perhaps react to very differently. Is it self-indulgent to read about survivors of an arctic expedition, whisperers to horses, dogs, and monkeys, to read memoirists and muckrakers of every description? Novels set in fifteenth-century Italy, nineteenth-century India, *fin de siècle* Austria, murder mysteries that take place in London, New York, or Paris? You bet it is. My counsel is to make the most of it. Reading for pleasure is delicious and well-deserved. The best instruction in letters comes by indirection.

As for my own private canon, let me say that my personal reading habits are haplessly eclectic and voracious. I devour whatever crosses my field of sight: books of poems, seed catalogs, novels, memoirs—especially of poets and other writers—literary journals, and editorial pages. At random on the long counter that serves as my desk are arrayed the current *Atlantic Monthly*, *The New Yorker*, *Organic Gardening*, *Smithsonian Magazine*, *Poetry*, *Ploughshares*, and *The Georgia Review*. Abutting these, *The American Heritage Book of English Usage* and *The American Heritage Dictionary*.

On the nearby shelf, Marianne Moore's *Selected Letters*, Eileen Simpson's *Poets in Their Youth*, Louise Bogan's *Journey Around My Room*, and Thoreau's *Walden* and *The Maine Woods*. In the reading stand cantilevered over my bed, Margaret Drabble's *The Peppered Moth* has just succeeded Rosa Shand's *The Gravity of Sunlight*.

In the past year I have gobbled up so many books of poems that I hesitate to single out particular names. Robin Becker, Carolyn Kizer, Jane Hirshfield, Marilyn Hacker, Enid Shomer, Philip Levine, Mark Doty, Hilda Raz, Sharon Olds, Stanley Kunitz, John Balaban, Carole Simmons Oles, Maurya Simon, Philip Booth, B. H. Fairchild, and Stephen Dunn represent the tip of the iceberg.

I am perfectly willing to stand still for an elusive, difficult poem; I think it is fair to give such a poem three readings with as unprejudiced a mind as I can muster. But I am just old-fashioned enough to expect some sort of narrative flow from a poem. When nothing coalesces for me after these efforts, I pass. This may be my loss, but I believe that poems made of blood and muscle, music and memory, are the ones that will endure.

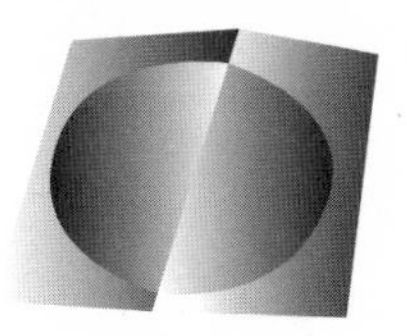

DAVID WOJAHN

From the Valley of Saying

Poetry "survives in the valley of its saying, where executives would never want to tamper": most us know these lines from Auden's elegy for Yeats, and all of us likely know the line which immediately precedes them, that famously blunt assertion: "poetry makes nothing happen." I imagine that when poets look at Auden's last stanza, they are less interested in the oratorical flatulence of the contention that poetry won't make anything happen than they are in determining how poetry survives in the valley of its saying. Where is that valley, and why do the executives want to steer clear of it? The trope is quintessential Auden, a rather loopy metaphor that on the other hand is instantly recognizable; in some alternate universe it is surely a well-worn cliché. And in fact, Auden implies that it is only *in* a kind of alternate universe where poetry survives, for the valley of its saying calls forth images of an obscure and inaccessible backwater, some Appalachian hollow where the inbred inhabitants still speak a kind of Elizabethan English, and not even a new satellite dish will distract the toothless populace from their dulcimers and back-porch banjo-picking. No wonder the executives won't go there. It is also perhaps a lost valley, where creatures thought extinct still roam, something out of the boys adventure books which the youthful Auden cherished—it is Conan Doyle's *Lost World*, Edgar Rice Burroughs's *Land that Time Forgot*.

And yet, whether from neglect or because it always will remain, for most of the world, a region unmapped and unexplored, the Valley of Saying is not often disturbed, and its odd little culture continues to survive, if not to prosper. Here a small number of inconsequential lives go on, lives devoted largely to useless activity. For poetic endeavor is very much akin to the great polar explorer Fridjof Nansen's definition of "polar endeavor." It is "about nothing, in nothing, for nothing...." And nothing, we know, will come of nothing, neither the nothing that is not there nor the nothing that is. In the Valley of Saying, the same old wearisome nothings prevail: there is no audience for poetry, no money in poetry, no respect for its virtues and nothing new for it to say. No wonder there's a brain drain in the valley: the real talent leaves as soon as it can: outside the valley there are novels to write, scripts to crank out, agents to contact; the dollar signs and memoirs of dysfunctional families beckon. The Real Talent boards the Greyhound, and it never looks back.

How strange, therefore, that in the Valley of Saying there exists so little envy, and those who choose to stay do not feel left behind. For uselessness exerts a powerful appeal. The poets in their uselessness know something that the Real Talent never suspects. It is the very uselessness of poetry, its economic insignificance, and political and cultural irrelevance that are in fact the sources of its greatest subversive power. Let us therefore talk uselessly awhile, let us, in the words of that supremely subversive figure, Walt Whitman, sit down awhile and loaf. Let us begin with a small, flawed, and quirkily exquisite poem by Kenneth Rexroth, likely written within a year or two of Auden's Yeats elegy, and published in his 1944 volume, *The Phoenix and the Tortoise*:

The Advantages of Learning

I am a man with no ambitions
And few friends, wholly incapable
Of making a living, growing no
Younger, fugitive from some just doom.
Lonely, ill-clothed, what does it matter?
At midnight I make myself a jug
Of hot white wine and cardamom seeds.
In a torn gray robe and old beret
I sit in the cold writing poems,
Drawing nudes on the crooked margins,
Copulating with sixteen-year-old
Nymphomaniacs of my imagination.

One could hardly imagine two poets more different than Rexroth and Auden. Yet in the early years of the Second World War the pair faced similar aesthetic crises, and addressed them in roughly parallel ways. The activist thirties were dead and gone; Marxism had lost its promise in the wake of the Moscow show trials, the defeat of the Spanish Republic, and the Hitler-Stalin nonaggression pact. And now the world was plunged into its second huge conflagration in less than thirty years. Auden flees to Manhattan, abandons the Marxist-inflected sloganeering of his early poems and instead ends embracing his new-found Christianity. The rhetoric of his poetry cools, the fiercely stentorian refrain of "Spain"—"today the struggle"—is replaced by the end of the low, dishonest decade with something which, in hindsight, we must read as a form of plea rather than as ultimatum: we must love each other or die, or so we are told in "September 1, 1939." In time, even this assertion was called into question by the poet. Now his poems, for all their didacticism, would venture inward, a transformation toward what Jarrell called "a vaguish humanitarian mysticism."

Unlike Auden, Rexroth had actually been a member of the Communist Party, but by 1938 his romance with the Left had also soured, and by the start of the Second World War he had sought conscientious objector status. He was reading a wide range of mystical literature, from Jakob Boehme to the Tao te Ching, and trekking for weeks on end in the Sierras. Now his subjects would be love and death and the changing of the seasons—or "bearshit on the trail of poetry," as one of Rexroth's later detractors put it. Perhaps confusion and ambivalence are the only proper response at this particular historical moment: the world is on the brink of war; the dream of world revolution has been betrayed. How could a cohesive artistic position be possible now, when the first order of business is to acknowledge the breadth of world violence, and the meaninglessness of activism? Auden and Rexroth are back to where Pound had been in 1917, witnessing the carnage from afar, yet with the same infuriated bile that animated his Mauberly sequence. Where does a poet turn when faced with conditions such as these? Pound of course turned to crank economic theories, a choice disastrous for both his poems and for his life. Auden turned to the church, a choice that seems equally dubious, at least as far as Auden's later poems are concerned. Rexroth made a third choice, following what one of his poems calls "the way of homesickness and exile"—a path of aestheticism and armchair anarchism. And to the Valley of Saying he went to live out his remaining years.

So let's return to "The Advantages of Learning." In the manner of T'ang Dynasty poems he would later translate, the poet begins with a deadpan account of his shabby condition: "I am a man with no ambitions / And few friends, utterly incapable / Of making a living, growing no / Younger. . . ." But in the context of the poem's title, the flatness of the statements and the terse enjambments give its opening a bitter irony, an irony made even more pronounced when we remind ourselves that Rexroth, for all his much-vaunted erudition, was an autodidact: in the world's eyes, his learning meant nothing, quantifiable by no advanced degree, no marketable skills. The poem quickly becomes tongue-in-cheek imitation of Li Po or Tu Fu, who themselves were adept practitioners of self-mockery. As the poem moves from statement to narrative, Rexroth trots out the familiar stereotypes.

> At midnight, I make myself a jug
> of hot white wine and cardamom seeds.
> In a torn gray robe and old beret,
> I sit in the cold writing poems,
> Drawing nudes on the crooked margins,
> copulating with sixteen-year-old
> Nymphomaniacs of my imagination.

I see far more whimsy here than I see self-pity. Rexroth characterizes himself as a bohemian out of central casting, up late to drink and write poems, sporting his beret while alone in the house. And of course, when it actually comes to writing poems, the speaker's been distracted; he's instead drawing nudes, and indulging in some male fantasies which are themselves as stereotypical as the robe and the beret. But the buffoonery isn't all there is. Something in the poem—perhaps it's the flatness and precision of the language and its detail—asks us to also see the speaker's plight as genuine. He traffics in clichés in part to reinvigorate their legitimacy. He is poor, solitary, and can't even finish the poems for which he has given up his hopes of worldly success. And no one is better able to see his ridiculous plight than the poet himself, who documents his condition with a kind of anti–ars poetica. It is a poem which conveys both conviction and detachment at once, and a detachment decidedly different from the lofty remove which permeates a good many of Rexroth's other poems. The tone instead recalls the dry, fastidious irony of contemporary Eastern European poets such as Herbert and Milosz: it is not the effete irony practiced so benumbingly by poets in the heyday of the New Criticism, but instead what A. Alvarez calls, in characterizing Herbert's poetry, "the irony of a vulnerable man." "The Advantages of Learning" refutes all the romantic precepts of lyric poetry: neither the poet nor poetry itself can make any special claims to significance. But the "advantage" of poetry is its capacity to allow the poet to dwell outside the parameters of significance, be they aesthetic or economic. The advantage of poetry, that dialect spoken in the Valley of Saying, is its uselessness. It is the argot, sometimes ironic, sometimes enacting the entrancement of detachment—what Bishop called "a perfectly useless concentration"—of the vulnerable men and women who dwell in the Valley. The subversive power and authority of poetry thus derives from two main sources, one linguistic—the idiosyncratic speech and regional accent of the valley dwellers—and one geographical or spatial, for the Valley of Saying is a *special* backwater, far removed from the bustle of the capital.

Special lingo, special perspective: from grade school onward we are told that this is what poetry is about. But these characterizations tend to come with valorizing strings attached. Poetry's "specialness" is somehow connected to notions of the sublime, of obscurity, of deadly earnestness. The popularizing of verse-writing through poets-in-the-schools programs and collegiate creative writing classes hasn't done much to dissuade the world at large from holding these notions. Nor has the legacy of literary modernism, and it's the High-Church Modernists who young readers are apt to first encounter. Eliot, Pound, and Yeats are still the gatekeepers, despite the efforts of anthologists to enlarge the canon. And it's Rilke, that Sultan of Sublime, who occupies the most shelf space in the poetry sections of Borders or B&N. The result of all of this, aside from making bad translations of *The Duino Elegies* a kind of cottage industry, is to reinforce a decidedly Victorian notion of poetry's mission: it is quaint, good for you in an oat bran sort of way, and above all domesticated. It is this declawed, spayed, or neutered version of poetry which causes the Language poets to rant against Official Verse Culture. Poetry which falls outside the parameters of these sanctioned norms tends to be neglected, or at worse, its practitioners are punished and silenced: witness the fates of Gumilev and Mandelstam.

The product of the Imagination's Party Line, whether a Yevtusenko ode to a new hydroelectric dam or a laureate doodle on something-safely-quotidian, is not the kind of writing which first attracts us to poetry. Tyro poets tend to be drawn either to poetry's subversive playfulness with language—to a hit parade which includes Hopkins, Roethke, and more recently James Tate and John Ashbery—or its postures of rebelliousness: this is why the Beats are still read, and why a talent as indifferent as Chatterton's could so inspire the Romantics. The Minions of Official Verse Culture (among which I reluctantly count myself), whether consciously or not, try to wean the kids away from these interests and these models. And in a short time they learn just enough to know they should regard these first poetic mentors with suspicion. Last year my then-colleague Dean Young taught a graduate seminar on Dada and surrealism, and apparently subversiveness and nihilism don't play well anymore. Stein, Breton, Cage, O'Hara: despite the students' knowledge of these writers' impact on postmodern thinking, they resisted them all, for lots of dutiful but inchoate reasons, all of them vaguely P.C. In one particularly puzzling conversation, O'Hara got branded as a sexist and racist (an accusation that certainly would have startled O'Hara himself). The class in essence reenacted the miserable tale of the surrealists' flirtation with international communism, with poor Dean playing the role of Breton and company, and the students the role of the Stalinist hacks, baffled and threatened by the convulsive transgressiveness of surrealist poetics, its call for "a revolution of the mind." And of course a revolution of the mind has little institutional value, whether it is debated around a seminar table or presented naïvely to the Comintern as a weapon for destroying the Beast of Capitalism. Revolutions of the mind are always useless, always subjective—and almost always poetry's first order of business. The revolution of the mind is for the young poet not some major upheaval, but a kind of initiation to the transformative properties of language, and of poetry's role in self-transformation. And yet, in the way of all revolutions, it is followed by a counter-revolution, a Thermadorian Reaction where a kind of aesthetic zealotry prevails; my friend Dean's students seem caught in the throes of such a reaction, for better or for worse, but they're not untypical. Some poets are trapped in that reaction—and the embitterment which accompanies failed promise and failed allegiances—for long and sorrowful stretches of their writing careers. It causes some to turn to silence, some to turn to new fidelities (Auden to the church, Wordsworth to the Tories). And some—at the risk of muddying my analogies—will pack their books and papers up, move off to the Valley of Saying, and come full circle, back to poetry's initiating thrall and vigor, its useless but astonishing delights.

An archetypal pattern, then? Maybe, but this sounds too grandiose. Yet I see my own career as following it, and I see it enacted in many of the poets I most admire, provided they live long enough, and escape the choice of punishment or silence. I am now forty-seven years old, Mandelstam's age when he was last sighted, scavenging a Gulag garbage heap in search of food, and the age when Paul Celan chose to leap from a bridge into the Seine. According to Dante, old age begins at forty-seven: you're a graybeard now, entering geezerhood: you can lay down your lyre and quill. But I'm lucky enough to feel persecuted only by myself, to have no suicidal inclinations, and to have no intention of putting down my pen. In the Valley of Saying, in the subdivision called Minor Poet in Mid-Career, there's still a great deal I want to say.

Oddly enough, the journey takes me again to Kenneth Rexroth, and again to "The Advantages of Learning." For in 1970 there were precisely three books of contemporary poetry to be found on the shelves of the Washington County Public Library's Lake Elmo branch. I was seventeen, and I'd been reading poetry with a sort of desultory avidness for a couple of years. Pound, Eliot, Stevens—I'd read them, but not closely, read them because my high-school English teacher suggested them to me, but frankly they left me cold. I sensed in them the same sort of mock-profundity and declamatory self-importance that I got from my Emerson, Lake and Palmer LPs (Stevens was, admittedly, a little more interestingly weird, more like Pink Floyd . . .). But the high modernists, in their loftiness, were high in the wrong way. I was ready for something else, and into my life there came—serendipitously, and thanks to the exquisite taste of an anonymous rural Minnesota librarian who no doubt spent a hefty portion of the little library's purchasing funds on three new poetry books—*The Collected Shorter Poems* of Kenneth Rexroth, *Silence in the Snowy Fields* by Robert Bly, and, most importantly, the 1971 *Collected Poems* of James Wright. I read them in precisely that order, and I read them and read them. Rexroth I liked, Bly I liked better, and Wright I adored. When the library books came due I bought my own copies, and battered they sit on my desk as I write this, paper yellowed, spines unglued, their dust jackets long-ago turned to shreds, worn like the woodworking tools my father kept in his basement shop. After all the years of reading and rereading this trio, it's hard to pinpoint what first attracted me to their work, but I know my love of them sprang in part from their attention to place, and in the case of Bly and Wright to a landscape that was my own: the snowy windswept fields were right before me, but suddenly they no longer suggested the dreary tedium of Sinclair Lewis and his purgatorial Gopher Prairie—after all, we'd read *Main Street* and *Babbitt* in English class, and I and my friends all suspected that real life occurred somewhere else. But now, in a single stroke, real life was happening right before me, and it was a mysterious, occult, and hugely sensual reality—"a cloister, a silence, / closing around a blossom of fire," as Wright put it in "The Jewel." "Frail shadows" everywhere, everywhere "cathedrals in the wind"—an exquisitely mystical vista of Swedenborgian correspondences, of shadowy hermetic revelation: "we are all asleep in the outward man," said Bly in his epigraph to *Silence in the Snowy Fields*, quoting Jakob Boehme. But the means to wake the inner man were all around you, if only you had the wherewithal to look—here "the moon drops one or two feathers in a field," and there "the dark wheat listens." I did not know in those days what pain and self-torture the poems of James Wright emerged from: that understanding of Wright would wait for later. In those days his were purely poems of ecstasy, poems which subverted the natural order through the revelatory astonishments of their imagery, and by rhapsodizing places and situations which I knew, but now saw x-rayed, revealing a hitherto hidden luminosity. A hammock in Pine Island, Minnesota, Indian ponies in a field off Highway 55 to Rochester, and on the South Dakota border, "where the moon is out hunting," at last we understand that we "are lost in the beautiful white ruins / of America."

Here you could voyage to the inner life, but you could also drive to it, as my friend Pete Mladinic and I did one afternoon, trying to locate that roadside field where Wright set "A Blessing." (Admittedly, we'd smoked a lot of hash that day....) Wright and Bly weren't trendy in the way the Beats were, but they still possessed some countercultural cachet. I knew they wrote in protest of the war, and Bly in his readings liked to wear a serape. They lauded the simple pleasures of doing nothing, pleasures which to me seemed a lot like getting high. I didn't know the hammock poem could be seen as a self-indictment, didn't understand its desperate homage to "The Torso of an Archaic Apollo." I read the poems as if they were ways to jump-start the inner life, and even at their most trivial they seemed profound. And it didn't hurt that no one else but my friend Peter seemed to get the point. My mother, who not many years earlier had banned all comic books from our house save those from the Classics Illustrated series, thought well of my interest in reading poetry, until one day she picked up my copy of *Silence in the Snowy Fields*. I'd dogeared a poem she found easy to judge:

Driving to Town Late to Mail a Letter

It is a cold and snowy night. The main street is deserted.
The only things moving are swirls of snow.
As I lift the mailbox door, I feel its cold iron.

There is a privacy I love in the snowy night.
Driving around, I will waste more time.

"Billy Shields could write better than that," she said, referring to the retarded kid who lived up the street. My mother valued learning, but she also had a cruel streak. The learning which this poem exemplified, a learning without quantifiable values, a learning whose purpose is sometimes to educate us in the value of useless pleasure, wasn't something her accountant's mind could grasp. It made me love the poem all the more.

But I also suppose that even then I knew in some vague way that Bly's poem was ultimately a trivial thing, a kind of Wordsworth Lite. The World That Is Too Much With Us is, in so many of the Deep Image poems which Bly and Wright spawned, very easy to reject in favor of atavistic symbolism and a fuzzy romantic pantheism, and there is no cost to pay. When you could so readily drive to the inner life, cruising at sixty in what Bly inanely termed "the iron solitude of the car," using barely a quarter tank of gas, revelation came to seem like a cheap thrill. Bly himself was shaken out of this sort of quietism by the Vietnam War, and the most enduring poetry of the Deep Image group—most notably Merwin's *The Lice*—sets the retreat into the self against a backdrop of Imperialist warmongering and the threat of atomic Armageddon. Yes, you can still drive to the inner life, but there are many roadblocks along the way, and when you get there you must face your own extinction; you see that in fact you have crawled off like a wounded animal to die: "It is March and black dust falls from the books / Soon I will be gone / The tall spirit who lodged here / Has left already," says Merwin in a poem from *The Lice*. No consolation here, and certainly no delight. But after book upon book of this sort of thing, Merwin's testimony seemed inauthentic.

But new models came, and two of them I want to speak of in detail, for their lessons apply here in ways which perhaps no others can. Both poets are provincials, writing in languages which, even in an era of diversity and multiculturalism, are apt to be branded as marginal. Tomas Tranströmer writes in Swedish, Constantine Cavafy in modern Greek. Their work comes to me infused with the distortions, inaccuracy, and feedback which attend any work of literary translation, for I have no knowledge of what their poems might sound like in their original form. Tranströmer will probably never be awarded the Nobel; for the Swedes to give the prize to one of their own would be an act of... provincialism. Cavafy, one of the last century's greatest poets, never issued a book of poetry during his lifetime, unless you count the stapled and mimeographed productions he'd from time to time put together for his friends. As an Alexandrian Greek, speaking Arabic in the cafés he frequented and English in his workplace—the Dantesque-sounding "Third Circle of Irrigation"—Cavafy spoke the tongue he wrote his poems in only occasionally. And *fin de siècle* Alexandria, once the greatest Greek city of all, was in his time neither Greek nor much of a city. One of the things which links these two very different poets is a stance which does not and cannot assume centrality: they must position themselves in the cheap seats, the outermost districts, far from the foci of cultural or political power. They cannot assume the roles of smiling public men, or pen aristocratic odes to Union or Confederate fallen. Yet they remind us that even in the sticks life goes on, and that distant vantage points are often the ones which permit us the most acute and truthful view: both of history and of ourselves, and sometimes of the ways in which selves and history must inextricably commingle. Like Chekhov's three sisters, they'll never visit Moscow, but in time the most fortunate of them learn to turn their very obscurity, marginality, and insignificance into their strongest assets. The process of this transformation is a complex one, and it entails more than writing diddley-squat epiphanies in Midwestern cornfields in the manner of Robert Bly, and yet—ironically—it was Robert Bly who helped to teach me this.

The lesson took place on a Monday in early November, 1972. Specifically, it was the eve of Richard Nixon's reelection, not the grimmest day in American history, but certainly a shameful one, and surely a time of profound and benumbing despair. Four more years of Nixon's criminality and our genocidal war in Asia seemed to loom before us, and nothing appeared to stop him or to slow him down. Marches and moratoria had failed, and the well-meaning earnestness of George McGovern would inevitably fail as well. I could say that times such as these are the ones in which we turn to poetry for solace, but I have to report that I wasn't thinking very clearly in those days. Yet somehow I found myself in an auditorium on the University of Minnesota campus, and before me and a few dozen others stood Tomas Tranströmer, flanked by his translator Robert Bly. Had I not been there that night, I doubt if I'd have continued to write poetry.

That only a handful of listeners had come to the reading was no surprise. Tranströmer was at that time represented in English by only two collections, a small *Selected* which Pittsburgh had issued, and an even smaller volume which Bly's Seventies Press had printed. I'd never read the Swedish poet's work; like most of the audience, I was there to hear Bly, whose manic delivery and marathon readings lasting hours had in those years taken on a kind of cult cachet. Bly didn't disappoint: he hulked and strutted about the classroom, punctuating his translations of Tranströmer's poems with speedy and pontificating between-poem banter. Tranströmer's presence was entirely different. Tall, thin to the point of gauntness, with angular Nordic features which made him look for all the world like Max Von Sydow, blond hair going to gray, Tranströmer looked quietly commanding, relaxed above the podium, but standing very still. He recited his poems in Swedish, but also read several of them in translation, slowly and in an almost accent-free English. Tranströmer and Bly were a study in contrast, but also oddly symbiotic. Bly paced, circled, and generally filibustered around Tranströmer at his podium, orbiting him like a wayward asteroid. Tranströmer presented a kind of Zenlike awareness, quietly attentive toward both his poems and the audience; he seemed strangely egoless, more like a shrink than a poet—listening and observing in an intense but nondirective fashion, and putting his poems under the same sort of benign scrutiny a therapist would give a client's self-appraisals. ("Were your needs being met by this metaphor?" "Do you still feel angry toward this stanza?" "Tell me more about the image of the horse's flank?") That night, as he introduced a poem entitled "After the Attack," I discovered that Tranströmer was, in fact, a psychotherapist, working in a boy's reform school. As the years passed, I came to understand that a stance of detachment that is at the same time utterly attentive was a principal source of Tranströmer's authority as a poet. In his famous poem about Vermeer, it is neither the painter himself nor his human figures which have the last word, but a ray of light, corporeal and incorporeal at once, which utters the poem's conclusion:

The clear sky has set itself against the wall.
It's like a prayer to emptiness.
And the emptiness turns its face to us
and whispers
I am not empty; I am open.

In this poem, as in so much of Tranströmer's work, the hidden world of inanimate and abstract things is invariably personified, sometimes consolingly, sometimes frighteningly. "Memories Look at Me" is in fact the title of an autobiographical sketch in Tranströmer's book *For the Living and the Dead,* and a passage in "The Gallery," a long and nightmarish lyric that functions as a kind of ars poetica, has this to say about the poet's creative process:

Often I have to stand completely motionless.
I'm the partner of the knife-thrower in the circus!
Questions I threw from me in a fit of rage
come whining back
don't hit but nail down my shape
in coarse outline
stay there when I've left the place.

Critics in Sweden, especially those with a Marxist bent, have condemned this stance throughout Tranströmer's career, seeing in it a kind of apolitical Olympian indifference—one of them went so far as to label him "a buzzard poet." And indeed, many of his poems do seem to arrive at an aerial perspective, or at the vantage point of someone who suddenly finds himself to be experiencing astral projection. One poem concludes with a vision of "islands [which] crawl like huge moths over the globe." In another the shadow thrown by an airplane covers a man at work in a field and "for a fraction of a second he is right at the center of the cross." These are not moments of potential rapture, in the way that even the most ambivalent images at the conclusion of many of James Wright's poems can be; they instead seem prophecies of conflagration, whether an annihilation of the self or destruction on a cosmic level; sometimes they point to both at once.

Certainly this is the case with the poem Tranströmer chose to read at the close of his reading:

The Open Window

I shaved one morning standing
by the open window
on the second story.
Switched on the razor.
It started to hum.
A heavier and heavier whirr.
Grew to a roar.
Grew to a helicopter.
And a voice—the pilot's—pierced
the noise, shouting:
"Keep your eyes open!
You're seeing this for the last time!"
Rose.
Floated low over the summer.
The small things I love, have they any weight?
So many dialects of green.
And especially the red of housewalls.
Beetles glittered in the dung, in the sun.
Cellars pulled up by the roots
sailed through the air.

Industry.
Printing presses crawled along.
People at that instant
were the only things motionless.
They observe their moment of silence.
And the dead in the churchyard especially
held still
like those who posed in the infancy of the camera.
Fly low!
I didn't know which way
to turn my head—
my sight was divided
like a horse's.

An unsettling poem, surely; despite its imagistic pyrotechnics, it is telegraphic and brusque. By line eight Tranströmer is out his window, once again becoming a buzzard poet. Yet the experience of being airborne is hardly that of a delightful flying dream, where our wings spread and we coast upon thermals. This final glimpse of the world beneath us permits no consolidating clarity—the poem ends abruptly, with a startling image of bifurcation: our sight is "divided / like a horse's." Although the image is striking, the poem seems to stop in mid-thought.

The audience greeted this with a stunned silence, and it took a while for someone to remember to applaud. A halting question-and-answer session began—not because Tranströmer seemed uncomfortable with English, but because the audience seemed puzzled by the oddness of perception and the quiet gravity of his poems. Yes, they were surreal, but the images seemed to derive from something far different from the slick romanticism of Deep Image verse. Bly tried to play ringmaster to this all, joking that he'd initially made a huge blunder in his translation, mistaking "rockerapparater," the Swedish word for electric razor, for "rocket apparatus"—thus his initial version of the poem had its speaker strap on some sort of Buck Rogers device and literally rocket out his open window. The audience lobbed some of the usual questions reserved for such events—asking Tranströmer about his influences and writing habits. But one question was openly hostile: the questioner was wearing a Mao cap, a red star in its center: "How, at a time like this, can you write such introspective poems? How can you be so apolitical? You're like an ostrich with his head in the sand."

Clearly Tranströmer had heard this sort of accusation before, and often. "I write poetry because I believe in the value of individual lives. By writing about my private life I hope to remind my readers of theirs. In a world such as ours, where the individual is little valued, this position seems to me a highly political one." The dignity and wisdom of this reply stunned me: it is of course the kind of statement that has been uttered in countless ways in the past two centuries; you hear it in Blake and Wordsworth as well as in the Language poets. But I'd never heard this sort of formulation before, and never again would I hear it without recalling that evening in 1972. Years later, during a winter in which Tranströmer stayed in Provincetown, I mentioned that Minnesota evening to him. He sheepishly confessed that he couldn't recall it, though he still agreed with the content of his statement. Some friends and I were chauffeuring him to a reading he was to give in Boston. On the way there, he asked to be driven on a side trip through Roxbury. He'd never seen an American slum before. The talk turned to politics, and he told me that he'd written "The Open Window" during the week of the Cuban Missile Crisis: the notion of having a final view of life on earth was at that moment not by any means a mere metaphor.

In some ways the most radical—or surreal—aspect of Tranströmer's poetry is its manipulation of spatial relationships, its willingness to suddenly alter our physical perspective—at one moment we are shaving, in the next we are flying high above the planet: tracking shots suddenly become closeups, and vice versa. We never are allowed to stay in a position long enough to grow comfortable with our point of view. These devices are wrenching and unsettling rather than simply virtuosic; it is not the frenetic jump cutting of an MTV video or the latest Lexus commercial that Tranströmer gives us, but a warning that we will never see *anything* from the best or the right perspective, and never do we remain at a single vantage point for long. Tranströmer asks us to stand in the way that E. M. Forster cannily noted that Cavafy stood—"at a slight angle to the universe."

Like Tranströmer, Cavafy sees displacement as the single thing which most characterizes the human condition, and yet he too finds in these states of exile and rupture the content of his most enduring poetry. This is of course a paradox, but Cavafy's oeuvre abounds in paradox. No other great poet—with the possible exception of Hardy—employs such a restrictive palette. Metaphor is nearly absent from his work, his language is spare and minimalist, and his themes are limited to three: memory, desire, and the failure of ambition. Yet the scope of Cavafy's poetry is immense; somehow the tilt of Cavafy's perspective—that vantage point comprised of views from café tables, a single apartment balcony, windows in homosexual brothels, and an untidy desk in the Third Circle of Irrigation—begat a body of work of tremendous vitality. It is peopled with a nearly Shakespearean variety of characters, but it is also autobiographical, infused with a self-reflective intelligence considerably different from the reportorial drabness of American confessional verse. Yet no other poet will ever sound much like him. No other poet of the modernist era speaks to us with such straightforwardly lucid intimacy; yet Cavafy remains unapproachable, even unknowable, a figure of baffling complexity and reserve. "Hidden Things," an early but crucial poem, offers up an aesthetic which is based upon a striking paradox, at once baldly direct and poignantly self-protective:

> For all I did and said
> let no one try to find out who I was.
> An obstacle was there that changed the pattern
> of my actions and the manner of my life.
> An obstacle was often there
> to stop me when I began to speak.
> From my most unnoticed actions,
> my most veiled writing—
> from these alone I will be understood.
> But maybe it isn't worth so much concern,
> so much effort to discover who I really am.
> Later, in a more perfect society,
> someone else made just like me
> is certain to appear and act freely.

It is easy to read this poem as a denunciation of the closet, but this is to oversimplify the intricacies of the dance between self-disclosure, impersonation, and self-concealment which lies at the heart of Cavafy's writing. It is not a question for him of being closeted or out, but of selfhood being permeable, malleable, vibrantly in play within the matrix of his trio of thematic concerns. And to some degree you need a highly educated theologian of Cavafyism to separate the attributes of this trio, for in the poetry of Cavafy memory, desire, and history often seem one and the same: historical monologues and recollective love poems occupy identical regions of the past.

The means by which art and politics commingle in Cavafy's world parallel those in which eros and memory are conjoined. Cavafy's historicizing impulses encompass the erotic life with a similar ruefulness. Memory's imaginative power derives not from comprehensive evocation, but from selectiveness, flattening to a kind of shorthand the ephemeral nature of erotic beauty as well as the tawdriness within which it is set. Memory is thus both the ash of experience and its base metal alchemized to gold, causing rapture and bitterness to alternate from line to line. "Days of 1909, '10, and '11" is one of the best examples of this strategy:

> He was the son of a harassed, poverty-stricken sailor
> (from an island in the Aegean Sea).
> He worked for a blacksmith, his clothes shabby,
> his workshoes miserably torn,
> his hands filthy with rust and oil.
>
> In the evenings, after the shop closed,
> if there was something he longed for especially,
> a fairly expensive tie, a tie for Sunday,
> or if he saw and coveted
> a beautiful blue shirt in some store window,
> he'd sell his body for a dollar or two.
>
> I ask myself if the glorious Alexandria
> of ancient times could boast of a boy
> more exquisite, more perfect—lost though he was:
> that is, we don't have a statue or painting of him:
> thrust into that awful blacksmith's shop,

> overworked, tormented, given to cheap debauchery,
> he was soon used up.

The acuteness and gruff realism of the portraiture gives way in stanza three to idealization, but only for a moment, and with the dual goal of insisting upon the young man's beauty while linking it to the long-departed glories of the Classical world. Yet memory has but one horizon: both the beauty and the glory are equally extinct. All that remains are chiseled letters weathered smooth, composed in a language which itself is dead. It is a poor and fragmentary metonymy, but in its flat insistence, in its ardor to preserve some essence in spite of these relentlessly eroding forces, Cavafy's cameo of the blacksmith boy is richly poignant. But he does not let us savor this poignance: the brutal closing lines have seen to that. Like Dickinson, that other great miniaturist, Cavafy refuses to dwell in a single emotive state for long.

When Cavafy was asked by friends why he had lived for twenty-five years in the same apartment, in a shabby neighborhood deemed unbefitting of an educated man with a private income, in an apartment above a bordello, looking out upon a decrepit church and a charity hospital, he famously replied that in fact his street had everything: "Where could I live better?" he said. "Below, the brothel caters to the flesh. And there is the church which forgives sin. And there is the hospital where we die."

What of this myth, beyond the poems, now remains? Our driver and our guide have been lost for half an hour, circling street after narrow street, from the waterfront to the coliseum ruins and back again. The Greek-speaking Alexandria of Cavafy's day has now been thoroughly Arab-ized, and the address we're seeking is no longer 10

Rue Lepsius, but its current incarnation, 4 Sharia Sharm Al-Sheikh. Hesham, our guide, knows Alexandria well, but no one's ever asked to visit the dwelling of a long-dead Greek poet. The guidebooks are of little help: the big *Blue Guide to Egypt* says nothing of Cavafy or his house; the *Knopf Guide* notes the existence of a Cavafy museum, but it's unstarred and without an address, Cavafy's poem "The City"—typeset as prose—appears beside a drawing of the poet. "Upon his death in the 1933," says the guide, "his apartment was converted into a museum." Here again the guide's mistaken. When the translator and Cavafy scholar Edmund Keeley visited here in the early seventies, the poet's apartment was a transient hotel, the Pension Amir, "each room a dormitory crammed with sway-backed beds and peeling wardrobes." The purchase of the apartment by the Greek consulate and its conversion to a museum happened much later. "Are you sure the house is in Alexandria?" asks our guide. "Perhaps it's actually in Cairo."

I'm starting to think the house is not just off the tourist maps, but that it may never have existed, is as mythic as the city of Cavafy's poems. It's been a long drive from Cairo. My wife and Hesham are growing impatient; they're ready for lunch. "I know it's near a Greek church," I say, "and maybe near a hospital." So we circle again, finding at last the Church of St. Shara, and then a winding street called Sharia Sharm Al-Sheikh, and on it number four, among a row of nineteenth-century apartment buildings, brightly colored in stucco, three and four stories high, bristling with TV antennae. The doors are flush with the sidewalk; it's like the French Quarter in New Orleans, but much worse for the wear. Beneath the paint's garish maquillage, the pinks and iridescent greens, the buildings are about to crumble. But several plaques have been affixed to number four, Arabic above, Greek in the middle, and English below: CONSTANTINE CAVAFY HOUSE. Below the plaques is a handwritten wooden sign: "open ten o'clock to three." And below it, a message has been stuck with masking tape: "asend the stare on top floor please ring bell." The door we push open is huge and weathered, carved with arabesques. Before us, a courtyard, cat-cradled with hanging laundry, line upon line of sheets and T-shirts, thick old-fashioned torpedo-pointed bras, men's white briefs with tears badly mended, semaphores of handkerchiefs and blue and red bandannas. Behind them, almost invisible, the stairway: *part these curtains and "asend."*

But we can never approach great writing by rising up. When reading poetry, Hélène Cixous insists, we always must descend, ever downward in a slow deliberate katabasis, down to the realm of the eloquent shades. So it's downward to the top floor, downwardly ascending to the bell, the gatekeeper telling us, in halting English, that "the most substantial poet of the modern Greeks" wrote only some one hundred poems; downward to the shuttered little rooms, slates of light on a rickety display case where the old man's death mask floats atop a purple cushion (weirdly garish, like the head of John the Baptist on its jeweled plate) beside a chapbook of his poems, a tattered mimeographed affair, bound with a stickpin—one of the "collections" he'd present to friends. Downward to a hulking writing desk, inlaid floridly with mother-of-pearl, to a rickety teak armoire and a huge Victorian four-poster; and beyond them, downward further, downward to the bottom-most place, the lowest rung, the deepest cavern, we step out on the balcony to the scalding Mediterranean sun, blinded and groping for our sunglasses. Car-horns and a distant siren, the dome of the church which forgives your sins, the hospital where you go to die. "You'll always end up in this city," says the poem. "Don't hope for anything elsewhere. / There is no ship for you, there is no road." There is only this crucible, inside which lies the city, this necropolis, this citadel. The Valley of Saying and its ancient capital.

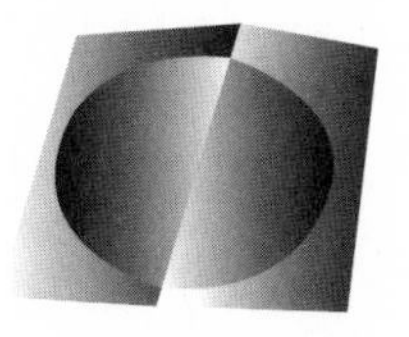

ADAM ZAGAJEWSKI

Young Poets, Please Read Everything

There is at least one danger here: discussing a way of reading, or simply producing a portrayal of a "good reader," may create the impression that I myself am a perfect reader. Nothing could be further from the truth. I'm a chaotic reader, and the holes in my education are more stunning than the Swiss Alps. Therefore my remarks should be seen as belonging to the realm of dreams, a kind of a personal utopia, rather than as part of the very small platoon of my virtues.

Reading chaotically! Some time ago I unpacked my summer-vacation suitcase. Let's see what kind of books I had with me in Switzerland, near Lake Geneva. I probably should have taken with me Jean Jacques Rousseau, Byron, Madame de Staël, Gibbon, and Nabokov, all of them somehow linked with the famous lake, but actually none traveled with me. Instead I see on the floor of my study

Jacob Burckhardt's *The Greeks and Greek Civilization* (yes, in English translation, a book I found in one of the Houston half-price bookstores); a selection of Emerson's essays, Baudelaire's poetry in French, Stefan George's poems in Polish translation, Hans Jonas's classical book on Gnosticism (in German), a volume of Zbigniew Herbert poems, and one of many volumes of Hugo von Hofmannsthal's *Collected Works* (*Gesammelte Werk*), containing his remarkable essays. Some of these books belong to different Parisian libraries; this tells you also that I'm a rather neurotic reader who often shuns the owner's responsibility and prefers the library books, as if reading a book that doesn't belong to me gave me a feeling of additional freedom (the library—the only venue where the socialist project has succeeded).

But why do I read? Do I need to answer this question? It seems to me that a poet would read for many different reasons. Some of them are quite plain and don't differ from the motives of any other mortal. Our reading stands mostly under two signs: under the sign of memory and under the sign of ecstasy. We read for memory (for knowledge, education) because we are curious about what our numerous predecessors produced before our own minds had been opened. This is something we call tradition—or history.

We also read for ecstasy. Why? Because. Because books—especially some poetry books—contain not only wisdom and well-ordered information, but also an energy that can be situated near dance and shamanistic drunkenness. Because we ourselves experience these strange moments when we are driven by a force that demands strict obedience and—sometimes, not always—leaves black spots on paper, the way fire leaves ashes behind (*noircir le papier*, as the French call the noble act of writing). And once you have lived a moment of ecstatic writing you behave like a drug addict and you want to have more of that. You would do anything to get more of it; indeed, reading doesn't seem an exaggerated sacrifice.

The books I read—if a confession is required or desired here—are divided into these two categories, books of memory and of ecstasy. You can't read an ecstatic book late at night: no sleep. You read history before falling asleep. You read Rimbaud at noon.

The relationship between the two, between memory and ecstasy, is paradoxical, rich and interesting; sometimes the latter grows out of the former and it's like a forest fire—an old sonnet found by a greedy eye can trigger a new poem. But often memory and ecstasy do not overlap. Sometimes they are separated by an ocean of indifference.

There are scholars whose memory is amazingly vast and yet they produce very little; sometimes you see in a library an old man bent under the weight of years, wearing a bow tie, and you like to think—this person knows everything. And indeed, some of these old readers wearing thick glasses do know a lot (perhaps not the old man you saw the other day); however it's a far cry from that to creativity. On the other side of the spectrum there are teenagers getting high on rap music, and yet we don't expect a fat artistic harvest from that enthusiasm.

Apparently memory and ecstasy need each other desperately. Ecstasy must be a little learned and memory would lose nothing if it were colored by strong emotions.

The problem of reading is so vital for us—us, poets, but also we who just like to speculate—because our education had been so imperfect. Liberal schools you attended (or communist schools I attended) did not care enough for the classics, nor did they care for giants of modernity. Our schools are proud of producing streamlined members of this Great Animal, the new society of proud consumers. It's true: we were not tortured like teenagers in nineteenth-century

England (or France or Germany, or Poland for that matter), we didn't need to memorize the whole of Virgil and Ovid. We must be self-taught; the difference in this respect between someone like Joseph Brodsky, who left school at the age of sixteen and later read everything he could get hold of, and someone who went through the complete cycle of American education and received a Ph.D. without leaving the ivory tower, is obvious.

We read mostly outside the campus and in the post-campus life; American poets I know are very well read, and yet I see clearly they have acquired their learning in the years between graduating and entering the zone of middle age. Most of the American graduate students know rather little, less than their European counterparts, but many of them will make up for this in the years to come.

My impression is also that many younger American poets today read in a somewhat narrow way: they mostly read poetry, and nothing or little else except for the criticism of poetry. There's nothing wrong with reading poetry from Homer to Zbigniew Herbert and John Ashbery, but it seems to me that this mode of reading is too limited. It's like having a biology student tell you he or she reads only biology. Or a young astronomer who studies only astronomy. Or an athlete who reads only the sports section of the *The New York Times*. Nothing terribly wrong with reading "only" poetry, and yet a shadow of a too-early professional attitude hovers over this practice. A shadow of shallowness.

Reading only poetry suggests that there's something rigid and isolated about the nature of contemporary poetic practice, that poetry has become separated from philosophy's central questions, from history's anxieties, from a painter's dilemmas, and from the honest politician's qualms—i.e., from the deep and common source of culture.

Actually, the way a young poet organizes his reading is quite crucial for the situation of poetry and other arts; it may determine—and not just for one person—whether poetry is a central discipline (even if read uniquely by the happy few), responding to the most important impulses of the given historic moment, or a somewhat interesting drudgery that for some reason attracts a few unhappy fans.

Perhaps it's the other way around: the choice of reading reflects our deeper, perhaps not completely conscious decisions, about the role of poetry in our lives. Will we be satisfied with the timid method typical of a "specialist" who has a sectarian and cautious approach to literature, or someone who agrees to be limited in his writing to a little story of a broken heart? Or will we take instead the generous stance of a poet trying to think, to sing, to take risks, to embrace generously and boldly the thinning humanity of our time (without forgetting the broken heart)?

So, young poets, please read everything, read Plato and Ortega y Gasset, Horace and Hölderlin, Ronsard and Pascal, Dostoyevsky and Tolstoy, Oscar and Czeslaw Milosz, Keats and Wittgenstein, Emerson and Emily Dickinson, T. S. Eliot and Umberto Saba, Thucydides and Colette, Apollinaire and Virginia Woolf, Anna Akhmatova and Dante, Pasternak and Machado, Montaigne and St. Augustine, Proust and Hofmannsthal, Sappho and Szymborska, Thomas Mann and Aeschylus; read biographies and treatises, essays and political analyses; read for yourself, read for the sake of your inspiration, for the sweet turmoil in your lovely head, but read also against yourself, for questioning and for helplessness, read for despair and for learning, read the dry and sardonic remarks of cynical philosophers like Cioran or even Carl Schmitt, read newspapers, read those who despise, dismiss, or neglect poetry, and try to understand why they do it, read your enemies and your friends, read those who flatter your sense of what's becoming in poetry and read also those whose darkness or malice or madness or greatness you can't yet understand because only thus you can grow and outlive yourself and become what you are.

THE EDITORS

Sharon Bryan is also the author of *Flying Blind*, her third collection of poems which appeared from Sarabande Books in 1996. The first two collections, *Salt Air* and *Objects of Affection*, were published by Wesleyan University Press. She is also the editor of *Where We Stand: Women Poets on Literary Tradition* (Norton, 1993). Her awards include an Academy of American Poets prize, the Discovery Award from *The Nation*, and two fellowships in poetry from the National Endowment for the Arts. She was poet-in-residence at The Frost Place in 1993. She teaches as a visiting writer, and lives in Port Townsend, Washington.

William Olsen is the author of three collections of poetry, *The Hand of God and a Few Bright Flowers* (Illinois, 1988), *Vision of a Storm Cloud* (TriQuarterly, 1996), and *Trouble Lights* (TriQuarterly, 2002). Olsen is the recipient of a NEA Creative Writing Fellowship, *The Nation*/ Discovery Award, a Texas Institute of Arts Award, a Bread Loaf Fellowship, and poetry awards from *Poetry Northwest* and *Crazyhorse*. His poems and essays have appeared in *The New Republic, Chicago Review, The Paris Review, The Southern Review, New American Poets of the Nineties, The New Bread Loaf Anthology of Contemporary American Poetry, Poets of the New Century* (Godine, November 2001), and many other magazines and anthologies. He teaches at Western Michigan University and in the MFA Program at Vermont College.

CONTRIBUTORS

Robin Behn is the recipient of fellowships from the Guggenheim Foundation and the National Endowment for the Arts. She has published three volumes of poetry, most recently *Horizon Note*, and she co-edited *The Practice of Poetry: Writing Exercises from Poets Who Teach*. She teaches in the MFA Program in Creative Writing at the University of Alabama.

The latest of **Marvin Bell**'s seventeen books of poetry and essays is *Nightworks: Poems 1962–2000*. He is a longtime member of the faculty of the Writers' Workshop at the University of Iowa. In the seventies and again in the nineties, he wrote an influential column about poetry and the creative process for *The American Poetry Review*. Bell lives in Iowa City, where he teaches one semester a year; Sag Harbor, New York; and Port Townsend, Washington. In the year 2000, the State of Iowa named him its first Poet Laureate.

Eavan Boland's most recent book is *Against Love Poetry* (W. W. Norton, 2001). She is co-editor with Mark Strand of *The Making of a Poem: A Norton Anthology of Poetic Forms*. She teaches at Stanford and divides her year between Dublin and California.

Madeline DeFrees's seventh collection, *Blue Dusk: Poems 1951–2001*, appeared from Copper Canyon. She has also contributed seventeen short stories, essays, and reviews to various journals. Her work has been recognized by a fellowship from the Guggenheim Foundation and a grant from the National Endowment for the Arts. She lives and writes in Seattle.

Stephen Dunn is the author of eleven collections of poetry, most notably *Different Hours*, which was awarded the Pulitzer Prize in 2001, and *Loosestrife*, a finalist for the National Book Critics Circle Award, 1996. Both books appeared from Norton. Mr. Dunn has received three fellowships from the National Endowment for the Arts, fellowships from the Guggenheim and Rockefeller Foundations, and an Academy Award in Literature from The American Academy of Arts and Letters, among many other awards. He is Distinguished Professor of Creative Writing at Richard Stockton College of New Jersey.

Reginald Gibbons is author of five volumes of poetry, most recently *Sparrow*, as well as several works of criticism, a short story collection, and a novel. He served as editor of *TriQuarterly* from 1981 to 1997. He is the recipient of several awards, among them a Guggenheim fellowship, a National Endowment for the Arts grant, and the Carl Sandburg Award. A native of Texas, he now lives with his family in Evanston, Illinois, where he directs the Department of English at Northwestern University.

Albert Goldbarth was educated at the University of Illinois-Chicago, the University of Iowa, and the University of Utah. He has taught at Cornell, Syracuse, the University of Texas, and Wichita State University, where he is Distinguished Professor of the Humanities. Among his numerous awards are fellowships from the Guggenheim Foundation and the National Endowment for the Arts, the National Book Critics Circle Award for both *Heaven and Earth: A Cosmology* (1991) and *Saving Lives* (2001), and the PEN Creative Non-Fiction Award for *Many Circles: New and Selected Essays*. His most recent books are *Combinations of the Universe* (2003), a collection of poetry, and *Pieces of Payne* (2003), a novel.

Beckian Fritz Goldberg holds an MFA from Vermont College and is the author of several volumes of poetry, including *Body Betrayer* (Cleveland State University Press, 1991) and *Never Be the Horse*, winner of the University of Akron Poetry Prize (University of Akron Press, 1999). She has been awarded the Theodore Roethke Poetry Prize, *The Gettysburg Review* Annual Poetry Award, and a Pushcart. Currently, Goldberg teaches in the MFA Creative Writing Program at Arizona State University.

Linda Gregerson's most recent book of poems is *Waterborne* (Houghton Mifflin, 2002). Her awards include an Academy Award in Literature from the American Academy of Arts and Letters, the Levinson Prize from *Poetry* magazine, the Consuelo Ford Award from the Poetry Society of America, the Isabel MacCaffrey Award from the Spenser Society of America, and grants and fellowships from the Institute of Advanced Study, the Ingram Merrill Foundation, the National Humanities Center, the Arts Foundation of Michigan, the National Endowment for the Arts, and the Guggenheim Foundation. She teaches Renaissance literature and creative writing at the University of Michigan.

Mark Halliday has published three books of poetry, *Little Star*, *Tasker Street*, and *Selfwolf*, as well as a critical work, *Stevens and the Impersonal*. He collaborated with Allen Grossman on *The Sighted Singer*, a book of interviews about poetics. Recipient of a Lila Wallace Prize and a Rome Prize, he teaches at Ohio University.

Edward Hirsch has published five books of poems, including *Wild Gratitude* (1986), which won the National Book Critics Circle Award, *Earthly Measures* (1994), and *On Love* (1998). He has also published three prose books, *Responsive Reading* (1999), *How to Read a Poem and Fall in Love with Poetry* (1999), and *The Demon and the Angel: Searching for the Source of Artistic Inspiration* (2002). He is a 1998 MacArthur Fellow, and teaches in the Creative Writing Program at the University of Houston.

Garrett Hongo is the author of *Volcano: A Memoir of Hawaii* and two books of poetry, *Yellow Light* and *The River of Heaven*. He has also edited *The Open Boat: Poems from Asian America* and *Under Western Eyes: Personal Essays from Asian America*. Winner of two NEA fellowships, The Lamont Prize from The Academy of American Poets, and a Guggenheim Fellowship, he is Distinguished Professor of Arts and Sciences at The University of Oregon in Eugene.

Richard Jackson received the 1999 Juniper Prize from the University of Massachusetts Press for *Heartwall*. He is also the author of four previous books of poems, *Alive All Day* (1992), winner of the Cleveland State University Press Award, *Worlds Apart* (Alabama, 1987), *Part of the Story* (Grove, 1983), and *Heart's Bridge: Poems Based on Petrarch* (University of Toledo: Aureole). His two books of criticism are *Dismantling Time in Contemporary American Poetry*, winner of the Agee Prize, and *Acts of Mind: Interviews with Contemporary American Poets*, a *Choice* award winner. Recipient of fellowships from the Guggenheim Foundation, the National Endowment for the Arts, and the National Endowment for the Humanities, he has also been a Fulbright exchange poet to Yugoslavia. Richard Jackson teaches at the University of Tennessee at Chattanooga, and is on the staff of the Vermont College MFA Program in Creative Writing.

Maxine Kumin is the author of thirteen books of poems, most recently *The Long Marriage*, preceded by *Selected Poems 1960–1990* and *Connecting the Dots*. She has also written three essay collections, including *Always Beginning: Essays on a Life in Poetry*, a collection of short stories, four novels, and an animal rights murder mystery, *Quit Monks or Die!* Among her many other awards, Kumin received the Pulitzer Prize in 1973.

Richard Lyons has published two books of poetry, *These Modern Nights* and *Hours of the Cardinal*. He is the recipient of an Academy of American Poets' Younger Poet Award. He directs and teaches in the graduate writing program at Mississippi State University.

Cynthia Macdonald has taught at Sarah Lawrence and Johns Hopkins University, and is now a professor at the University of Houston, where she founded the creative writing program in 1979. She has received many grants and awards for her work, including the O. B. Hardison Poetry Prize, given by the Folger Shakespeare Library. She is also a graduate of Houston-Galveston Psychoanalytic Institute and is now a member of that faculty. The most recent of her six books of poems are *I Can't Remember* (1997) and *Living Wills: New and Selected Poems* (1991), both from Norton.

J. D. McClatchy is the author of five collections of poems: *Scenes from Another Life* (Braziller, 1981), *Stars Principal* (Macmillan, 1986), *The Rest of the Way* (Knopf, 1990), *Ten Commandments* (Knopf, 1998), and *Hazmat* (Knopf, 2002). His literary essays are collected in *White Paper* (Columbia, 1989), which was given the Melville Cane Award by the Poetry Society of America, and *Twenty Questions* (Columbia,

1998). He has also edited several other books, including James Merrill's *Collected Poems* (2001), and edits the acclaimed series *The Voice of the Poet* for Random House AudioBooks. Since 1991, he has served as editor of *The Yale Review*. A chancellor of the Academy of American Poets and a member of the American Academy of Arts and Letters, Mr. McClatchy is Professor of English at Yale. He lives in Stonington, Connecticut.

Campbell McGrath is the author of five books of poetry, including *Spring Comes to Chicago* (Ecco, 1996), *Road Atlas* (Ecco, 1999), and *Florida Poems* (Ecco/HarperCollins, 2002). Among his awards are the Kingsley Tufts Prize, and fellowships from the Guggenheim and MacArthur Foundations. He teaches in the MFA Program at Florida International University, and lives with his family in Miami Beach.

Jacqueline Osherow is the author of four collections of poetry, the most recent of which is *Dead Men's Praise* (Grove, 1999). She is the recipient of fellowships from the National Endowment for the Arts, the Guggenheim Foundation, the Ingram Merrill Foundation, and was awarded the Witter Bynner Prize from the American Academy and Institute of Arts and Sciences. She is Professor of English at the University of Utah.

Carl Phillips is the author of six books of poetry, including *Rock Harbor* (Farrar, Straus, & Giroux, 2002). His awards include fellowships from the Guggenheim Foundation and Library of Congress, and an Award in Literature from the American Academy of Arts and Letters. Phillips teaches at Washington University in St. Louis.

Stanley Plumly is Distinguished University Professor and Professor of English at the University of Maryland. His work has been honored with the Delmore Schwartz Memorial Award, an Academy Award in Poetry from the American Academy of Arts and Letters, and nominations for the National Book Critics Circle Award, the William Carlos Williams Award, and the Academy of American Poets' Lenore Marshall Poetry Prize. His most recent book of poems is *Now That My Father Lies Down Beside Me: New and Selected Poems, 1970–2000* (Ecco, 2000).

J. Allyn Rosser has published two volumes of poetry, *Bright Moves* (winner of the Morse Poetry Prize) and *Misery Prefigured* (winner of the Crab Orchard Award). Recipient of a National Endowment for the Arts fellowship, she teaches at Ohio University.

Mary Ruefle is the author of seven books of poetry, the most recent of which is *Among the Musk Ox People* (Carnegie Mellon, 2002). She is the recipient of a National Endowment for the Arts fellowship, a Whiting Writers' Award, an Award in Literature from the American Academy of Arts and Letters, and a Guggenheim Fellowship. She teaches in the MFA Program at Vermont College.

David Wojahn is the author of six collections of poetry: *Icehouse Lights*, which was a selection in the Yale Series of Younger Poets and also winner of the William Carlos Williams Book Award, as well as *Glassworks* (1987), *Mystery Train* (1990), *Late Empire* (1994), *The Falling Hour* (1997), and *Spirit Cabinet* (2002)—all published by the University of Pittsburgh Press. A collection of his essays on contemporary poetry, entitled *Strange Good Fortune*, appeared from the

University of Arkansas Press in 2001. He teaches at Virginia Commonwealth University, and is also a member of the faculty in the MFA in Writing Program at Vermont College.

Adam Zagajewski is the leading Polish poet of his generation. He was born in Lvov in 1945 and studied philosophy at Cracow's Jagiellonian University. He lives in Paris and teaches each spring in the writing program at the University of Houston. His most recent book of poems is *Without End: New and Selected Poems* (Farrar, Straus, & Giroux, 2002). He has also published two books of prose in English: *Two Cities* (1995) and *Another Beauty* (2000).

WORKS CITED

"In the Music Room" by Robin Behn

Understanding Fiction, Cleanth Brooks and Robert Penn Warren
How Does a Poem Mean? John Ciardi and Miller Williams
Under Milk Wood, Dylan Thomas
Nude Descending a Staircase, X. J. Kennedy
Death in the Afternoon, Ernest Hemingway
Collected Lyrics and *The Collected Poems*, Edna St. Vincent Millay
Tender Buttons, Gertrude Stein
Music, the Brain, and Ecstasy, Robert Jourdain
View with a Grain of Sand: Selected Poems by Wisława Szymborska, translated by Stanisaw Baranczak and Clare Cavanagh
Natural Classicism, Frederick Turner
Four Quartets, T. S. Eliot

"Required Reading" by J. D. McClatchy

Collected Poems, Wallace Stevens
Lectures on Literature, Vladimir Nabokov
In Search of Lost Time, Marcel Proust
Water Street, James Merrill
Aeneid, Virgil
The Tale of Genji, Murasaki Shikibu
The Pillow-Book, Sei Shōnagon
The Waste Land and *Four Quartets*, T. S. Eliot
Collected Poems, W. H. Auden

"Reading Poetry" by Jacqueline Osherow

Astrophel and Stella, Philip Sidney
Don Juan, Lord Byron
Requiem, Anna Akhmatova

"First Principle" by Albert Goldbarth

The Divine Comedy, Dante
Penthouse Magazine
On the Nature of Things, Lucretius
Vanity Fair, William Makepeace Thackeray
Bleak House, Charles Dickens
Finnegans Wake, James Joyce
A Gentle Madness, Nicholas Basbanes
The Book on the Bookshelf, Henry Petroski

"Someone Reading a Book Is a Sign of Order in the World" by Mary Ruefle

Madame Bovary, Gustave Flaubert
In Search of Lost Time, Marcel Proust
The Waves, Virginia Woolf
The Return of the Native and *The Mayor of Casterbridge*, Thomas Hardy
The Scarlet Letter, Nathaniel Hawthorne
Notebooks, George Seferis
The Seven Pillars of Wisdom, T. E. Lawrence
Les Chants de Maldorer, Lautréamont
The Notebooks of Malte Laurids Brigge, Ranier Maria Rilke
Collected Stories, Franz Kafka
The Rings of Saturn, W. G. Sebald

"Another and Another Before That: Some Thoughts on Reading" by Carl Phillips

The Joy of Sex, Alex Comfort
Selected Poems, W. H. Auden
The Adventures of Tom Sawyer, Mark Twain
The Call of the Wild, Jack London
The Joy of Cooking, Irma Von Starkloff Rombauer
Areopagitica, John Milton
The Old Testament and Apocrypha
The Salt Ecstasies, James White
Seven Greeks, Guy Davenport
Odes, Pindar, translated by Lattimore
The Golden Bowl, Henry James
In Search of Lost Time, Marcel Proust
The Waves and *To the Lighthouse*, Virginia Woolf
Memoirs of Hadrian, Marguerite Yourcenar
The Art of Eating, M.F. K. Fisher
The Temple and A *Priest to the Temple*, George Herbert
Sermons on the Psalms and Gospels and *Devotions upon Emergent Occasions*, John Donne
English Renaissance Poetry, John Williams, Ed.
Poetry of Meditation, Louis Martz
Love and Fame, John Berryman
Ariel, Sylvia Plath
Bright Moon, Perching Bird, Li Po and Tu Fu, translated by Seaton and Cryer
Navigable Waterways, Pamela Alexander
Too Bright to See, Linda Gregg
Lugging Vegetables to Nantucket, Peter Klappert
Bad Boats, Laura Jensen

The Arrangement of Space, Martha Collins
The Woman at the Washington Zoo and *The Lost World*, Randall Jarrell
Hermetic Definition, H. D.
Meditations, Marcus Aurelius

"One Life, One Writing" by Edward Hirsch

Collected Poems, 1937–1971, *The Dream Songs*, and *Recovery*, John Berryman
The Complete Poems 1927–1979, Elizabeth Bishop
The Collected Prose, Elizabeth Bishop, edited by Robert Giroux
The Poems of J. V. Cunningham, J. V. Cunningham
The Complete Poems of Emily Dickinson, Emily Dickinson, edited by Thomas H. Johnson
Selected Letters, Emily Dickinson, edited by Thomas H. Johnson
The Opening of the Field, Robert Duncan
The Poetry of Randall Jarrell, Suzanne Ferguson
Elizabeth Bishop: The Biography of a Poetry, Lorrie Goldensohn
Collected Poems, Robert Hayden, edited by Frederick Glaysher
The Complete Poems and *Poetry and the Age*, Randall Jarrell
Randall Jarrell's Letters, edited by Mary Jarrell
Becoming a Poet: Elizabeth Bishop with Marianne Moore and Robert Lowell, David Kalstone
The Collected Poems of Weldon Kees, Weldon Kees, edited by Donald Justice
Modern Poetry after Modernism, James Longenbach
Collected Prose, *Day by Day*, and *Selected Poems*, Robert Lowell
Randall Jarrell, 1914–1965, Robert Lowell, Peter Taylor, and Robert Penn Warren, Eds.
Lost Puritan: A Life of Robert Lowell, Paul Mariani

Effort at Speech: New and Selected Poems, William Meredith
Recitative: Prose, edited by J. D. McClatchy
Opening the Hand, W. S. Merwin
Manic Power: Robert Lowell and His Circle, Jeffrey Meyers
The Maximus Poems, Charles Olson, edited by George F. Butterick
Randall Jarrell: A Literary Life, William Pritchard
The Collected Poems, Theodore Roethke
On the Poet and His Craft: Selected Prose of Theodore Roethke, edited by Ralph J. Mills, Jr.
Straw for the Fire: From the Notebooks of Theodore Roethke, 1943–1963, edited by David Wagoner
Out of Silence: Selected Poems, Muriel Rukeyser, edited by Kate Daniels
Selected Poems: Summer Knowledge (1938–1958), Delmore Schwartz
The Collected Poems, Dylan Thomas
Part of Nature, Part of Us, Helen Vendler

"Reading Autumn" by Stanley Plumly

Hyperion, John Keats
The Seasons, James Thomson

"Caveat Lector" by J. Allyn Rosser

The Faerie Queene, Edmund Spenser
Mountain Interval, Robert Frost
Paradise Lost, John Milton
Poetic Meter and Poetic Form, Paul Fussell
The Canterbury Tales, Geoffrey Chaucer
The Divine Comedy, Dante
Swann's Way, Marcel Proust
Molloy, *Malone Dies*, and *The Unnamable*, Samuel Beckett

The Ambassadors and *The Golden Bowl*, Henry James
Iliad, Homer
Dombey & Son, Charles Dickens

"Prosody & Reciprocity (On Reading)" by Marvin Bell

Spring & All, William Carlos Williams
Collected Poems of William Carlos Williams, A. Walton Litz and Christopher MacGowan, Eds.
Imaginations, edited by Webster Schott
Tape for the Turn of the Year, A. R. Ammons
Silence in the Snowy Fields and *The Light Around the Body*, Robert Bly
Drowning with Others, *Helmets* and *Buckdancer's Choice*, James Dickey
Poems (first collection), Alan Dugan
The Lady in Kicking Horse Reservoir, Richard Hugo
Flower Herding at Mount Monadnock, *Body Rags*, and *The Book of Nightmares*, Galway Kinnell
Not This Pig and *They Feed They Lion*, Philip Levine
Ghosts of the Heart, *Spring of the Thief*, and *The Zigzag Walk*, John Logan
The Moving Target and *The Lice*, W. S. Merwin
Ariel, Sylvia Plath
Diving into the Wreck, Adrienne Rich
All My Pretty Ones and *Live or Die*, Anne Sexton
At the End of the Open Road, Louis Simpson
West of Your City, *Traveling Through the Dark*, *The Rescued Year*, and *Allegiances*, William Stafford
The Branch Will Not Break, *Shall We Gather at the River*, and *To a Blossoming Pear Tree*, James Wright
For Love, Robert Creeley
Say Pardon, *Figures of the Human*, and *Rescue the Dead*, David Ignatow

With Eyes at the Back of Our Heads and *The Jacob's Ladder*, Denise Levertov

The Materials and *This in Which*, George Oppen

Some Trees, *The Double Dream of Spring*, and *Three Poems*, John Ashbery

Stand Up, Friend, with Me, Edward Field

Thank You and Other Poems, Kenneth Koch

Meditations in an Emergency, Frank O'Hara

Gasoline, Gregory Corso

A Coney Island of the Mind and *Starting from San Francisco*, Lawrence Ferlinghetti

Howl, *Kaddish*, and *Wichita Vortex Sutra*, Allen Ginsberg

The Opening of the Field, Robert Duncan

The Distances, Charles Olson

A Range of Poems, Gary Snyder

Homage to Mistress Bradstreet and *77 Dream Songs*, John Berryman

The Lost World, Randall Jarrell

Life Studies, Robert Lowell

The Lost Son and *Words for the Wind*, Theodore Roethke

Questions of Travel and *Geography III*, Elizabeth Bishop

The Hard Hours, Anthony Hecht

The Summer Anniversaries, *Night Light*, and *Departures*, Donald Justice

Water Street and *The Fire Screen*, James Merrill

Selected Poems, Howard Nemerov

Heart's Needle, W. D. Snodgrass

Bone Thoughts and *White Paper*, George Starbuck

Love Calls Us to the Things of This World and *Selected Poems*, Richard Wilbur

Another Republic, Charles Simic and Mark Strand, Eds.

Postwar Polish Poetry, Czeslaw Milosz
Roots and Wings: Poetry from Spain 1900–1975, E. Ward
Sunflower Splendor: Three Thousand Years of Chinese Poetry, Wu-Chi Liu and Irving Yucheng Lo, Eds.
One Hundred Poems from the Chinese and *One Hundred Poems from the Japanese*, Kenneth Rexroth
The White Pony, Robert Payne

"The Cattle Raid" by Campbell McGrath

Coleridge, Richard Holmes
Civil War, Shelby Foote
Civilization and Capitalism, Fernand Braudel
The Invisible Universe, David Malin

"Poetry and Murder" by Beckian Fritz Goldberg

Life Support, Tess Gerritsen
Cemetery Nights, Stephen Dobyns
The Egyptian Book of the Dead
Portrait of a Lady, Henry James
Body Criticism, Barbara Maria Stafford
Literature and the Body, Elaine Scarry
Classic Descriptions of Disease, Ralph Major
Red Dragon, Thomas Harris

"Reading List for American Poets of the New Millennium" by Garrett Hongo

Ion, Plato
Poetics, Aristotle
The Critique of Judgment, Immanuel Kant

Aesthetics, Hegel
Lyrical Ballads, "Preface," William Wordsworth
Feeling and Form, Susanne Langer
The Prison-House of Language, Frederic Jameson
The Wretched of the Earth, Frantz Fanon
The Colonizer and the Colonized, Albert Memmi
The Prison Notebooks, Antonio Gramsci
Lenin and Philosophy, Louis Althusser
Orientalism, Edward Said
Imaginary Homelands, Salman Rushdie
The Location of Culture, Homi K. Bhabha

"Perverse Reading" by Mark Halliday

Great Expectations, *Bleak House*, and *Our Mutual Friend*, Charles Dickens
The Waste Land, T. S. Eliot
Hamlet, *King Lear*, *Macbeth*, *Measure for Measure*, *Othello*, and *Antony and Cleopatra*, William Shakespeare
Paradise Lost, *Paradise Regained*, *Samson Agonistes*, John Milton
The House of Mirth, *The Custom of the Country*, and *The Age of Innocence*, Edith Wharton
Despair, *Lolita*, and *Ada*, Vladimir Nabokov
Between the Acts and *Mrs. Dalloway*, Virginia Woolf
The Man Who Died and *Women in Love*, D. H. Lawrence
When She Was Good and *Portnoy's Complaint*, Philip Roth
The Moving Target, *The Lice*, and *The Carrier of Ladders*, W. S. Merwin
Iliad and *Odyssey*, Homer
Metamorphoses, Ovid
The Divine Comedy, Dante

Essay on Man, Alexander Pope
The Prelude, William Wordsworth
Leaves of Grass, Walt Whitman
Gravity's Rainbow, Thomas Pynchon

"A Loose Net: Some Meditative American Poets"
by Richard Lyons

An Atlas of the Difficult World, Adrienne Rich
Trappings, Richard Howard
Letters from a Father and Other Poems, Mona Van Duyn
Country Music, Charles Wright
Geography III, Elizabeth Bishop
In the Badlands of Desire, Beckian Fritz Goldberg

"The Compass of Association" by Cynthia Macdonald

Metamorphoses, Ovid
Don Quixote, Cervantes
The Pillow-Book, Sei Shōnagon
Reflections, Walter Benjamin
The Guinness Book of Records
A *Child's Garden of Verses*, Robert Louis Stevenson, Ed.
The Poet's Notebook, Deborah Tall, Stephen Kuusisto, and David Weiss, Eds.
The Compleat Angler, or the Contemplative Man's Recreation, Izaak Walton
Vermeer and the Delft School, Walter Liedke

"A Few Cells in the Great Hive" by Reginald Gibbons

Collected Poems, T. S. Eliot

ABC of Reading, Ezra Pound
Howl, Allen Ginsberg
The Burden of the Past and the English Poet, Walter Jackson Bate
The New Oxford Book of Sixteenth Century Verse, Emrys Jones
Forms of Discovery, Yvor Winters
Collected Poems, William Carlos Williams
The Voice That Is Great Within Us, Hayden Carruth
American Negro Poetry, Arna Bontemps
Every Shut Eye Ain't Asleep: An Anthology of Poetry by African-Americans Since 1945, Michael S. Harper and Anthony Wilson, Eds.
Cracking Up, Christopher Bollas
Yeats at Work, Curtis Bradford
Selected Essays and Reviews, Hayden Carruth
Rootprints and *Three Steps on the Ladder of Writing*, Hélène Cixous
The Complete Works of Isaac Babel, Isaac Babel
The Story and the Fable, Edwin Muir
The House of Breath and *Had I A Hundred Mouths*, William Goyen
Letter to an Imaginary Friend and *The Movie at the End of the World: Collected Poems*, Thomas McGrath
What Is Found There and *An Atlas of the Difficult World*, Adrienne Rich
The Enemy's Country, Geoffrey Hill
How to Kill a Dragon: Aspects of Indo-European Poetics, Calvert Watkins
English Versification, 1570–1980: A Reference Guide with Appendix, T. V. F. Brogan
Go Tell It on the Mountain, James Baldwin
Mythologies, Roland Barthes
Gathering Evidence, Thomas Bernhard

A Street in Bronzeville, Gwendolyn Brooks
Southern Road, Sterling A. Brown
The Poem Itself, Stanley Burnshaw
The First Man, Albert Camus
Articulate Energy, Donald Davie
Shooting the Works, W. S. DiPiero
Selected Poems, Robert Duncan
Identity and the Life Cycle, Erik Erikson
Bakkhai, Euripides
The Truth of Poetry, Michael Hamburger
Hourglass, Danilo Kiš
The Life of the Poet, Lawrence Lipking
Thomas McGrath: Life and the Poem, Reginald Gibbons and Terrence Des Pres, Eds.
The Witness of Poetry, Czeslaw Milosz
The Complete Essays of Montaigne, Michel de Montaigne, translated by Donald Frame
Speak, Memory and *The Gift*, Vladimir Nabokov
Orality and Literacy, Walter J. Ong
Pale Horse, Pale Rider, Katherine Anne Porter
Swann's Way, Marcel Proust
The Radetzky March, Joseph Roth
Confessions, Jean-Jacques Rousseau
Out of Silence, Muriel Rukeyser
The Street of Crocodiles, Bruno Schultz
The Emigrants and *The Rings of Saturn*, W. G. Sebald
Oedipus Tyrannus, Charles Segal
The Man Died, Wole Soyinka
View with a Grain of Sand, Wisława Szymborska

The Tree of Man, *A Fringe of Leaves*, and *The Solid Mandala*, Patrick White
The Country and the City, Raymond Williams
Black Boy and *American Hunger*, Richard Wright
Anthology of Modern American Poetry, Cary Nelson, Ed.
Anthology of Twentieth-Century British and Irish Poetry, Keith Tuma, Ed.
The Making of a Poem: A Norton Anthology of Poetic Forms, Mark Strand and Eavan Boland
Glossary of Literary Terms, M. H. Abrams

"Reading: Preparing the Mind for Possibilities & the Soul for Tenderness" by Stephen Dunn

The Razor's Edge, *Of Human Bondage*, and *The Moon and Sixpence*, W. Somerset Maugham
Nine Stories and *The Catcher in the Rye*, J. D. Salinger
On the Road, Jack Kerouac
The Amboy Dukes, Irving Shulman
Peyton Place, Grace Metalious
Wuthering Heights, Charlotte Brontë
Martin Eden, Jack London
East of Eden, John Steinbeck
The Naked and the Dead, Norman Mailer
An American Tragedy, Theodore Dreiser
Billy Budd and *Moby-Dick*, Herman Melville
The Fountainhead, Ayn Rand
The Brothers Karamazov, Fyodor Dostoyevsky
Don Quixote, Cervantes
The Education of Henry Adams, Henry Adams

One Hundred Years of Solitude, Gabriel García Márquez
Blindness, Jose Saramago
Given Sugar, Given Salt, Jane Hirshfield
Collected Poems, Wallace Stevens
The Hard Hours, Anthony Hecht
Hope Against Hope, Nadezhda Mandelstam
King Lear, William Shakespeare
The Reader, Bernard Schlink

"Pleasure Dome" by Madeline DeFrees

Kenilworth, *Waverley*, *The Heart of Midlothian*, and *The Bride of Lammermoor*, Walter Scott
Middlemarch, George Eliot
Joy, Georges Bernanos
Thérèse Desqueyroux, Francois Mauriac
The Dyer's Hand, W. H. Auden
Dictionary of Phrase and Fable, Brewer

"Dancing As If Free: Reading, Imitation, and Influence" by Richard Jackson

The Lice, W. S. Merwin
Rime, Petrarch
Other Traditions, John Ashbery
North of Boston, Robert Frost
Odes, Horace
Imitations, Robert Lowell
With Akhmatova at the Gate, Stephen Berg
Touchstones, Robert Pack
The Freedom of the Poet and *The Dream Songs*, John Berryman

The Poetics of Space, Gaston Bachelard
Poetry, Language, Thought, Martin Heidegger
The Nine Gates, Jane Hirshfield
Lectures on Shakespeare, W. H. Auden
Sonnets, William Shakespeare
Essay on Criticism, Alexander Pope
Paradise Lost, John Milton
Song of Myself, Walt Whitman
Astrophel and Stella, Philip Sidney
La Vita Nuova, Dante
The Book of the Dead Man, Marvin Bell
Elegy, Larry Levis
Odyssey, Homer
Civil War, Lucan
Love Poems, Propertius
On the Nature of Things, Lucretius
Metamorphoses, *Amores*, *The Art of Love*, Ovid

"Peripheral Vision" by Maxine Kumin

Mother Nature, Sarah Hardy
The Making of a Poem, Eavan Boland and Mark Strand, Eds.
Patterns of Poetry, Miller Williams
Strong Measures, Philip Dacey and David Jauss, Eds.
Selected Letters, Marianne Moore
Poets in Their Youth, Eileen Simpson
Journey Around My Room, Louise Bogan
Walden and *The Maine Woods*, Henry David Thoreau
The Peppered Moth, Margaret Drabble
The Gravity of Sunlight, Rosa Shand

"From the Valley of Saying" by David Wojahn

Selected Poems, edited by Bradford Morrow
The Collected Shorter Poems, Kenneth Rexroth
Kipling, Auden & Company: Essays and Reviews 1935–64, Randall Jarrell
Zbigniew Herbert: Selected Poems, translated by Czeslaw Milosz and Peter Dale
The Duino Elegies, Ranier Maria Rilke
Silence in the Snowy Fields, Robert Bly
Collected Poems, James Wright
Selected Poems, W. S. Merwin
Selected Poems 1954–86, Tomas Tranströmer, edited by Robert Hass
New Collected Poems, Tomas Tranströmer
Collected Poems, C. P. Cavafy
Cavafy's Alexandra: Studies of a Myth in Progress, Edmund Keeley
Knopf Guide to Egypt

"Young Poets, Please Read Everything" by Adam Zagajewski

The Greeks and Greek Civilization, Jacob Burckhardt
Collected Works, Hugo von Hofmannsthal

OTHER TITLES IN THE WRITER'S STUDIO SERIES

The Writer's Studio features books that challenge, stimulate, and support the writer of poetry and short fiction. These titles are not how-to books, but books for writers who already know how to write well and are looking for further stimulation, or to deepen and expand their sense of community with other writers.

They Have a Word for It:
A Lighthearted Lexicon of Untranslatable Words and Phrases
by Howard Rheingold

A Fine Excess: Contemporary Literature at Play
Edited by Kirby Gann and Kristin Herbert

Passing the Word: Writers on Their Mentors
Edited by Lee Martin and Jeffrey Skinner